Bull of the Woods

Bull of the Woods
The Gordon Gibson Story

Gordon Gibson
with
Carol Renison

Douglas & McIntyre
Vancouver

Copyright © 2000
First paperback edition 1982
First POD edition 2011

All rights reserved. No part of this book may be reproduced, stored in a retrieval system or transmitted, in any form or by any means, without the prior written consent of the publisher or a licence from The Canadian Copyright Licensing Agency (Access Copyright). For a copyright licence, visit www.accesscopyright.ca or call toll free to 1-800-893-5777.

Douglas & McIntyre
An imprint of D&M Publishers Inc.
2323 Quebec Street, Suite 201
Vancouver BC Canada V5T 4S7
www.douglas-mcintyre.com

Cataloguing data available from Library and Archives Canada
ISBN 978-1-55054-781-8 (pbk.)
ISBN 978-1-926706-49-8 (ebook)
ISBN 978-1-77100-017-8 (POD)

Cover design by Peter Cocking

We gratefully acknowledge the financial support of the Canada Council for the Arts, the British Columbia Arts Council, the Province of British Columbia through the Book Publishing Tax Credit and the Government of Canada through the Canada Book Fund for our publishing activities.

*To all those who have found themselves
on a different wavelength
from their teachers*

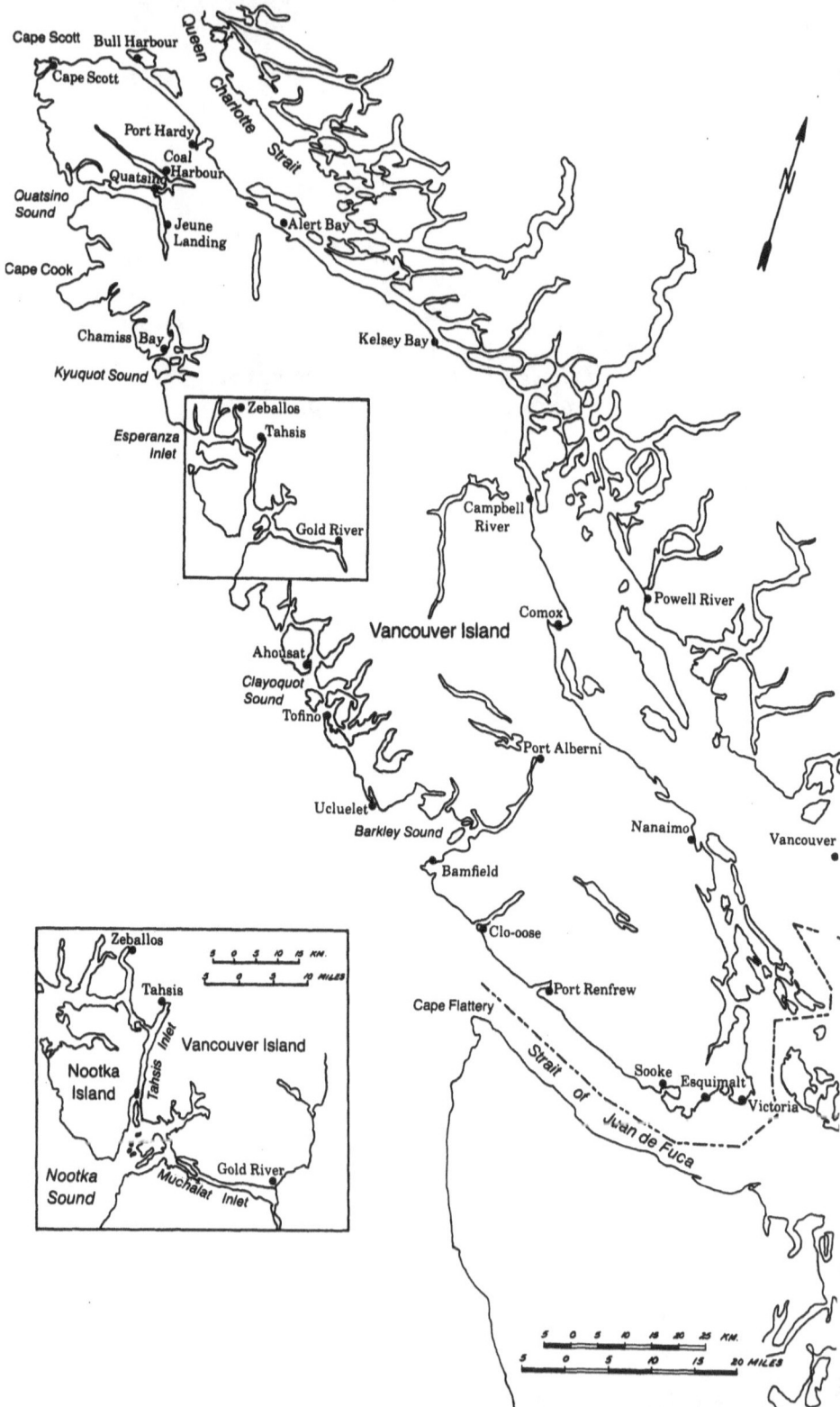

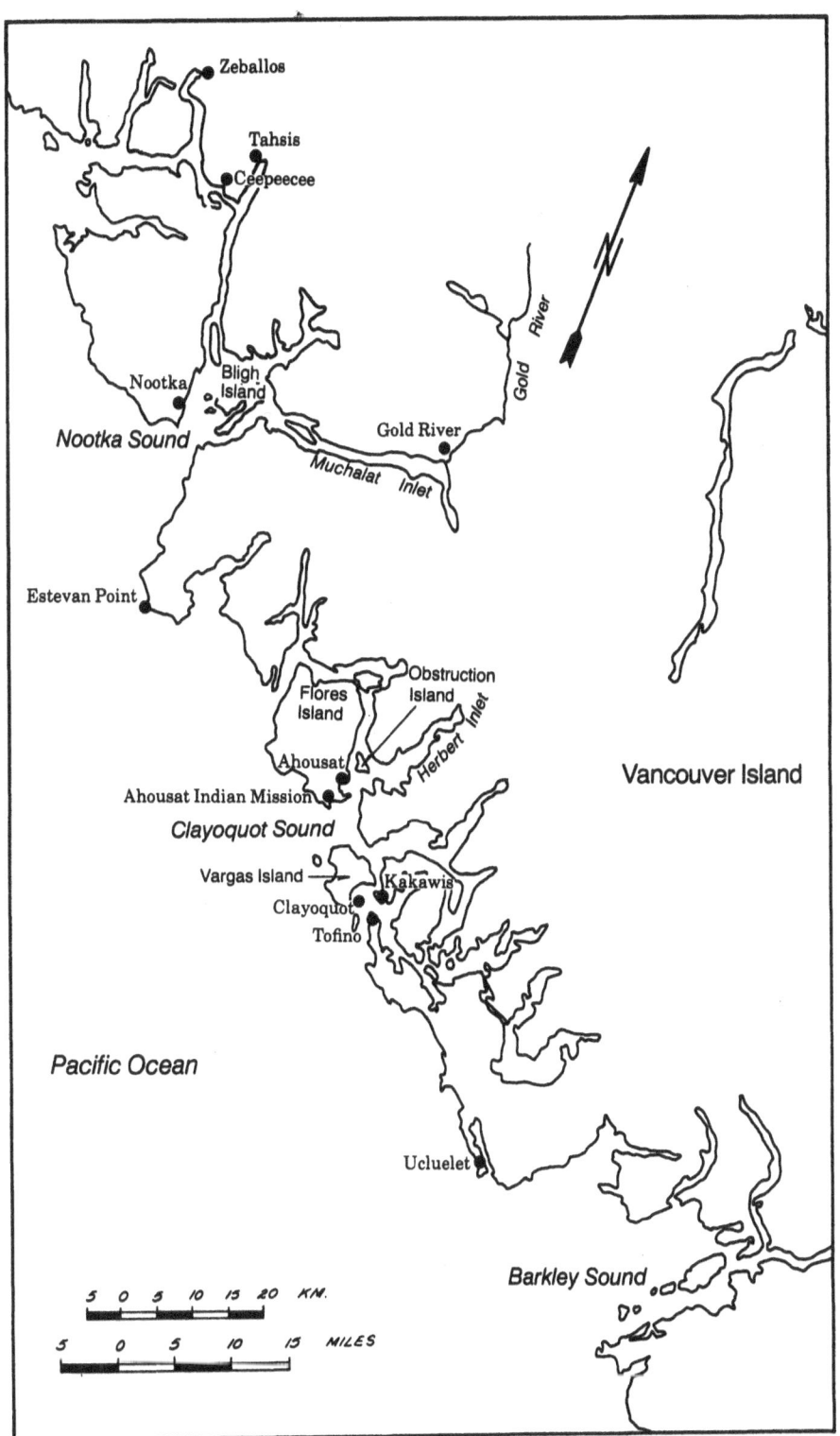

INTRODUCTION

I hadn't opened my copy of this book for years. I'd even forgotten the inscription: "To you Gordon. I'm very proud of you. Dad." Well, no one could be prouder than I am of him. I wish he were here today to sign this book for you.

Bull of the Woods was first published in 1980. I was only forty-two then, a relatively young man with a strong and famous father and all the privileges and problems that entails. Dad passed away in 1986. Even after all of these years, never a month goes by that I don't hear a new story about this fabulous man, though the survivors of his time become fewer.

Many children, getting on in life themselves, have the time to take the full measure of their parents before they die. My mother was too young for me to fully appreciate—gone at only sixty. And though my father lived to eighty-two, he was too immense to fully encompass even after that time. I often wish I had had the chance to ask him about famous people he knew or more details of his adventures. Perhaps such regret is part of the human condition.

But this book captures a good part of a wondrous life. Reading the pages again, I alternated between gales of laughter and incredulous cries of "Jesus!" at one or another of my father's fantastic escapades (for I learned his salty vocabulary well).

This is the story of a man whose kind is literally not made any more, for he was the product of the hard and isolated life from which most people these days are spared. It wasn't just lack of money—as he said, "Although we had no money we were considered well-to-do by local standards. Our neighbours were more broke."

Even more importantly, after the humiliations and failure of the only six years he spent in school, he had a lifelong drive to succeed. In his words, "I came out of school a loser, my teachers having told me repeatedly that I was a hopeless student."

Many years later, my guess is that his alleged dullness in school was really a moderate deafness—Dad had a great, booming voice to compensate—and a mild form of dyslexia. It certainly wasn't a lack of wit or spirit. When one of his teachers remarked that he had a dog at home brighter than my father, Dad replied, "Who did you get to teach your dog?" My father was expelled.

While his brothers carried on with school in Vancouver, Dad went to the west coast of Vancouver Island with his father, W. F. Gibson, a small-time entrepreneur and timber cruiser. Dad, born in Dawson City during one of W. F.'s quests for fortune, an unsuccessful try for a piece of the Yukon gold rush, became at twelve the rejected kid who lived the life of a frontier adult from then on. There was no choice, which in a way made the decision easy.

The little enterprise went broke, and went broke again. On one occasion, a receiver stepped in and offered the tiny assets of the backwoods operation to the neighbours in a fire sale: "He sold everything the Indians had the cash to buy—even the window panes out of my bedroom."

Life on the west coast was tough and simple. When they got too far inland to cut and drop trees directly off the steep slopes into the saltwater inlets, Dad and W. F. got a couple of bulls to help with the haulage. The young bull gored the old one, which then had to be put down. In Dad's recollection, "We salted down the old bull and later ate the son-of-a-bitch." (There was nothing disrespectful in his swearing. SOB was almost a term of endearment.)

The west coast in those days consisted of a few Indian villages and isolated logging and fishing camps. Characters tended to the rougher side. You had to be tough to survive, especially as a kid in charge of increasingly larger crews of older men. In one hilarious incident, after a crew of Italian shingle cutters chased my father to his boat brandishing axes over a pay dispute, he left them on the beach for a week, stating, "You bastards will starve to death. You don't even know where you are." As is a common theme of this book and of his life, everyone ended up on good terms, because Dad was a fair man—hard as nails, but without a mean bone in his body.

My father loved the ladies all his life, and he was a great favourite in the small settlement social events. But there weren't many women in the wilderness and the rare exceptions could cause trouble. A worker in one of Dad's camps had brought his lady along, and went off on a week's assignment. On returning early, he found another man in bed with his wife. My father managed to talk the aggrieved husband out of his shotgun plans, and then noted in an aside, "To be honest, I was glad he had not arrived home a day earlier."

Dad met my mother on a fishpacking trip to Seattle. She was there working as the secretary to a railroad vice-president, in the fanciest offices in town. My father talked her into marrying him through a combination of charm and false pretenses. I've often wondered what she must have felt upon arriving on the desolate west coast of Vancouver Island.

I do know that, until the day she died, my mother had a good deal of indignation, not all of it mock, about the time she and I (as a one-year-old infant) and our floathouse were blown out to sea by a storm. Returning on his boat from up the inlet, Dad sized up the situation and spent the next few hours retrieving the scattered boom of logs that was the total family fortune at the time. He only picked us up after that, having calculated that we were not in serious danger.

But life was like that. Often decisions had to be made on the spur of the moment. Twice my father kidnapped entire logging camps to deal with emergencies, towing one to sea in the middle of the night. As he recounted the story, "The crew were all asleep in their bunks and had no idea they were headed for a real adventure." He lived the maxim that it is easier to ask forgiveness than permission.

Dad once told me that the family never knew the Depression was on. The west coast was so poor it made no difference, and the fish were still there for the eating. But through their hard work in the woods, he and his brothers were making a respected name for themselves by that dreadful decade. He recalled, "Our father died in late 1933, and we brought his body down from Ahousat to Vancouver on the *Otter*. Every CPR boat slowed down and lowered its flag as we passed." My father was not yet thirty.

The family went into the fishing business in addition to logging, and oh my, did they acquire boats. The vessels they could afford were invariably old, decrepit, sometimes unseaworthy, and very, very cheap. But boats were central to the west coast, not just for fishing but for towing and even socializing. There were no roads.

To my father, boats were much more than transportation. They were a symbol of how he wanted to live his life. "Any man who is master of his own little boat can go where he will," he claimed, "and is far more fortunate than the man who can hire another to be his captain, even if he can afford the finest stateroom on the *Queen Elizabeth*." All his life he wanted to be free and in charge, at least of himself, and owning a boat delivers that independence.

Some of Dad's tales are truly hair-raising, and anyone who knows the sea will understand not only that my father was a great sailor but that he was a very lucky one. One time, while sailing the *Malahat*, an aging 250-foot long, five-masted schooner converted to a barge, he was caught in heavy seas and zero visibility. He soon glanced off a hazard known as Paddle Rock: "We touched and slipped down the side with the kiss of a mermaid." The distance between drowning and fortune can sometimes be measured in inches.

The little family empire kept growing. During World War II, Dad was too old for military service, but he built several airfields for the government and gained a distaste for bureaucratic procedures, which never left him. During the same period, he and his brothers bought a failing airline, which they later sold to Canadian Pacific for a large profit, after charging the company an extra $10,000 over the agreed price for a taxi ride they had had to take in Winnipeg.

The forestry operations gradually became a big money maker. No other outfit had been able to make a buck on the rugged west coast, and the Gibsons' just kept growing. Dad built the huge lumber complex at Tahsis, saw the main mill burn down with no insurance (they were still negotiating over rates), and had the pile drivers working to rebuild the plant before the embers were cool. He was the resource-industry version of the Terminator—nothing could stop him. He just picked up and carried on.

By 1951, Dad and his brothers sold out to the East Asiatic Company of Denmark, and for the first time he had some real money, which he used with the same flair as he used the freedom of poverty. He went into politics and became a member of the Legislative Assembly (as a Liberal, but he was really always an Independent, as was formally my uncle, Member of Parliament Jack Gibson, another fabulous character).

His "money talks" speech, which is famous in B.C. history, had him ejected from the legislature when he refused to withdraw allegations of bribery. Much later, the accused cabinet minister went to jail on exactly that charge, but in the meantime, Dad was defeated in a by-election after he resigned his seat to take the issue to the people. Of that by-election, he said, "Every baby within a radius of twenty-five miles was kissed at both ends" by Socred ministers. The government had pulled out all the stops and all the road-building machinery to beat its nemesis.

He was re-elected in 1960 and was one of the best-loved members of the legislature until 1966. To this day, one-time premier Dave Barrett talks fondly of debates and late-night Chinese dinners with my father. Legislative sessions away from home can be terribly hard on families. Dad also spent at least some of his evenings dictating the recollections that make up much of this book.

During his political career, Dad began the hotelier phase. My parents had bought a large chunk of ground on Maui and built a winter home. Although the book doesn't tell this story, the property became a hotel as a result of a long-running rivalry with my mother. She was a real-estate flipper of some note, building the allowances she got from Dad into a sizable portfolio. On these matters, my father was kept completely in the dark, and it drove him nuts.

On Maui, she had quietly acquired a parcel with hotel zoning. When Dad found out through a mutual friend, nothing would do but that *his* property—the winter home—must get hotel zoning too. The county authorities required that an actual hotel be built in exchange, and that was the start of the Maui Lu Resort, visited by literally hundreds of thousands of Canadians over the years.

Mother died in 1967, and Dad became a changed man. Always a prodigious drinker—this habit having had much to do with some of the most outrageous and hilarious tales in the book—his daily intake escalated to two bottles. His favourite beverage was Seagram 83 rye, distinguished by the fine characteristic of being in an oval bottle and thus guaranteed not to roll around in the glove compartment.

Then, one day, he stopped. He talked to himself: "Gordon, you big son-of-a-bitch (that term of endearment again), you'll never take another drink as long as you live." And he didn't.

He learned by experience all his life and was big enough to change his ways. He was always an outdoorsman, and in the early days hunted for food. When he was older and didn't need to hunt, he shot a magnificent moose for sport. He didn't like what he had done. Years later, he recalled, "I have not shot a moose since, nor do I ever want to. It was a cowardly act, one I am not proud of."

Dad remarried, to Gertrude Gibson whom he had met at the Maui Lu, and she helped him run it for many years. The hotel became the centre of his life. He sailed the huge yacht *Norsal* to and from Hawaii, with inexpensive, amateur crews. They nearly sank on the return voyage, and the ship limped into harbour without electricals or hydraulics, its engines incapacitated and most of the furnishings a total writeoff from water damage. His verdict? "I wouldn't have missed it for the world."

There are some sea stories that remain untold. On the much smaller, 65-foot *Cape Beale*, a converted seiner with a fireplace that I have the fortune to run today, Dad's personal parsimony (he was famously generous to others) once drove his crew of four guests to flag down a fishboat for extra food. He was also known to bang into things from time to time, and on one occasion, he hit a dock with a boatload of seniors, toppling one surprised woman right off the toilet seat she was on at the time. And other times, on land, his long-time secretary, Helen Richards, solved more than one minor car accident with a side-payment for repairs to the other party.

My father was a giant of a man, but more than that; he was a good man, a kind man and a generous one. He had a great, rambunctious joy in living, which was infectious to all who came near.

He could also be a hard man, because sometimes life is hard. He wasn't dealt many cards, but they were good ones: strength of body, quickness of mind and a wonderful share of luck. He lived his life the way he did in order to be himself and to succeed, and nothing was more important than that. "Although I was delighted to have two children," he once said, "I saw little of them until they had finished school and married." He was out in the bush doing his job as the family provider. He was also having a hell of a good time.

This is a wonderful book, an ode to joy in print. It is an inspiration, in particular for kids not well favoured in their beginnings. My father had a great life, one that touched innumerable people and made them happy, one that was successful by any measure at all. Until the day he died, he was always scrambling, always trying to prove that those Grade 6 teachers were wrong. But he won on his terms. He lived life his way.

To his children, me and my sister, Louanne, he was a force of nature. It was a genuine shock that in the end he could actually die. How can the winds cease to blow or the rivers to run? I was called to his bedside, and I hugged and kissed him, but he was gone. Many years later, it's good to have this book.

Enjoy.

Gordon F. Gibson, 1999

CHAPTER 1

When I left school I was told I was such a dog that someone would have to feed me for the rest of my life or I would surely starve to death. It was then I determined in my mind that I would never again be at the bottom.

We have been called by many names in our day, but by God, no one has ever said we were lazy! My three brothers and I have been in every kind of business except running liquor or owning a whorehouse. We have had opportunities for adventure as few other men of our generation, in gold mining, fishing, logging, construction, whaling and later politics. No small sideline was our interest in the ladies who brought a little grace and beauty into our lives.

We have owned or sailed some of the finest wooden ships ever built including the *Maid of Orleans*, 104 feet long with tremendous beam and two masts, a notorious "blackbirder" built in 1882 and first used to smuggle black labour from the Solomon Islands to the sugar plantations of Queensland; and the famous *Malahat*, a 245-foot five-masted schooner, which had been the mother ship of the rum fleet during the American Prohibition years and was converted in our heyday in the 1930s to a log-carrying vessel.

We have had our fair share of disasters, too, like the night a gale blew the belly out of the *Malahat*'s sails ripping them to shreds as we drifted onto a reef; or the fire at our mill in Tahsis that nearly destroyed the results of half a lifetime's sweat in a matter of a few hours. Those were just two of the many occasions when we were broken financially and had to start all over again with just a little hope and a lot of damned hard work.

Our struggle, above all else, was to simply survive. I was forty-eight years old on my way out of this life before I ever had more than a few dollars to spend. Within three months of that birthday my three brothers and I were each worth more than a million.

There is little doubt that we come from hardy stock—survivors—travelling long and light. Our father came from a farm in Ontario and worked his way as a carpenter and sawmill operator from Chicago to Kananaskis, Alberta, before he was twenty. Dad was a great promoter and free enterpriser and when the mining fever started in British Columbia, he came to Lillooet and staked some claims. On one of his trips to civilization, he met our mother, Julia. Her father had died in Quebec and her mother came out west when Julia was very young. When her mother died a few years later, Julia went to work looking after the two children of a very strict Presbyterian family in Vancouver.

After they were married in 1902, Dad went to the Yukon in search of that elusive gold, while Mother waited patiently in Vancouver for the birth of her first baby. This was Clarke, born in 1903.

Mother accompanied Dad to the Yukon the next year, living in a log cabin which in later years she described as the house she loved best. While Dad worked his mine, she looked after the entire crew of ten men as well as her own family under that one roof. I was born in the cabin on 28 November 1904, Mother being assisted by Margaret, the wife of my father's partner, Jack Keefer. Their mine was called #5 and located four miles upstream from Discovery, the first rich gold mine to be found in the Goldbottom area.

Our mother came out of the Yukon in December 1905 because she was expecting a third child and conditions were becoming too tough for a pregnant woman with two babies, although she cooked for the crew until the day she left. In later years Mother regaled us with stories of her week-long trip with two small children from Dawson to Whitehorse in a cold sleigh, coping with feedings and soiled linen in log roadhouses at night. She was grateful to the only other passengers, several dance hall girls, who befriended her during the journey.

Cash was virtually unknown to my family at this time, and the crew could not be paid until the cleanup in the spring. One of the problems of Dad's mine was that a shaft had to be dug to bedrock and a steam pipe vented down to soften or thaw the gravel. The rock containing the gold was then dug out and hauled to the surface in buckets. There was no way of separating any quantity of gold until the spring runoff when water was available to put the gravel through a sluice box.

By early 1906 Mother was getting pretty desperate for money and Dad sent her a cheque for $125 with the following letter:

> 5 January 1906,
> Goldbottom
>
> Dear Julia,
>
> Your letter of the 7th arrived just yesterday. I wish you had told me sooner that you were getting short of money. I am sending you my policy out to get a loan on it as it is much cheaper than to borrow up here. . . .
>
> We have all been very short. It costs quite a lot to run this crowd to spring. No end to credit but cash is something that we don't know anything about.
>
> It does not seem like living to be away from all that is dear to me. I thought sure that I would get a picture of the children before Xmas.
>
> Dear love, take care of yourself. I am glad that you have found some nice rooms and I wish I could come out for the birth but it is impossible. Now Julia you know how hard it is to get money at this time of the year so I don't need to say anymore, but if you see you are getting hard up you can tell these people that I have to carry everything here for another six months until clean up without getting a cent for our work.
>
> Well Dear, if you were here I could talk to you for a long time but I don't know what else to write. If you were not expecting, it would be different, be sure. Write often and tell me everything. Lots of love and kisses to your dear self and to those good Boys.
>
> Yours,
> W.F.G.

Dad came out of the Yukon in 1906 after his dreams of a Klondike jackpot had faded completely. The value of the cleanup was $3,700, which after paying wages, expenses and grocery debts was split between Dad and Jack Keefer. The crew was paid in gold. There must have been a little left because Dad was able to pay his way to Vancouver, where he took on various jobs including working in the Hastings Sawmill. His payment was mostly in lumber and shingles out of which he built us a home at 1222 Keefer Street, and another house next door which he later sold. By building this second house, he was able to pay for the first.

Jack was born in that little house in 1906. In 1908, Earson, the baby of the family, became the fourth child in six years to hang about our mother's skirts.

In 1907 our father started timber cruising the west coast of Vancouver Island. The government had initiated a policy that anyone could stake a square mile of timber provided certain conditions were met. The Crown timber lands were thrown open and Dad staked claims, then sold them to speculators who hoped to sell the claims later at a good profit. A large number of these timber claims were in the Clayoquot Sound area and on Flores Island where our family later settled.

In 1912 Dad borrowed $1,000 from his sister-in-law, Lucy Brett, for passage on the *Carmania* to England to try to interest British investors in the B.C. timber business.

By lucky chance, he was invited to meet the Lord Provost of Glasgow, and when Dad was showing him pictures and maps of the timber stands, the Lord Provost asked if there was any place in that wilderness for his son, who was an alcoholic. Evidently, the Provost had hired a tutor to keep an eye on his son but the tutor had become an alcoholic too! So the Provost was looking for a place where liquor was not available.

As a result of this conversation, Dad brought the Provost's son back to Vancouver, and helped marry him off to the daughter of Dr. Sleeth, a veterinarian. After the wedding Dad arranged for them to file a preemption of 160 acres in Hesquiat Harbour on the west coast of Vancouver Island. The couple raised a large family up there, and the young bride became known as the "cougar woman" in later years, for shooting these animals.

When Dad's business in England was finished he planned to return home on the *Titanic*, which was touted by the English press as luxurious and unsinkable, but as his funds were getting low he opted for the *Carmania*. The *Carmania* picked up the survivors of that great sea disaster on her return trip.

Dad decided in 1915 to join the Forestry Corps because of his training as a lumberman, for there he could make the best contribution to the war effort. The standard pay for a private in World War I was $1.10 a day, 90¢ of which was assigned to Mother, leaving 20¢ a day for him to buy tobacco. The Patriotic Fund gave us an income of $37 a month which was added to Dad's contribution, making a grand total of $64 a month for our mother to manage the house and feed and clothe four little children.

During the time that Dad was in the army we boys went down to False Creek every morning to trap muskrats, using Japanese orange boxes as traps. We sold our catch to a friend of Dad's who owned the Whittaker Fur Company, getting as much as $1.25 for a muskrat skin, which was a fortune in those days. Mother would dry the skins on a board behind our wood stove in the kitchen. Sometimes they smelled a little high but it was the odour of prosperity so we learned to put up with it.

If I made a dollar I gave to Mother, and she might give me back ten cents, but I would never dream of keeping the dollar. Not one of us would think of going to Mother and asking her for money to buy candy.

Mother ruled our household in most matters, and it was her attitude to hard work and her fine character that made a lifelong impression upon all of us.

She was 5 feet 9 inches tall and absolutely square shouldered. Even at the age of ninety she could still bend down and touch her toes. Years later I remember her saying to my son, Gordon, "Straighten up, you're more stooped than I am," to which he had the quick wit to reply, "But Grandmother, you've had eighty years now to practise being tall and straight."

Even up the west coast you would seldom see her in anything but a clean white apron as if ready for work. On one occasion a girl who was married to one of the crew arrived at our camp wearing a very short dress, with bare legs and rolled-down socks. She was smoking a cigarette, and my mother said, "That young one looks worse than the women I knew up in Dawson—she shouldn't be allowed off the boat. She'll do this camp no good." That was what our mother was like.

In Dawson, there were three types of females—respectable married women, semirespectable single ladies, and sporting girls. Mother often praised the last for their kindness to her during the sleigh ride from Dawson to Whitehorse. She was honest enough to be broad-minded.

We have always been a very close family, principally because we were taught the need for each other. Today, children don't need their families because they are told at school and by their peers that society will look after them. They don't believe that they need religion either because there are other things, like money, to take its place. Our only sources of help were ourselves and our parents. Great harm has been done today by the belief that someone else should look after you. That only robs a man of his real character.

Mother taught us to pick up the heavy end of the stick and do more than our share, to be honest and deal with honourable people. No man would think of swearing in front of her. She set a standard for our behaviour that as grown men we truly wanted to uphold, and I would never dream of behaving as other than a gentleman in her presence—not just for her sake but for my own. Her faith in her sons was complete and no man can afford to lose that kind of affection.

She was beloved by many of our friends, and when she died H. R. MacMillan sent this note to Clarke: "I wish to express to you and your brothers my sympathy on the passing of your mother and to add my words of appreciation upon her great service to the Yukon and to the frontier of B.C. Her like will not be again."

After Dad returned from the Forestry Corps in 1916, he worked for a short time on the Coughlin Road, near Aldergrove, B.C. He dug out ship's knees, the huge knee-shaped roots that were so vital in the construction of the old wooden sailing ships, as they were used for right-angle joints connecting the deck beams to the ribs. In the summer of that year Jack and I went with him up to Clayoquot Sound where he had contractors falling timber for telephone poles. Occasionally he would let Jack and me fall one, and we helped him skin off the bark. In the Christmas holidays of 1917 I was sent up the coast to drive a team of horses pulling ship's knees to the railroad tracks. It was a few months later that an incident occurred which changed the course of my life.

Clarke, Jack and Earson were great students, graduating from high school with their matriculation papers. The only paper I ever got in my life was a diploma for two years of regular and punctual attendance at Sunday School. For ten years, starting when each of us reached age five, Mother walked us the twelve blocks to church, and in those years we rarely missed a Sunday.

I've wasted only six years of my life—the years between six and twelve when I went to school. Perhaps one reason I was not a complete failure is that I wasn't handicapped by other people's ideas, and had freedom from the age of thirteen to think for myself so that I could develop what little brain I had.

I came out of school a loser, my teachers having told me repeatedly that I was a hopeless student and would never learn to spell. The fact that I'm not a good speller doesn't bother me any more, although when I spoke at the Sloan Inquiry into mismanagement of government funds and the court clerk asked me to spell a word I had used, I blustered, "I'm making this speech, it's your job to do the goddamned spelling!"

One of my teachers told me that he had a dog at home who was brighter than I was, and I said, "Well, Sir, who did you get to teach your dog?" My answer was a protective reflex but I meant that I didn't think much of him either! That was the first time I ever looked down on someone who was in a superior position to mine. I had been taught to look up to my teachers—to revere them—but that man abused my trust and tried to make me out to be a worthless person. I never forgot that incident.

On one occasion the class was asked, "Does anyone know how to determine which is the right-hand bank of a river? Do you look upstream to the source or downstream in the direction the river is flowing?" I was the slowest boy in the class and sat right at the very back. Finally I put up my hand and answered, "You look upstream, teacher." She replied, "You're wrong, Gibson. Why did you say that?" I kind of smiled as I said, "I didn't know the answer but if I had been right I would have had one chance in two of being the smartest kid in your class."

Two weeks before examinations my class went up Grouse Mountain for a picnic. I was the biggest and strongest boy in my class so I was the leader of the group. My girlfriend and I wandered away in the snow from the rest of the kids to hide for half an hour for a little fun and loving. We didn't have brains enough to know that our footprints would lead the principal right to us. We were lying under a tree, and I guess we were trying to do what should come naturally, when a couple of teachers grabbed me as though I was a criminal and took her away. From what I hear, the kids are doing it today just the same as back then.

The upshot of this episode was that I was not allowed to return to school until I had apologized to the girl and her parents. I didn't go to see them; I just stayed away from school and missed my examinations. When I failed, my mother went to see the principal who, to his credit, never told her the story. He recommended I quit school, pointing out that I had very little scholastic ability. Mother agreed because she felt I would be too big to repeat the grade. My parents encouraged me to have some sense of myself by giving me work driving a team of horses to pull out ship's knees. Later in 1918, I joined Dad in Alberni, a strapping youth of fourteen nearly 6 feet 2 inches tall. My hands, feet and ears were so outsized that I was just this side of being downright homely.

God knows what would have happened to me if I had stayed at that school. I'm sure it would have handicapped me for the rest of my life as I felt so low in my mind. Not only had my teachers told me that I wasn't very bright but also that someone would always have to look after me—that I would probably starve to death if my father or brothers didn't keep me in food. I think I determined then that I would prove their judgement wrong.

Having started my life with such a great inferiority complex, I said to myself, "Gordon, you can't ever be second, you must try to be first when you can." Not for the reward but for my self-respect. For the rest of my life I would never accept being at the bottom of the barrel. I would have something that I could be in charge of even if it was merely a wheelbarrow. Put it down to ego, or perhaps it was truly pride, but I had to prove I had some worth. Nor was it just the idea of "challenge" which seems only to ask "could you"; I had to say "I will."

More than anything else I had the ability to start a project and get men to help me follow it through. Invariably, in any kind of work, there was one man with better qualifications than I had. I would promote him to foreman right away, merely watching him afterwards and moving on to another camp or another business. There wasn't one thing I ever did that I was as good at as the best man I had working for me, but if that man decided to quit, everyone knew the work would go on regardless.

I suppose I have some ability to manage people because I know what it is like to be on the other end of the stick. After my teacher's sneer about his dog I swore I would never tolerate abusiveness from anyone in my personal life or in my work. It's helped me avoid any real labour trouble, of course, and my brothers and I were always on the job five minutes before our workers and half an hour after they left. If there was a heavy end of the log we generally picked it up.

We always believed we were responsible to the people who were dependent on us: as captain of the *Malahat* I was responsible for ensuring that our men didn't drown and that they got a chance at promotion. I was responsible for their total well-being, and they became a part of me. But if a man fished against me in another boat, I tried like hell to catch more fish than he did. If someone started a logging camp and bid timber against me, I'd try to outbid him and certainly wouldn't co-operate with him. I always had to dominate.

God made people so that their first instinct is survival. The second instinct is self-esteem, which makes us take a pride in our work. My mother, my father and all my experience have taught me that the closer I am to doing right, the more successful I will be in my own mind and in the minds of everybody else.

If a man does a truly good act he feels better because of it but if a man does a mean act and knows it, he keeps remembering it and thinks less of himself. The regret drags him down. A man has to use common sense and obey the natural laws of the world. If you cheat you lose in the long run because all you have to sell is your confidence in yourself— and other people's confidence in you. And when you cheat you know that you didn't win legitimately. So the winning doesn't make you feel better, nor does it make you the person you really want to be.

The first time I got a little confidence was up the west coast when I found that I was able to run a little faster, jump a little higher than the others. I got more when I taught some Indians how to pole-vault. I had to recognize some individual qualities in myself that other people didn't possess before I found a little faith in myself.

By confidence I don't mean ego; I mean the ability to make reasonable decisions about one's own life. So many people seem to lack this kind of confidence and that is because they were taught improperly at school and lacked affection at home. My greatest luck in life was being thrown out of school young enough that I had to develop myself through taking a lot of hard knocks. Since then no one who has sneered at me has been able to make me feel insignificant.

With failure I am unhappy: that defines me right there. Most of my life has been happy because usually I have been successful, but sometimes that success has taken a few days or months or years to get. When I'm not happy, I'm never able to blame anyone else except myself. If I don't get done one day what I want to do, then I might lose a lot of sleep trying to plan what in Christ I'll do about it the next day.

Success can come in a lot of different ways. Every man must share in some fashion in the fruits of his labour. He can be paid with money or better working conditions; rewarded with extra courtesy, or promotion, or simply in self-satisfaction and thanks for a job well done.

Success has little to do with excellence—there are so damn many excellent failures. Ninety per cent of the men I've worked with were excellent at something that I was not, but they lacked the drive to succeed. Give me a man who is poor at doing something but has the desire to do it, for he will be ten times as good as the man who has the ability but lacks the desire or doesn't have as much.

There is only one person in this world that you must live with and impress, and that's yourself. If the rest of the world thought you were great and you went through life thinking you were a nobody, you would be a failure. God made every one of us a unit completely unto himself with an individual fingerprint and an individual brain.

I wanted to be liked and admired by women. Men were the competition. I had close male friends whom I respected for their character and their ability to work. But women provided me with warm companionship. I was always comfortable with them, in telling stories and in being a man. Women brought all the good things into my life. Of the fifty people I loved the most, respected the most, needed the most, forty of them would be women.

When I found a lady who was special, I pursued her like a hunter after a special set of antlers. Winning her was an accomplishment. Later our relationship would become a full-blown friendship. I don't know any woman who, according to the way I used her or she used me, wouldn't be considered a lady. I never wanted a masculine woman nor did I necessarily want a very efficient woman. I think I judged them by their ladylikeness and their depth.

I need a lot of affection. I'll fight for respect but I like to get affection voluntarily. A man can earn respect, but for some reason he can't earn affection quite as easily. Affection just has to come naturally.

There was once a man who was asked if he slept in his pyjama trousers or just in the jacket or if he slept in the nude. His answer was, "Depending on where I am, and who I am with." I think that love cannot be confined to one or to ten, and I've loved pretty well in ratio to the affection that was shown towards me and my need for it. My first wife, Louise, who died of cancer, was the mother of my children and went through a tremendous lot with me; and Gertrude, my wife, has sustained me in every way through my later years. But first there was my mother, whom I needed more than anyone—every man can appreciate that.

CHAPTER 2

Too much schooling is apt to make a man take for granted that what he was taught is right. Horse sense comes more readily to a man who has had to rely on natural instincts and his past experiences.

A ship's knee comes from a tree whose main taproot has been forced to form a right angle to the trunk because it cannot penetrate a layer of hardpan under the surface of the earth. In order to find which trees had such a root, Dad would scout around until he found a tree that was approximately 18 to 24 inches diameter on the stump.

We cut a face on each side of the root up to about 14 to 16 inches across by 4 feet out on the toe and 5 feet up the tree. After shaping, we cut away the main root at the end of the toe and any other anchor roots so that the tree would fall over, and lift its main root out of the ground. The rest of the tree was not wasted as we would square it into 45-foot-long timbers to make the big deck beams for the ships. All the lumber was then sent down to Victoria.

In 1917 when the contract for ship's knees was completed, Dad took on another contract to take out airplane spruce. This meant making our headquarters first on Trout River, and a year later at the head of Herbert Arm, halfway up the west coast of Vancouver Island. By this time I had been working with Dad for a couple of summers, but after I was kicked out of school I remained up the coast with Dad all year.

Dad had bought a boat in Vancouver called the *Meander* and that summer he and Clarke brought her up to our camp. The *Meander* was 36 feet long with a 14-horsepower Frisbee engine. Her cabin ran pretty well the whole length of the ship and contained cooking and sleeping quarters for six men. She was a fine boat, certainly one of the best in the district at that time, and was to be our only method of transportation for years. We used her until her engine gave out, after which we sold the hull to the Indians. Our only other connection with the outside world was the Canadian Pacific steamer, *Princess Maquinna*, which brought up all our provisions and occasionally a load of workmen. Many evenings we would go out on the *Meander* to unload our freight from the *Maquinna* and then make the fifteen-mile journey up the inlet to our camp.

About this time we were joined by Jimmy Livesley from Greenwood, B.C., who became Dad's foreman. He was a twenty-five-year-old ex-hockey player who had broken his leg and been forced to give up the sport. Even the army had turned him down because of this leg injury. We were all to become close friends in the following years.

Jimmy chose Captain Heater's Saltery and Fish Baiting Plant at Riley's Cove as one of our rendezvous on weekends. This was where the sealers and halibut fishermen would come in to get their herring bait, and Captain Heater was clever enough to bring out fifteen single, good-looking Scottish girls to this part of the world where there were ten men for every woman. That was the real bait for the fishermen, and the men from our logging camp couldn't get there fast enough on the weekends. I was a tyro in these matters but I'm glad to say I was rescued from such innocence before long.

The spruce trees we were to fall had to be over 6 feet in diameter in the butt so they could be cut into 24- or 32-foot lengths then split into six pieces before the heart was taken out. Only the outside 18 inches of round was used in the main structure of fighting aircraft for the air force. To split these trees we used a battering-ram technique. After the tree had been chosen, felled and cut into proper lengths, we took steel wedges 12 inches long and rammed these home with a 10-pound sledge hammer working from the outside to the centre and driving straight through. This would open a slight crack down the tree which we would split wide with strong wooden wedges made out of hardwood split from local trees—usually crab apple or yew. These wedges were 6 feet long and about 1 inch thick and sharpened to a point.

We made a tripod consisting of three round cedar poles which were lashed together, 24 feet high and about 6 inches on the butt and 3 inches at the top. From this, we hung a rope to which we tied a battering-ram weighing close to 200 pounds. It was made of a piece of hemlock or fir, about 12 to 14 inches in diameter and 6 to 8 feet long.

It took three men to operate the battering-ram, swinging it at the right height to hit each wedge. The hardwood wedges would be forced 2 or 3 inches deeper into the trunk with each blow until a 10-inch split appeared at one end. One man would walk the length of the tree using a steel spud—a bar 6 feet long with a sharp 2-inch chisel on the end—to cut the holding fibres. Gradually the tree's resistance was worn away and the two pieces fell apart. We would repeat the process until the entire tree was split along the grain and it was reduced into six equal parts around the central core called cants.

In those days there was no power to help us haul the logs to the CPR. Since we couldn't afford steam donkeys to take out the scattered spruce logs, we first tried two bull oxen from the same herd, yoked together forward and chained together aft to stop them from fighting.

Two bulls just naturally battle, and these goddamned animals were no exception. The young bull had never been allowed to breed because the big bull figured he should have complete rights in this department. I had driven them for about two weeks before the little one gored the old bull, wounding it so badly that it was useless for any work. It was impossible for us to log with just one bull so we made a great decision: we salted down the old bull, and later ate the son of a bitch. The younger bull was returned to the herd. Dad went to town and brought back a team of horses. That seemed to be the solution to our whole problem—something really modern! The horses were brought up on the *Maquinna*, loaded onto a float and towed to our camp by the *Meander*.

That first night the horses were turned out on the little pasture found at the head of most inlets in British Columbia, but the next morning our plans had gone all to hell: one of the horses had eaten poison parsnip which bloated him up to four times his ordinary girth and finally killed him. None of us had known about the danger of poison parsnip. Horses that are around this plant seem to know enough to leave it alone, but these animals were from the city and had lost their natural instinct. Again we were left with just one animal which could not pull our cants, and we certainly could not afford another team.

By this time we had made the acquaintance of another pioneer family called the Darvilles, who worked even harder than we did. Mr. Darville was a great mechanic, but like our father had absolutely no capital. He was operating a very small shingle mill, a one-machine affair run by waterpower. Everything in his mill was homemade, and he had even managed to build his piping out of lumber as well as constructing a water wheel to run the machine. Our two families worked quite closely together because we considered ourselves neighbours though we lived twenty miles apart.

Darville had made a small winch to take about 500 feet of ½-inch line on a single drum, powered by a 7-horsepower coal oil engine from Norway. It was just a hot head engine with no spark plugs that had to be heated up with a torch. He loaned this to us; I'm certain we did not buy it since no one had any money. Dad and I worked the engine along with our horse which was to pull the line fastened to the cants. The engine was put in gear and slowly pulled the cant ahead to the river. The horse helped on the way out with the load, stepping over the line and pulling it clear of the stumps. I must say that horse soon became a very capable logger. It would take fifteen minutes to pull out each log. Today this could be accomplished in half a minute.

The government took a long time to pay us for our aircraft spruce and Dad tried to cut down even further on the expenses since there was not enough money to pay our crew. We just carried on hoping that things would get better. One old fellow of about seventy was so forgetful that he would lose his saws, wedges and hammer one after another, and sometimes spent the rest of the day trying to find them. Dad tried in a dozen different ways to get rid of John but I guess the poor old guy had nowhere else to go.

He told us he didn't care whether or not he got paid because we were all the family he had.

Flash floods were common at the head of the inlets where the rivers ran down from the mountains. One night the water flooded so high through our camp that we all had to climb on the roof until the water receded the next day.

That winter a flash flood came close to ending my life. An Indian by the name of Bennett went with me one morning to go timber cruising about six miles up a river. It had been raining heavily as only it can in that area between the mountains, sometimes as much as 4 inches in one night. On one side of the river we came to a rocky bluff and so decided to cross the river on a windfall log that ran pretty well across the creek. Bennett, who was ten years older than I, went across first, jumping off in a few feet of water before making the shore. When I jumped off the log, I stumbled and was swept down the river to a sandbank about 300 feet distant. The river was running so fast that Bennett had to run down the bank and pull me out before I was washed away.

We decided to light a fire and make camp rather than try to cross the river again that night. By the next morning the river was 4 feet higher.

We spent the day going up and down the river trying to find a place to cross back, but twenty-four hours later the water had not receded an inch. We had had nothing to eat and were beginning to get a bit anxious. Bennett and I decided the best idea under the circumstances would be to cut down another big tree to make a bridge. Our only gear was a small cruising axe, and it took us until three o'clock to fall a tree 4 feet thick. It fell perfectly across the river. We were just ready to run across on it when the goddamned thing began to swing free and was carried away by the torrential water. I must admit we were feeling pretty bloody desperate by this time. By noon the next day the two of us managed to fall another tree and ford the river. Three days without food had passed since we had left camp.

Bennett had been carrying matches with him in a waterproof container and it was these matches and the little axe that really saved our lives. In those days there were no search parties to go out and pick a fellow up. You either got back on your own or it was the last that was seen of you.

By this time we had cut enough spruce to load a small barge, and we therefore arranged with a towboat to drop a barge for loading and return for it about a week later. The barge was not more than 160 feet long, with a steam donkey aboard and a one-drum winch for loading. We learned to rig a boom from the mast so that logs could be stowed aboard, and it was this experience that stood us in such good stead fifteen years later when we converted the *Malahat* to a logging barge.

The war came to an end in August and we received a letter from the government instructing us to stop logging. As a settlement, they granted us a concession which gave us all the spruce cants that had already been cut. These were lying in the water and it would have cost five times as much as they were worth to ship them down to Victoria. Dad decided that the only possible way to salvage any money out of the situation was to build a small sawmill and cut these cants into oar stock, the choicest straight-grained wood, strong but light, for the Vancouver market. V. M. Defoe, a boatbuilder, had offered Dad sixty dollars a thousand for just such a project, and we secured a contract to that effect.

Our headquarters were moved to Ahousat, on a beautiful, well-sheltered bay on Flores Island, where we started to build our mill and where we spent the next fifteen years of our lives in a real struggle for survival.

It was a tough life, not only for us but also for the crew who worked for us. Dad and I, a Chinese cook and ten men were living in a building built out of split lumber shakes. The shack was added to as lumber was cut in the sawmill.

I guess one of the reasons I survived as a kid was the fact that above anything else I had dominance, verbal and physical, over most of our crew. Everyone knew I could stay up later, work longer and run harder. God gave me all those things and with them the ability to recover from fatigue quickly.

CHAPTER 3

> *I am monarch of all I survey,*
> *My right there is none to dispute;*
> *From the centre all round to the sea*
> *I am lord of the fowl and the brute.*
> *Oh, solitude! where are the charms*
> *That sages have seen in thy face?*
> *Better dwell in the midst of alarms,*
> *Than reign in this horrible place.*
>
> William Cowper

This verse would come to me while I stood alone at the head of some desolate inlet. I had no companions of my own age except a couple of Indian boys who occasionally spent an hour or two with me. There were no white children, no white men—not even my father. That's when I started to ask myself if there was not some way I could beat my way out of an existence that was so lonely and dreary and fight to the top.

Nineteen eighteen was the year of the great flu epidemic when people all over the country died including many up the coast, and I guess the only reason none of us got the germ was because the cracks in the walls and the floor were at least half an inch wide. In some places a man could very nearly fall right through the floor, and on stormy nights the one calendar we owned stood out straight from the wall in the wind. No germs could survive in these conditions.

One thing we did know was how to make a little fun for ourselves. I remember having gone for a swim one night just after work and coming back feeling full of life. Most of the crew were resting in their bunks. The fire was fairly hot in the big round stove that had been made out of a gasoline barrel. I started to take some playful punches at Jimmy Livesley, challenging him to a boxing match without gloves. Jimmy was ten years older and I expect he was not in a very good mood. He got out of his bunk, squared off and hit me so hard I tumbled over the stove, burning my backside as I went ass-over-applecart. I got up and said, "Jimmy, when you get older and I get older I'll give you a licking for that." He stayed with us for forty years and thank God we never fought again.

A young friend of mine, Johnny Babcock, and I were the butt of many jokes played by the older men in the bunkhouse and we decided to play a trick on one of them. We placed a full pail of water on the top of a door that was partly ajar. We hid and waited for our victim to come in and be drenched with water, but instead, the pail fell down and hit him on the head putting a 6-inch gash in his scalp and knocking him completely cold. That little joke got me a good dressing-down as the poor man had to be rushed to the doctor. It also taught me that there are lots of practical jokes that aren't so very funny.

The split spruce cants that had been dumped into Trout River before the government ordered us to stop cutting had to be brought through a bit of open water to our new headquarters in Ahousat, using an Indian boat to pull a bag boom of a hundred logs encircled by boom sticks. David Jacks, one of the Indians, left with me for what should have been a two-day job.

It was about a twenty-mile tow; perhaps five miles were in outside waters where the seas could be very rough. Because it was winter and the weather could be changeable, we waited for a good day. We set out down the inlet hoping to swing around and go up the ten miles into Ahousat. Just as we were manoeuvring the point our boom broke up, most of it drifting onto a little island farther out to sea. Fortunately, we still had the boom sticks intact. Only one chain had been broken and we were able to fasten the ends together again. We anchored our boat and went ashore with a canoe to gather up the cants and pull them out to the boom. Nearly half of them had been recovered when the tide changed causing the seas to become much bigger. At about four o'clock an enormous wave swamped us and we were thrown back on shore.

It was bitterly cold and by this time we had taken a lot of abuse in the icy waters. We tried several times before it became dark to get back to our boat, but our clothes were soaked through and our muscles were becoming numb. The island was only about forty feet across and a couple of hundred feet long; it lay so low and had so few trees that a strong north wind blew the spray straight across it. David and I huddled together all night without food, fire or any sort of protection.

The next morning at daylight we were nearly unconscious. By luck, the sea had gone down and the tide had changed; dead tired and exhausted we managed to launch our canoe in the water and get back to our towboat. The air was so bitterly cold that it was now not a case of saving the cants but rather of saving ourselves. The Indian was in bad condition and I was very little better. We decided to cut our boom loose and head for home. David Jacks passed out on the two-hour run and died the next day from exposure.

Our social life was a little tough too. The solitude was hard to endure. One close friend of mine was trying to make enough money to go back to England and get married. One night he came to see me and said, "Gordon, I'm going to marry one of the Indian girls." He was a pretty good friend and I said, "Don't be a damn fool. I won't let you throw away all your plans. Why in God's name are you marrying her?" and he said sadly, "She's expecting a baby and it could be mine."

I argued that there was just one chance in a hundred it might be his, but he was so lonesome he seemed to want the honour. The health of the Indians then was poor, for tuberculosis was prevalent among them. Against all advice, my friend married the young lady, but his health could not stand up to the environment and he was dead within a year.

Our contract to cut spruce for oar stock came to an end in 1918 because there was no market for ordinary lumber. We had run out of money and opportunity. We had to let most of our crew go, even our foreman, Jimmy Livesley. Dad went to town to find extra work and I stayed up at Ahousat by myself.

Christmas came and there were no supplies. Jimmy came back because he couldn't find work in town. All we had for dinner was a goose that we shot and ate before it was cool. Things were so tough we had to get a box of shotgun shells on credit from the Indian store. Those shells were so valuable to us that we never took a chance of shooting a bird on the wing, and not even a bird running around on the mud flats. We would hide in the bush above high water and wait two or three hours until a flock of ducks or geese came in with the tide; then we would get them lined up figuring on at least three birds to a shell. Birds were plentiful, shells were scarce and money absolutely unknown. On one occasion Jimmy Livesley and I ate five mallards between the two of us. We had already eaten two birds each but I was so hungry that, eyeing the fifth bird keenly, I asked Jimmy if he wanted the last one. He declined rather generously, and I gobbled up that duck raising my total at one sitting to three.

The *Meander* reached the end of her days of usefulness when the engine wore out, and we sold her to an Indian. Our next boat venture turned out badly. We still had one horse and this sad beast was eyed by Mr. Millar, the head of the Indian mission run by the United Church. He had a boat, a homemade affair built by the Indians, with a 10-horsepower 2-cycle engine, and we decided to trade the horse for his boat. But I had not run that goddamned boat more than two hours when one cylinder started to miss and the engine died completely. We should have been warned by the boat's name, *Coffin*, for I found a hole about the size of my thumb in one of the cylinders between the water jacket and the cylinder. Being a kid I thought it was bad luck, and it wasn't until years later that I found out from one of the Indians at the mission that I had been traded a boat whose engine had been filled with iron cement because of corrosion from salt water. No wonder the damned thing lasted only two hours! But we had not lost any cash and the parson had his horse. I guess in those days even parsons had to be fairly sharp to get by.

By now we had lost both the *Meander* and Mr. Millar's boat, and we were getting pretty desperate because it was essential to have a boat to go anywhere at all. When Dad wrote that he was buying a steam tug I imagined something about 50 feet long with maybe 50 horsepower. It was a steam boat alright, but it was a 30-foot captain's gig. It was good for little more than a two-mile run to shore with a full head of steam as it needed to be constantly stoked with coal to keep it going.

The *Evelyn R* had been built in England to be carried aboard a British battleship. The day my Dad arrived with it was one of the most disappointing of my life, yet that little toy was to be our marine power for the next two or three years. It turned out to be hardier than I realized because you didn't need a dollar to run it—just hard work. It could be run with nothing but fresh water for the boiler and fir kindling and bark for the fire. Stoked up you could get about 10 horsepower out of it. My fondest memories of the *Evelyn R* are the few times when I towed logs in the evening after work. Occasionally one of the young ladies from the district would travel with me, and I admit that many a night I could have got in two or three hours earlier. In fact, there were times when the fire under the boilers went out completely.

When it became impossible to make money in the lumber business, we decided to try fishing for spring salmon. Clarke was up again for the summer, and we made a deal with an old Indian fisherman who spent the next few months with us. We fished steadily, loading our boat with wood and bark to keep the engines running. Clarke and I would get up at four in the morning, light the fire in the boiler, sail at five o'clock after breakfast and meet the Indian with his canoe off the beach. We would be at the fishing grounds before seven. When we started this venture, I was so delighted with our catch that I wrote to Mother telling her we would never be poor again.

On a few occasions we caught as much as 200 to 300 pounds of salmon which we sold for ten cents a pound, but in the stormy weather our average was not good—and the take had to be split three ways. That summer in the fishing business taught us a great deal, and when we bought the *Anchorite*, our brother Clarke was able to pay off her debt in one season through his marvellous fishing ability.

It was during this time in Ahousat that I met a very

lovely young girl whom I admired and wanted to get to know. She was on the staff at the Indian mission. Her family was strict, as was mine, and we weren't given much of a chance to be together. Social life at that time was limited and much less open than today. This young lady lived quite a distance away; in fact, to get to her house I had to make a one-mile boat trip, then a walk of about a mile through an Indian village and along a trail through the woods. I have been a pretty hard worker all my life, and with the ladies I've certainly held my own. One night I became very ambitious and, waiting until everyone was asleep, I crept out of our house. I rowed our boat a fair distance before I dared to start the engine. As I sneaked through the Indian village dogs started to bark everywhere. I followed the trail to her house, and stood below her bedroom window, looking up, and wondered if I had gone plum crazy. There was a ladder at the barn a couple of hundred yards away and I ran for it and put it up to the window. Happily, none of her family woke up and our friendship continued for over two years. But that was a hard way to court a girl. It meant staying up all night, rowing, running through a village with dogs barking at me, climbing a ladder, getting home again and working the next day as if I'd had a good night's sleep!

A few years later when I was sixteen my mother arrived in Ahousat. She was concerned that my brothers had received an education and I had not. Mother sent a very hard-earned $100 to the Lasalle Business Management School towards a correspondence course for me. The cost was $500. The books arrived in two big boxes: there was more reading in any one of the twenty-four volumes than I had managed in my whole life. But Mother was ever hopeful and for a few evenings at least, I tried to develop into the student she felt sure I was. It was usually eight o'clock at night before I had a chance to begin my homework. After starting work at six o'clock in the morning and putting in ten hours of heavy labour it was difficult to study for even two or three hours. I just could not grasp the subject at all. After a week I said, "Mother, it's no use. We'd better send the books back. I'm sorry but we'll have to lose that hundred dollars." Mother was heartbroken but she could see that the task was beyond me; so we returned the books in the same box with just one opened. The advertisement had said that satisfactory results were guaranteed. It might work for everyone else but I was certainly the exception!

Mother sent a nice letter to the company saying that they could keep the books and the $100 as we had made a terrible mistake. In about ten days a friendly letter came back from Lasalle saying that they had run into types like me before and in the long run we made the best students. All I needed was a little extra time and they were prepared to extend our payments. It was a three-year course but they would allow me to take six years because men like me with no education at all had become great business executives after taking their course. All the books came back a few days after their letter. But I was a stubborn son of a bitch, even in those days, so we again returned the books. A month passed and a collection agency from Vancouver sent a dunning letter that said I must continue the course and pay the remaining $400 because the books were now mine by contract. I guess that part of the agreement was in very fine print since we had never read it.

In any case, I made the first business decision of my life and wrote to the president of LaSalle:

Sir,

I read your advertisement and sent you a hundred dollars. I believe that your advertisement meant something and that you were an honourable firm. I find that you are neither. You may think I have wasted my hundred dollars, but I will tell you here and now you will never get the other four hundred dollars. I have got the maximum value out of your course and that is never to deal with unreliable, sheister outfits that will not stand behind their name.

They had guaranteed results, and from that day on I swore never to deal with other than honourable people. Perhaps Lasalle has changed its policy by now. Needless to say, I never had another letter from them and I am sure I have stopped a thousand people from taking that course by retelling this story.

CHAPTER 4

I'm at my best when I'm in trouble. God help the man who gets in my road if I'm in a bad enough jam.

In 1920 Dad formed the Gibson Lumber and Shingle Company with Tommy Atkins who had been one of his associates in the timber and real estate business prior to the war. Considerable improvements were made to our sawmill and two very modern shingle machines installed. We wanted to change over to the manufacture of shingles because the costs of shipping raw lumber to the Vancouver market were prohibitive—ten dollars a thousand at this time—and handling costs took over forty per cent of the selling price. The freight cost for shingles took about a third of the selling price and this allowed us two-thirds for our operation.

A shingle bolt is a rough piece of split wood that has been sawed into 60-inch lengths from a cedar tree after the tree has been bucked and split into pieces with wedges. These bolts were taken to our shingle mill and sawn down to either 16 inches for 3X shingles or 18 inches for perfection shingles. Eventually we manufactured only 18-inch shingles as they were worth considerably more on the market than the 3X, which were much thinner and of a poorer quality, although the transportation costs were the same for both sizes.

My duties included looking after a crew of Chinese shingle bolt cutters who had taken a contract to split shingle bolts on Obstruction Island about eight miles from our mill. Our living conditions were even tougher than the Chinamen were used to, and ten of them gave up after about six months. Dad went to town and got another set of contractors. This time they were Italians; only one of them could speak English.

We towed the shingle bolts from the island to our sawmill, kept their camp in provisions and scaled their shingle bolts. These were bought by the cord which averaged about twenty-eight bolts. To ensure that a uniform size was maintained, one cord out of ten had to be piled 4 feet high and 8 feet long between uprights. If the crew picked the largest shingle bolts for this making the average bolt in the other piles smaller, our company would lose money. Therefore, to keep everyone honest, the contractor and I would each pick a bolt and one of the Italians would measure them between the uprights. If the contractor picked a large bolt I would pick a small one.

On one of the scaling tests, a real row started when I threw in a couple of undersized bolts and the contractor threw in very large ones. One of the Italians took a swing at me. I was fine as long as there was just one of them having a go at me, but he called for reinforcements and in a few minutes the odds were eight to one.

We were in the woods about 300 feet from shore. My boat was tied up at the end of some boom sticks. All of a sudden I saw six of the Italians coming at me with pickaroons—iron spikes about 8 inches long mounted on axe handles. I made the greatest hundred-yard dash of my life; even so there was only about 15 feet between me and my closest pursuer when I got to the end of the second boom stick where my boat was moored.

By God, we were very natty on the logs though we were only kids and didn't have caulk boots. I can remember those bastards coming after me yelling at the top of their lungs. I turned at the end of the boom stick and started rolling back the logs. As each Italian came at me I would roll him into the water. When the six of them were in the water I had about half a minute to untie my boat and shove clear. I yelled, "You bastards will starve to death. You don't even know where you are."

The Italians had been working at the camp for about two months by now but because it had been dark when they landed, they had no idea where they were. I left them there for nearly a week and when I came back they were a very subdued crowd. Four of them had started out in a dugout, taken the wrong inlet and lost their way. We found them camped in an old Indian shack.

Those were really tough days for the men but things were just as tough for our family too. I am happy to say we settled our differences after this and that crew of contractors kept on for several more months. Considering the low standard of living, shingle bolt cutters were happy to make about five dollars a day. Incidents like that in my life hardened me and made me completely dependent on myself.

In the summer of 1921 Jack came to work in the sawmill during the school holidays. It was wonderful to have his companionship for two months. On the evening of his departure for Vancouver, Jack and I rowed over to Ahousat village in a canoe and walked over the trail to the post office at the Indian mission. As it grew dark we could see the lights of the *Maquinna* about ten miles up the channel. We picked up the mail from the missionaries and took it out to the ship. A north wind was blowing that night. I felt a little sad as Jack climbed the Jacob's ladder onto the *Maquinna*. With one quick stroke I turned my canoe towards the shore and headed back. I was to spend most of the next year by myself.

In 1921 there was a sudden recession in the lumber business and the price of 3X shingles dropped from $5 to $3 per thousand bankrupting the Gibson Lumber and Shingle Company. A man called Harrison paid around $500 to the receiver for the assets of our company and proceeded to Ahousat to take possession of our camp. Upon arrival, he presented me with the authority from the receiver to sell everything to the Indians that wasn't nailed down. I was alone, for Dad had left to find work elsewhere. We were so hard up I ran after Harrison demanding that he at least pay me some wages for being watchman. The son of a bitch sold everything the Indians had cash to buy—even the windowpanes out of my bedroom.

Jack went with Dad and his old friend, George Bower, to the Bank of Toronto. Mr. Bower gave a note to the bank for $2,500 on Dad's behalf, and with the money Dad was able to buy back all the remaining assets of the Gibson Lumber and Shingle Company. In later years we were able to pay off those creditors that had suffered a loss by our bankruptcy.

We contracted with a few Indians to bring in cedar logs which we bucked up with a drag saw. The Indians split these into shingle bolts at 35¢ an hour. By now we were sawing in the mill as well as using the shingle mill as often as we could. We didn't pull any money out, just enough for wages and our grocery bill. The hardware bill alone was crippling, often $200 to $300 a month because saw teeth and belts constantly need to be replaced. If we made $1,000 or $1,500 gross a month, chances were we just broke even. The great secret to our family success was that we never paid wages to ourselves.

After six years up the coast I got a chance for my first holiday when Dad gave me a hundred dollars for a trip to town. The fare was about twenty dollars each way and with the rest I had to buy a suit of clothes and have some fun. Our only transportation at that time was the *Maquinna*, which made three trips a month to Victoria and Vancouver. If I took a return trip travelling with the ship the whole way, I would have only three days in port. If I got off at Port Alberni and crossed the island on the Canadian Pacific train to Nanaimo and then caught the ferry to Vancouver, I could have thirteen days in Vancouver by missing one trip of the *Maquinna*.

Just as I was going up the gangplank Dad came over to me and said, "Gordon, how long will you be away?" I answered, "Well, Dad, three days in town doesn't seem like much after six years. I'll try to get back on the next trip—that means thirteen days." Dad took off his hat and with a look of great disappointment said, "Son, remember you only have a hundred dollars: never waste time and money too. Try and get back on that first boat." That was my three days' holiday!

It's just as well I didn't plan on thirteen days or I certainly would have been broke. Landing in Alberni and not knowing a soul, with just eighty dollars left in my pocket, I called a taxi and went to a place called the Old Goat Ranch on the outskirts of town. It was a combination bootlegging joint and dance hall with all the amenities thereto. That was where thirty dollars went. Then I went over to Vancouver and bought a suit with two pairs of pants for twenty-two dollars. A week later I was back in Alberni to catch the *Maquinna* home.

I'm reminded of the logger who was arrested for vagrancy. He had a stake of $500 when he arrived in town five days before. The judge asked him what he had done with his money. He said, "Well, your Honour, I spent a hundred dollars or so of it on liquor. I spent another couple hundred on some girls, and when I think it over, Judge, I'm willing to admit that I must have spent the rest of it kind of foolishly."

Whenever we could find extra hours, we worked on our first home, building it from the shell of an old store in Ahousat. When finished it consisted of a big living room with a dining room adjacent to the kitchen; upstairs were our parents' bedroom, a dormitory containing beds for the four of us and a few extra beds in case of visitors. The bathroom was very up to date for such an isolated area, having a toilet, bathtub and washbasin. Our family was very proud of this room and we showed it to everyone whether or not they had any use for it.

In the summer of 1922 my father had a heart attack. While rolling logs at the mill, he put too much strain on a peevee and it broke from the stress. I can remember guiding him up to the house: that was when the pains of angina pectoris started. He never really recovered his strength again.

Just before we rebuilt our mill in 1923 we were selling shingles through a broker named Timmins in Vancouver who settled up with us at the end of each month. It took ten days for his cheque to get to us, another ten days to reach our bank, and then ten more days for our notification of funds. One month our bank informed us that his cheque had not been honoured. That was a real disaster for us, because not only did we lose the little savings we had but we also owed a few thousand dollars in wages and bills. That cheque was for $2,500, which would have been worth well over $20,000 today.

Somehow Dad made arrangements with our creditors and borrowed enough to pay our crew. We never stopped working; we couldn't afford to give up.

We did, however, at least have a roof over our heads, and fuel and game were plentiful. Our mother carried on through all those blows. She had great strength and would simply not give in. In that little home in Ahousat, Mother and Dad instilled true family spirit in us and convinced us that if we stayed together we would succeed. They figured it out on the principle that four multiplied by four equals sixteen, but one multiplied by one is still one, and a thousand times nothing is still nothing. Dad was very philosophical: he said if we stayed together we could not be beaten. In the long run I am sure he was right. None of us would have succeeded individually. So we had lost only money and not each other. The closeness of our family has always kept us from the feelings of loneliness and desperation that seem so common now. We could always go to our parents or our brothers for help. That is one of the difficulties our wives have had: we were so close, they could never infringe on the fraternal side of the Gibson brothers. There is still a great bond between us which runs deep yet is seldom seen by outsiders.

We didn't have any crystallized business philosophy at that time but we would often hold discussions while we were towing logs and wondered how on earth people like the Weyerhaeusers had become millionaires because the margin of profit in logging was so minimal. But we would take on any job that brought in money. Clarke and Jack once went down to Clayoquot to pick up 500 cases of dynamite for the Sidney Mining Company, for which we got $100—a lot of cash then. We were also selling considerable quantities of lumber to that same mining company for mine props. We got $24 a thousand for lumber delivered to Sidney Inlet, which was about eighteen miles from our sawmill. Making a living was very tough and we pretty well lived hand to mouth.

Our cousin, Cecil Brett, the two Walker brothers and R. E. Brinckman asked our father if he would allow them to cut shingle bolts and sell them to our mill. They had been working as bookkeepers for the B.C. Telephone Company in Vancouver and were getting about $125 a month as clerks. Brinckman had been left a legacy of $10,000 worth of shares in Coates Thread Company of Scotland by his mother, who was a Jamieson of Irish whiskey fame. I guess these men thought they would make their fortune in the great outdoors. They arrived in the summer of 1923 with an old 6-horsepower boat called the *Cecic*.

They were not used to the hard work demanded by shingle bolt cutting, which involved falling great cedar trees and bucking and splitting them into bolts, nor had they the considerable skill necessary. But they were enthusiastic and worked hard at White Pine Cove. After a few months Brinckman was still determined to carry on, but his friends left for Vancouver slightly disillusioned and happy enough to go back to their sedentary employment. They had found that conquering the wilderness was beyond their capacity.

The more tenacious "Brinck" became a favourite with our mother, and he came to live with us almost as a brother and slept with us in the dormitory. He had been in an entertainment troop similar to the Dumbells during the war, and brought a completely new dimension to our lives. He was a music buff and a fantastic cartoonist. He was also an avid reader and had a standing order with a bookstore in Vancouver to send him novels as soon as they were available. It was through him that Jack was introduced to the operas of Gilbert and Sullivan, the books of Michael Arlen, P. G. Wodehouse and Arnold Bennett. Some evenings we had a singsong accompanied by "Brinck" at the piano or we listened to the gramophone. But most of the time we were too exhausted to do more than talk for a while before going to bed.

Brinckman was a man of artistic talent and imagination, but with his background he found it difficult to adjust to the rigours and isolation of the coast. He was a good worker, taking his turn at getting up in the morning to light the cookhouse fire, but like most Englishmen he had never learned to cook so we never trusted him much in the kitchen. But he tried hard in the sawmill, and though he was inept in many ways, he was such a gracious man that all of us were grateful for the warmth and new interests he brought into our lives. Many years later he got a job as a watchman at the Tofino Lifesaving Station and died there of pneumonia before the days of sulpha drugs.

Jack was the shingle packer and I was the shingle sawyer at our little mill. On a good day we could cut 20,000 shingles or a hundred bundles, which were loaded on the *Maquinna* for shipment to Vancouver. It took five bundles to make a thousand which was worth five dollars, or a dollar per bundle. We were fortunate if we made a shipment once a month because although shingles were the largest part of our production, we were also selling a little bit of lumber locally: 2,000 feet to one settler; 500 to an Indian; maybe another 2,000 feet sent up the coast to build some trapper's shack.

The *Maquinna* couldn't tie up close to our dock so we would load our shingles on a huge float 50 feet by 140 feet which we had bought up in Bear River, then we would tow it out to be anchored about a mile down the bay. We would pass the shingles from the float onto the 'tween deck of the *Maquinna* a good 5 feet up from the water line.

This would take four or five hours, usually at night, by which time we were soaking wet from the rain or salt water or sweat. My father and brothers—Jack, Clarke, myself and later Earson—would then make our way home, have a hot meal and fall into bed for a few hours' sleep before starting to operate the mill the next morning. After a few months of towing the float out to the *Maquinna* we decided to secure the raft to shore, and take a chance that Captain Gillam could bring the *Maquinna* in to us.

We drove in some piles and I reinforced the lashing, putting in stiff-legs—poles about 80 feet long—to keep the float offshore. We used cables that had been brought down from an old mine which had been started before World War I at the head of Bear River. Fastening 1,000 feet of this cable firmly to the float at each corner, we secured it to stumps on the shore. Now as we cut our shingles we were able to pile them on our float ready for shipment, eliminating that terrible towing trip. Because the engine in our boat had less than 10 horsepower we had to go down the bay with the tide and sometimes wait for six hours for another tide to make the return trip. Captain Gillam came in to look at our mooring and decided that he would risk bringing the *Maquinna* alongside it. She tied up to this float six times a month for many years, docking three times going north and three more times on her return trips.

CHAPTER 5

The people of the west coast of Vancouver Island, both native and white, were a special breed. We had a great camaraderie, especially in times of trouble, and without this none of us would have survived.

We attended dozens of potlatches given by the Indians of Ahousat. Some of the guests would come from as far away as Nootka. These gatherings were based on the principle that if I give you a present I rather hope that you might give me something better in return. It was a barter system based on honour.

Ten to twenty families came to a potlatch, a visit that lasted three or four days. They ate and drank all they could, each trying to outdo the other in giving presents and in being gracious. Lots of white men work on the same principle. The visiting chief would make a presentation to the Ahousat chief; then the best hunters and the best fishermen on each side would exchange gifts, and so on down the line.

For the most part the gifts would be practical ones such as a fine canoe or some smoked salmon. In the past the potlatches had become so extravagant that the federal government banned them to protect the Indians, for on several occasions a chief had been so overcome by the occasion that he had given away too many of his people's possessions.

The Indian longhouses were approximately 40 feet wide by 80 feet long. They were centred on 16-foot cedar poles with smaller 6-inch poles used for stringers along the side. Split shakes were fastened to the stringers. The walls were constructed from the best cedar split into 12-foot lengths, 1¼ inches thick and at least 12 inches wide. It was possible to see through the cracks in the walls since the boards didn't overlap. The dirt floor was raked smooth, and a little light came through holes made in the roof for the smoke from the fire to escape by. Three separate cooking fires were often needed for a big potlatch.

The Indian had little sense of time. A potlatch might start at eleven o'clock in the morning and still be going strong at noon the following day. Some guests would be sleeping while others were dancing, singing or swapping tales. It rained so much in the area that conditions were ideal for partying, which in later years consisted mainly of drinking. The Indians at Ahousat didn't drink heavily until they started to make their own home-brew, although that never made them nearly as drunk as the white man's whiskey.

The chief had more grace than many hosts today: he rarely said anything. He'd just acknowledge all the credit given to him, and if he was called the world's greatest hunter or warrior, he would just nod approval. Not like our politicians who never miss an opportunity to blow their own horn. In the heart of the Indian the only praise worth having was that of his peers.

An Indian on the coast would spend the minimum of energy to live unless he was very ambitious. Salmon was plentiful and easily caught then. In summer the fur seals would go to sleep on the top of the water, and an Indian could paddle right up to one and quite effortlessly club it and toss it aboard his canoe as he glided by. The Indians sold the skin and ate the carcass. Nothing was wasted. They were great clam eaters, and occasionally they shot a few deer. But fish made up ninety per cent of their diet and the oily smell seemed to permeate their hair and clothing.

God made things so easy for these people that they often didn't live as long as the interior Indians who had to walk a little farther and work a little harder just to find food and survive the elements.

Coast Indians spent much of their time in a canoe and developed extremely strong arm and shoulder muscles. Their canoes were made of cedar logs some of which were as long as 24 feet. An Indian war canoe could hold from twenty to thirty warriors. When our family arrived in Ahousat most of the canoes were small family vessels. The kloochman, or squaw, sat in the back using a steering paddle. A few canoes still had a figurehead nailed or bolted onto the bow—usually some kind of bird symbol sticking 2 or 3 feet over the water.

The first Indian canoe I owned was given to me by my father when I was fourteen years old. I had more pride in that boat than any we have owned since. It was so tender that if I put up my sail about 2 feet down from the first bow thwart, I could tack close into the wind and shoot back and forth across the inlet regardless of the wind's direction.

All the Indians sold their fish by canoe. The *Meander*, our first gasoline-driven boat, was a marvel to the native people. It was not long before many of them exchanged their canoes for power boats up to 30 feet long.

There was little sense of rivalry among these fine people; food was abundant, and there were plenty of women so they didn't have to fight over sex. Domestic arrangements were quite open and free; if a woman lived with a man she was considered to be married to him. No one made a fuss if a man was away for a month and his wife slept with someone else, but contrary to some ill-founded beliefs, Indian women were far less promiscuous than many of the white women in that area, and most preferred to stay within their own family group.

The few whites who lived with Indian women stayed on the outskirts of the village. A white man was accepted fairly well if he was an asset to the band in the sense of having given more than he received from the girl's family. But any who lived among the Indians was expected to work much harder than they did: a white man would not be accepted unless he had something outstanding to offer to the band as a whole.

The Indians were far more fatalistic than the white settlers. Perhaps this was because they knew that their numbers were dwindling. They did not seem to expect to live long lives and many of them died before the age of forty, some in childbirth. Many suffered from tuberculosis, constantly coughing and spitting up blood, and unfortunately they bought every kind of "canned heat" or wood alcohol to put down their throats in the belief that it would cure them. Over the years that we were at Ahousat the medical teams from the Department of Indian Affairs made attacks on this problem and finally reduced substantially the incidence of fatal tuberculosis among them.

We had few white friends during our first years at Ahousat, but by 1921 our small community had started to grow. Late one night we were called to pick up from the *Princess Maquinna* some missionaries who had come to help Mr. Millar, the head of the Indian mission at Ahousat. There was a Miss McCallum from Scotland, who was in charge of the housekeeping and food; Miss Chambers, the government nurse; and young Ella Herd, an assistant matron. Mr. and Mrs. Millar ran the religious end.

I was taking them by boat to the mission about four miles away when the engine broke down and we drifted in rough seas for two or three hours. Miss McCallum must have thought she had come to the end of the world because while we were tossing about in the storm-dashed water she said, "Couldn't we write a note and put it in a well-corked bottle? Maybe someone will find it one day after we have all drowned in this godforsaken place."

In spite of that inauspicious beginning our family came to know these people well during the next five years, and they were guests in our house at least twice a month for a dance or other social affair.

A couple of evenings a week I would spend a few hours at the mission. Ella Herd was about my age and we became fast friends. She carried scars on her face and on one side of her body as a result of a candle that had ignited a Christmas tree and set her dress afire when she was a child. But she was so likable and friendly that you soon forgot her disfigurement and saw only the lovely side of her face. She was one of the most charming girls I have ever known. We spent many evenings together in the mission home having tea, but for the two of us at our young age it was all rather confining. There was little opportunity to talk privately together so we would occasionally take a boat trip or a walk along the shoreline. Our friendship developed into warm and sincere affection. I still remember those times as some of the most pleasant of my life. Some years later, Ella went to Vancouver where she married.

We saw a lot of Miss Chambers, the government nurse, because she had become central to the life of our community. I was asked to take her by boat into one of the little Indian villages where she made her rounds. One morning she found a mother well into labour with her first child and we took her aboard to rush her to the mission. Halfway down the run, Miss McCallum calmly came forward saying, "You can slow down now, Gordon, it's a girl."

The Ahousat community started to grow with the arrival of a family from Los Angeles in 1923. The father was a great promoter and one of his gimmicks was to sell shares in a copper mine adjacent to our sawmill, half of whose profits were to be donated to a religious group in Los Angeles. In fact, he hustled money from his parishioners in that city for shares in the mine, and had the happy arrangement of being the sole benefactor of God's share of the profits. He sent his family up the coast to Ahousat, and to hear them tell the tale, that copper mine sounded a little too rich to be true.

When funds from his congregation ran out the children came to work for our family. Emily, the daughter-in-law, was a tremendous help to our mother. All of them were endowed with great buoyancy and optimism, qualities without which no one could survive up that coast.

Mr. and Mrs. Millar of the mission ultimately retired in 1925, to be replaced by a Mr. Jones. He was all out for high moral standards and against any liquor and he fought a great fight lest any faithful fall into sin. I remember one night an Indian boy of about fifteen had scrambled around the eavestroughs on the second storey of the boys' dormitory and was caught entering the girls' sleeping quarters. The hair-raising climb was worthy of a skilled mountaineer: the boy had to jump from one roof to the other and then slowly pull himself up hand over hand to reach the next building. The young lady must have been his accomplice since all the windows opened from the inside, so that there was little likelihood of rape. Mr. Jones wanted to send the young man to jail, but I urged that instead of being locked up he should be given a medal for his initiative!

Every year we had a sports day on the sandy beach at

Clayoquot for the Indian and white families of the area. One year Mr. Jones and our family arranged to hold the festivities in Ahousat on the agreement that there would be no drinking allowed whatsoever, for alcohol was not permitted on Indian reserves.

One of our guests was a man who worked in a cannery. About two o'clock in the afternoon we noticed that he was more than a little under the influence. I helped him to his boat which was moored about a quarter of a mile away. He was so drunk that he fell off the dock into the water and I had to pull him out and put him to bed.

The sports day had been most successful but Mr. Jones decided he would have to call in the Mounted Police and charge this man with drunkenness. I attended the trial at Tofino as a witness. Mr. Jones put forward his case saying that the man had been drunk and had fallen into the water. Worse still, he was guilty of being drunk on an Indian reserve which was off limits to the whites then.

The defendant was a young Norwegian who could speak very little English, so on his behalf I took the stand and told the judge that as far as I knew the man had just been ill. I told him that I had not smelled any liquor on his breath and had merely given him my arm to help him back to his boat. I had noticed no sign of intoxication, and he had gone to sleep very sweetly with no complaint.

In his summation Judge Gobal said something like, "Mr. Jones, I see nothing in your evidence to prove that this man was drunk and as long as the man can walk, albeit with assistance; if he can fall into the water and get out again; use no abusive language; and allow himself to be put to bed; I cannot find against him. I believe you have been very narrow-minded." Then he turned to me, "As for you, Mr. Gibson, the whole evidence in this case makes me believe that you're using the truth very carelessly in favour of the accused."

Even if things were pretty tough up the coast we knew how to enjoy ourselves in simple ways. We had built quite a nice home and danced almost every Saturday evening in our big living room with the ladies from the mission. Occasionally we would go by boat to Tofino twelve miles away to enjoy a little company there. If it was a rainy, stormy night a dozen of us would crowd into the little boat cabin and have a rousing singsong while someone accompanied us on the accordion. We usually took a few mattresses with us and if the weather was good on the return trip, everyone would lie out on the afterdeck and sleep during the two-hour run home.

On the way back from one of the Tofino dances I remember making a date with a young girl who was staying at George Nicholson's hotel. After taking her to the hotel and saying my good-byes, I chatted with a few of my friends who were sitting around in the lobby. Before leaving, I took a chance and slipped the bolt on one of the windows on the first floor. Later, certain that everyone was asleep, I sneaked in the window and stole upstairs. I suddenly realized that I had made the mistake of not asking her room number, so I crept along the hall and picked a door that seemed about right. Opening it very quietly and crawling on my hands and knees over to the bed, I felt about the covers to make my presence known to the young lady. In about one minute the room was filled with confusion and profanities. I shot down the front stairs with the Chinese cook after me screaming blue murder.

My friend Jimmy Livesley was sleeping on a couch in the lobby and I quickly crawled in behind it. George Nicholson got up and bawled the hell out of Jimmy, at first believing him to be the culprit. He looked everywhere for the troublemaker but never thought of searching behind that couch. I waited until everything had quieted down and George had gone back to bed. Then I tried again, stealing up the stairs without a sound, absolutely certain that this time there would be no more mistakes; but when I got to the head of the stairs I ran straight into George who was looking damn suspicious. That was the end of my fun that night. I made it out the window in three jumps, ran down to my boat, and ended up spending the night in my own bed, quite alone.

During the Depression years Dad had us cut lumber to build a sidewalk two planks wide running a few miles up the shore of the inlet to a hot spring behind our house. We then cut a trail and put the planks through to the outside beach.

In the summertime the *Maquinna* would bring groups of tourists up the coast, arriving at our place about six in the afternoon. All of us young bucks were tickled to death to take the tourists for a walk to the outside beaches, often building a campfire for a singsong. Naturally, we were most anxious to escort any of the attractive young ladies. After the walk we took everyone back to our home for coffee and a dance.

It was during these years up the coast that our mother's firmness of character was shown. I've never seen a man with nerve enough to say a word out of place, or to take a drink in front of her, because one look from our mother and the biggest of them would shrivel up and acknowledge that he had met his match.

CHAPTER 6

Success would be my price. Success, not money, and not anything associated with that word other than something within that said, "Gordon, your reach must exceed your grasp or what's a heaven for?" So I have my price—feeling good about myself. I've got to win.

In 1923 we made our first big venture into the fishing business. My brother Clarke bought the *Anchorite* from the Sooke Packing Company of Victoria for $2,500, the amount of money Dad had inherited from his father's estate. We put $750 down and thereafter paid $750 a term until our debt was cancelled. The *Anchorite* was 52 feet long with a heavy-duty Corliss engine that provided three times the power we had in any other boat. The *Anchorite* carried good luck. Clarke took her out for the fishing season the first year and made a couple of thousand dollars. In the summer she was a fish boat and in the winter we harnessed her for jerking logs out of the woods and towing them to the sawmill.

We were running a small logging camp at Ahousat then, with a two-drum donkey run by steam and the smallest crew possible. Jack was fireman, engineer and boom man and I was chief logger and whistle blower in the woods. We had an Indian who was three-quarters blind and his squaw cutting wood to steam the donkey, which was on a float held offshore by a stiff-leg. They were paid five dollars a canoe-load which gave us sufficient fuel for a day. Clarke and Dad ran the sawmill together with a few Indians, the Baldwin brothers and Brinckman.

In the morning while the steam was getting up on the donkey engine, big coils of ½-inch haul-back line would be yarded off the drum by Jack. I would pull the line onshore recoiling it 500 feet before moving up the hill about 400 feet to thread the line through the two large haul-back blocks.

The line was then drawn back to the floating A-frame and attached with the choker to the main hauling line.

Jack would return to the donkey, and I signalled to him to go ahead on the haul-back to send the rigging out to the woods. After setting the chokers on the logs, I waved to him to pull them in. When the logs were in the water Jack removed these chokers and sent the rigging back to me. It was a two-man show the way we did it but today it would require a crew of at least six men to get the same number of logs because we worked longer and harder. A day's cutting was not finished until we had enough logs for the next day's run at the sawmill.

Every second or third day, after we had cut from 5,000 to 10,000 feet of wood, we would tow our logs back to the sawmill getting in after midnight. This went along fine for about six months until one morning after a tremendous storm from the north we arrived at camp to find that our float had been so weighted down with ice that it had turned upside down and our steam donkey had dropped to the bottom in 50 feet of water. We didn't have time to try to salvage it then as that would have been a two-week job but continued by logging only those trees that could be felled with their tops near the water's edge.

Jack and I would leave the sawmill by six in the morning with two fallers, chokerman and deckhand and have breakfast aboard the *Anchorite* on the way out to the woods. The fallers would be put ashore in a canoe, and the deckhand would throw a heaving line to the chokerman on shore so that he could pull in our cable and fasten it to the fallen tree. When our line was fast, we would go full ahead with the boat, getting up our speed to about 2 m.p.h. so that the cable would tighten sharply. We jerked the logs free into the water with the momentum of the *Anchorite* which we loaded with 10 tons of rock for ballast. Occasionally we would break our towline if the logs became snagged behind a rock or some other immovable object, and everything would come to a sudden stop. At those times you had to be braced or you would fall flat on your face on the deck.

We never knew who owned the timber and in those days I must admit we did not much care. That year a couple of well-intentioned forest rangers came up the coast, and when they found us logging in this fashion they imposed a penalty which seemed heavy at the time—about $1.50 per thousand logs!

Once we had filled our contract for lumber in Barkley Sound we set to work pulling up that damned old donkey. The lines to the float were still attached to a tree in the woods so we knew exactly where the donkey had gone down. A 1-inch line was made into a cowboy's lasso and dropped down around the donkey engine, then we tightened it up by reefing it onto the boat. We took a scow alongside the *Anchorite* and ran two 12-inch by 12-inch timbers between them so that we could tighten the float cables a little at each low tide. There was a difference of 10 to 12 feet between high and low tides. At the first low tide we winched in the cables attached to the steam donkey and then waited until high tide to raise the donkey 12 feet. The lines were tightened at low tide and the process was repeated as we gradually moved in towards shore. It took ten tides to bring the bloody engine within 20 feet of the surface. Then we towed it eight miles to the sawmill and used our steam winch to right it onto its sleigh while it was still in the water and to pull it onto the beach with a ten-to-one purchase on the line. Apart from the smokestack being smashed, the machine was as good as ever. Even the water glass in the steam gauges was unbroken, and before another week passed we were again ready to log.

If we had not harnessed the *Anchorite* as a logging machine to pull out logs from anywhere along the coastline, our little enterprise at Ahousat would have gone broke and a number of people would have been out of work. We had a lot of orders on hand to cut fish boxes for packing salt herring to China and because this was the only income we had in the winter it was vital to keep a supply of logs going to our little mill. In the summer we fished and ran the sawmill.

In the fall of 1924 for the bargain price of $1,000 Dad took over the assets of the Ucluelet Sawmill. This was a water-powered mill owned by the Sutton Lumber Company, itself a subsidiary of the Seattle Cedar Company, and we were able to increase the number of salt herring boxes that we could manufacture. We didn't have an edger in our original sawmill which we needed for making fish boxes; this purchase brought us one as well as a carriage and head and top saws.

Although we had no money we were considered well-to-do by local standards. Our neighbours were more broke. The Darville family, who were using waterpower in their sawmill, were delighted with the excellent water turbines that we gave them as we had no use for them in our mill.

The dog salmon or chum came after the pilchard runs in the spring and summer and could be caught in shallow water with a very inexpensive net about 400 feet long and 40 feet deep. The Indians fished for them in their seine boats, and a crew as small as three were often able to catch 1,000 salmon twice a day. Sometimes they got a full load with one set of their nets. The Indians were making about ten cents a fish which was very good money in those days.

At first the dog salmon was sent to canneries in Nootka and Barclay Sounds to be salted and canned for export so in the off season we began to manufacture salmon boxes to supplement our larger production of herring boxes. We got sixty cents for a herring box and seventy-five cents for the slightly larger salmon boxes which were 4 feet by 2 feet by 1 foot high and held about 400 pounds.

After a year we gutted and cleaned our own fish. The first catch of salmon was landed fresh on the dock around noon and more loads would be brought in until eight at night. About 10,000 to 20,000 salmon would be cleaned and salted down before the next morning by twenty to thirty women from the village. This threw a little prosperity into the community during the winter months.

After the herring had been caught it was cured in big canvas tanks in a hundred per cent salt solution for six days before being drained, packed in salt and shipped out on the *Maquinna*. The herring was a staple for the Chinese coolie class, and the salmon was exported to the Japanese who considered it a delicacy.

We also built a general store containing a post office and we started a contracting and pile driving business. Consequently, we diverted our sawmill from the manufacture of fish boxes to the production of structural timbers and planking for fish plant construction.

In 1925 unusually large schools of California sardines or pilchards started to hit the west coast of Vancouver Island. A pilchard is a little bigger than a herring and has a very high oil content. In December of that year we received an order from Northwest Fisheries for 20,000 feet of fir lumber for scow construction and this was the first indication to us of the pilchard reduction plan boom that continued until 1929. We did very well supplying lumber for construction, and pile driving for pilchard plants over the next four years. Our competition from Vancouver and Victoria were unionized so that we were extremely competitive. We took on all contracts by simply adjusting our price to whatever the market would bear. With Jack and Earson running the pile driver rig we supplied and drove piles for the construction of the Northwest Fisheries reduction plant in Matilda Creek, logging the piles ourselves for ten cents per lineal foot. We charged twenty-five dollars per day for the labour of three men, the pile driver and steam donkey, and we supplied all the lumber for the project at twenty dollars per thousand board feet. We thought we were doing well at that because we also got lunch at no cost! We drove an average of thirty piles per day at what I think is the all-time west coast record for low-cost work.

In 1925 our family took contracts to build three plants—Shelter Arms Fisheries, Riley's Cove Fisheries and East Bay Fisheries.

At the Shelter Arms Fisheries we learned a very special lesson. We owned our own 1,600-pound pile driver and had it ready to start on the job but on landing at the site we found a 2,800-pound pile driver hammer that had been abandoned some years before. It was rusty, but we cleaned it up and found that it could be used in the same leads as our own hammer. We were earning five dollars a pile and it made sense to trade our light hammer for the heavy one so we would take advantage of the extra speed in running the pile driver.

After our contract was over, the owner of Shelter Arms

Fisheries found out that we had used this abandoned pile driver hammer for the 500 piles we had driven and docked us a dollar a pile—$500.00.

It is a strange road that has no turning, and I waited to get even. Less than six months later a fishing boat belonging to the same company had made an unusually large catch of 100 tons. The boat was equidistant from their plant and ours, about twelve miles, and because of a heavy fog the fish boat captain was unable to locate their scow and tender to put his fish aboard.

So that the entire catch would not be lost, we went alongside with our scow, which was large enough to carry their excess 75 tons. A skipper was not allowed to dump excess fish and had to turn them over to another scow if he could not carry the entire cargo to a reduction plant. If it had not been for the memory of the $500 cut from our pile driving contract, I would have simply given the skipper the use of our scow for nothing, a favour I would have granted to anyone caught in this way. Instead I made a deal with the captain that we would take the excess fish to our own plant and pay his crew $3 a ton, which was the full price that they would have received from the Shelter Arms Fisheries. That excess fish was worth $25 a ton to the plant after they had been processed. The captain and the crew suffered no loss and the owner of Shelter Arms Fisheries never knew about the incident. But we recouped that $500 loss four times over.

The owner of East Bay Fisheries tried to impress us young yokels with the money he had, but we soon found it difficult to get any money out of him while we were constructing his plant. He kept telling us to wait until our bill was over $1,000 as anything under that amount was too small to be bothered with.

The night we tendered our third bill he invited my brothers and me to play bridge with him. He had trained his wife well, and just before we opened with our first bid she said, "I don't know whether you have heard but my husband is considered one of the best bridge players in the world." We found out later that he was a fourflusher in business as well as in cards, and couldn't pay us for our work. When we asked him for an advance of $50, he said he didn't have anything smaller than a $100 bill. Clarke and I began to get a little suspicious, figuring that he was bluffing. It took months to get any money out of him and every dollar was hard fought for.

This contract cost us a lot of time and money but we learned a very important lesson. Talk is cheap and doesn't put food on the table.

It was a lonely life for most of the men who worked on the construction of these plants since few women lived near the sites. In one of our camps the husband of a very attractive young woman was continually being sent out by his boss under one excuse or another, usually to scout for new sites. Invariably he would be away for at least three days.

On one occasion his boat developed engine trouble and he came back two days early for repairs. When he returned to his house he found that his wife had his boss for company. The outraged husband told him, "Get out of that bed," and the boss replied, "Would you just step outside the door while I put on my clothes." That upset the poor fellow even more and he threatened to get a gun and shoot the boss where the bullet would do considerable damage.

The husband rushed over to my cabin and shook me awake. "Gordon, the boss is in bed with my wife and I'm going to kill him." I became quite nervous but managed to calm him down. To be honest, I was glad that he had not arrived home a day earlier!

I am quite certain that he would have indeed shot the man if I hadn't said, "Look here, he is no more guilty than a dozen men around this camp and I don't think you want to shoot all of us."

He saw my point, divorced his wife and later married a very fine girl.

In the spring of 1926 the pilchards were plentiful around the north end of Vancouver Island, near Cape Cook on an inlet called Ououkinsh. Dad, Clarke and I took the *Anchorite* about a hundred miles up the coast to Ououkinsh to look for a site to build our own fish reduction plant. While we staked the ground I dreamed of how rich we would all become.

When we arrived home again we made our plans to build

the plant, the whole family sitting around the kitchen table. We decided on the type of machinery, the design of the plant, the fish boats we would use—carrying on for at least two and a half hours. Everyone was fired up with enthusiasm.

In our minds we had the plant all ready to operate that next year, but my mother being the practical one in the family at last got tired of hearing all our gab. She had been listening to plans like this for years; she stood up at the end of the table shaking her apron and said, "You all make me tired. Here you sit around talking about spending $100,000 and I know you are well over $99,000 short. Let's wash the dishes and get to bed."

Mother was right, but not for long. That same year, although we did not build at Ououkinsh, we did build a fish reduction plant at Ahousat. Until then we had been contracting for other companies. We knew that we would make a lot of money if we could get into the business for ourselves. Robert Grosse, the president of Grosse Packing Company, was prominent in the fishing industry in those days, and seeing the tremendous possibilities he came to us with a proposition that he supply the machinery and we supply the power, the site and the fish. It was a fifty-fifty deal and in 1926 Robert Grosse formed a company with us known as the Matilda Creek Fisheries. Construction of a fish reduction plant started immediately. Clarke was appointed the general manager while Earson, Jack and I were to run the boats. I had some experience because the season before I had been learning the business as a deckhand—the only white man in a crew of eight—on our Indian fishing boat, and in 1927 I became a skipper.

The cook on the boat was an Indian named Shamrock, one of the real old-timers who didn't bother to wear any gumboots but worked in his bare feet. He weighed about 250 pounds and was a most jovial man. His cooking could be called tasty. It was a casual occupation with him, and cleanliness was just a side issue. We all chipped in for our meals which consisted of potatoes, boiled fish and sometimes fried fish; for a change, perhaps a little deer meat which we shot along the shore. Bacon and eggs and grub that cost money we simply forgot about. It was a fine diet once you got used to it, and we especially enjoyed boiled fish cheeks which we considered a real delicacy.

The *Anchorite* was too small to carry any substantial amount of fish so we also used a boat called the *Gibson Girl* to tow a small scow. She had a 20-horsepower engine, the same as that in the *Anchorite*.

The fish travelled in schools and could be spotted by the flash of their tails flipping on top of the water or by the dark shadow that they made under the surface. The schools varied in size from 100 feet across to 2 or 3 acres. The fish would travel at a speed of about ¼ mile an hour while feeding, and 5 or 6 miles an hour when the water was clear of plankton.

After deciding on the speed and direction of the school a skiff man would jump into the small boat that had been tied to the stern of the seine vessel. If the fish were moving slowly the seine boat would circle them with 2,000 feet of net suspended from a ½-inch cable about 600 feet deep. If the fish were travelling fast we would go alongside or just a little ahead of the school and set our net up forward in a huge circle. The ½-inch cable at the bottom of the net was slowly pulled in when the boat had completed the circle back to the skiff.

The idea was to make a kind of basket or purse so that the fish could not dive under the bottom of the net and escape. As the cable at the bottom of the net was tightened the fish struck the net, and finding no escape were forced to turn back up to the surface. As the skiff made its large circle the two top lines were fastened to the ship to make a complete barrier. Both ends of the purse line would be taken into the winches through a davit with two blocks on the side of the ship for fair leads to the drum. As the net was pursed in, the fish were forced up towards the surface into the bunt, a heavier-gauge net that could carry up to 100 tons of fish caught in a good set. A fisherman who pursed in rapidly could trap a school of fish in ten minutes, which at five dollars a ton gave a fair return.

The fully loaded ships would then head for their plant which might be ten miles or a hundred miles away, docking alongside a wharf having a big marine leg—a high-speed vertical conveyor with lots of buckets. The fish would be shot out of the hold with fire hoses into the buckets, which held 20 pounds of fish apiece. Within an hour up to 100 tons of fish would be in holding bins.

At our plant, the fish went from the bins into steam cookers at a rate of 5 tons an hour, gradually moving through 50 feet of cooker before being dumped into a press. The water and solids went through a machine much like a meat grinder. The solid residue would be shot out of the grinder after all the water and oil had been squashed out. The residue liquid was pumped into big settling tanks where the oil could be extracted from the watery emulsion by flotation. From each ton of fish 30 to 50 gallons of oil were extracted. The oil was shipped around the world to make soap and paints; the solids were put through big driers and processed as fish meal for cattle.

In the winter of 1927 we returned to logging and helped build more pilchard plants up the coast both for our own family and for other people. The following summer we went fishing for pilchards and acquired another boat called the *Walter M*, which we chartered from Vancouver and which would become our pride and joy for the next year. It had a 50-horsepower Atlas Imperial engine. Our crew consisted of my two brothers Earson and Jack, one Indian boy, Herbert Peter, and Ray Baldwin and Wallace Grant from Tofino. I was a skipper with just one season's experience, and most of the others had never fished before in their lives. We were certainly the youngest crew up the coast but what we lacked in knowledge we tried to make up in hard work, and we usually caught our share of fish.

In 1928 we took a step forward and chartered the *Talmasso*. She was one of the fastest boats on the coast, carrying about 75 tons with a 110-horsepower diesel engine. She was twice as big as our other vessels and could travel about 10 knots an hour. We rounded out our little fishing fleet with another boat, the *Roseanne*, which carried about 60 tons.

The galley on the *Talmasso* was fitted with sliding, heavy hardwood-frame windows for fresh air. On one trip a man called Billy Luckovitch was acting as cook. One day when he lifted the window it dropped down into its slot very neatly biting off the end of his thumb. Now losing an inch off the end of your thumb when a ship is at sea is not very serious but it can be very painful and unpleasant. We took about half an hour to patch up Billy's thumb and then I said to him, "Come into the galley and show me how in the hell that happened." He gave me such a good demonstration that in lifting up the window and showing me what had happened to his right thumb he lost control of the frame and it came down and took off the end of his other thumb! Although I do love a well and enthusiastically told story, I think the poor guy got carried away in this instance.

Up until 1928 most of the pilchard fishing had been done in inside waters where there is little swell. Now the boldest skippers of our group ventured into open seas, beginning at the mouth of the inlet and then fishing progressively farther into the open ocean to get bigger catches of pilchards.

When the pilchard season came to an end that year I went with an Indian crew to learn how to seine salmon while Jack, who had been engineer on the *Talmasso*, went ashore to take over the store and become the postmaster at Ahousat. We managed to build up our finances a little by being prepared to do anything. We logged and ran our mill in the winter, as well as shipping salt salmon to China, and we went fishing for pilchards in the summer. In October 1931, just after the equinox, came a solid seething mass of pilchards about 2 or 3 miles wide ranging from one end of the coast to the other. There were literally millions and millions of tons of fish and every boat in the area loaded up.

One night a storm blew up, and no boat dared to venture out for three days. When they did, there was not a fish to be seen. Fortunately, it was the end of the season and most of the fishing boats had made a good profit. In fact, the season had been so successful that we decided to invest more capital in our operation over the next year.

The fall storms came and all the plants closed down for the winter. In May 1932 we started to get ready for the fishing season, which started about the first week of July. We had spent at least $20,000 to get ready: nets were prepared and hung, boats chartered and crews brought in.

July passed, then August, and no fish came. There were a couple of hundred boats with 1,000 or more crew aboard as well as 400 men at thirty-five fish reduction plants scattered along the coast from Barkley to Quatsino Sound. The government sent out its fishing patrol boat, the *Givenchy*, with six skippers including myself, to locate the pilchards. We ranged as far south as the Columbia River, zigzagging back and forth, making about a 1,000-mile run searching for the fish. We didn't find them, and pilchards have never come back to the West Coast in quantities that are economical to harvest. According to Indian legend the "tsepin"—the Siwash name for pilchard—disappeared for long periods, and are one of the continuing mysteries of the sea. There is no explanation for the summer of 1932.

It was a tragedy for the industry. Our company could not pay its debts and Jack called a meeting of creditors, some of them itching to foreclose, but the credit manager of Shell Oil, Neville Skill, stood behind our company. Shell Oil held the biggest account and Neville talked the rest of our creditors into waiting another year to give us a chance to earn some money. For the last thirty years our company has bought only Shell Oil products in gratitude for Neville backing us when we were really down and out. A year or two later our bills were completely paid and we were ready to start again. Robert Grosse retired after the pilchards stopped running and we continued the business by ourselves.

Through the following years fishing continued as one of our interests and by 1940 we had built a cannery and a reduction plant in North Vancouver called North Shore Packing, not for pilchards but for herring caught in the winter.

We had some wonderful skippers during our fishing days; one of the leading was Walter Carr, a self-made man who had come as a boy from a Mediterranean fishing village. When I first met him in 1931 he was shovelling fish on contract out of the hold of a ship into an elevator. A year later he had a crew together and was skipper of a very successful boat. It was not long before he owned his own vessel and contracted with our North Shore Packing Company. He became our top fisherman and was a great credit to both himself and our company. Other great captains we knew during our days with the *Otter* and the *Malahat* were to become legendary figures: Dan Backie, Charlie Clarke, John Dale, Bill Olsen and Harold Arnett.

Dave Wilson, one of the best cannery men and managers the coast has ever known, was our partner and manager of North Shore Packing. Unfortunately, almost every year there were strikes in the fishing industry and inevitably our company had labour trouble. Each year we lost half our season because of strikes, and the fishermen lost half their season, too. Soon they couldn't make money and neither could we, and when an opportunity came to sell our cannery we decided to get out of the business. In any case, we were being forced out of North Vancouver because some people objected to the little smell associated with our plant.

Around fish plants a little smell is a sign of prosperity. As Will Rogers once said when someone corrected his grammar, "I have noticed a lot of people who ain't using the word 'ain't' ain't eating very well either." It was the same with a fish plant: it had to smell to be successful.

CHAPTER 7

It was my ambition to make the Otter *into the largest seine boat on the coast. I loved her and we became as one to survive the storms and seas. I guess I came to trust her faithfulness more than I have that of most men.*

In the early years we would buy any craft that stayed afloat if the price were right and if there were even a remote possibility that we could dream up a way to make a dollar.

The *Otter* was built in Victoria by the Canadian Pacific Navigation Company for the passenger and freight trade in the Gulf Islands. She had been owned by Canadian Pacific Steamships from 1901 to 1931 when we bought her, and had run faithfully from Victoria around the Gulf Islands and back to port. The *Otter* was in the hearts and souls of all those who lived in the Gulf Islands and, like the old *Maquinna*, she served the people well. Real credit should be given to the management of the CPR for carrying on these two runs, which were operated mainly for the benefit of the pioneers of those districts. Clarke and I grabbed the chance to buy her when she was offered for sale and struck a bargain with Captain Neroutsos of the CPR for $2,500.

A change in the ownership of any vessel necessitates a steamship inspection. Perhaps the government Steamship Department had been overly kind in the past to the CPR as far as safety precautions on the *Otter* were concerned; we could see from their attitude to us that they thought it was time to rectify any past oversights. On her last trip for the Canadian Pacific, the *Otter* had carried a crew of seventeen—a captain, two mates, two quartermasters, four deckhands, two engineers, two firemen, a purser, a chief steward and his two assistants. We were going to run a fish packer with just four crew aboard and it seemed most unfair to impose on us a different set of regulations than were upheld when there were a hundred passengers aboard.

The inspection went badly indeed. The lifeboats had been set in place by a crane and were 4 feet too long, making it impossible to launch them between the davits. We fared no better in the boiler room, where our boilers were condemned because of their age. The anchor was so antiquated that it had to be put overboard with a davit!

"If you condemn our boilers," I threatened, "you will have raised more hell than you know how to handle. We'll find out whether or not the Canadian Pacific is controlling our Steamship Department."

This worried Captain Neroutsos so much that CPR offered to call the deal off and give us our money back. We declined, saying that it was their problem to deal with the inspectors, and sailed out the next morning. A bitter feud developed between us and the Steamship Department which continued for three years and caused us plenty of trouble after we purchased the *Malahat* in 1934.

The following morning, with a strong westerly blowing, we sailed out of Victoria Harbour with only a crew of three—my brother Clarke in the engine room, myself at the wheel, and one man below. We had not had an opportunity to check out a very tricky reverse gear. I tried to swing up the starboard but the ship could not buck the strong westerlies. Clarke was unable to reverse the engine, which was a one-crank affair called a steeple compound, with a high-pressure cylinder and a low-pressure cylinder below; both operated by a single crank. To change direction, the engine had to be barred over to position when Clarke threw the steam to it. If we had any headway it was impossible to reverse the engine since it was directly connected to the propeller, and that engine would keep going in the same direction. Because of our hasty departure we had not learned how to operate her.

When we could not make starboard past the paint works, I put the helm hard over to port and took a swing at the harbour. About three-quarters round the circle, Hospital Rock was coming up dead ahead of us. I rang for "stop," then "astern." It was impossible to reverse those bloody engines, and as it was too late to drop anchor we headed straight for Hospital Rock, which is the beacon lying on the far shore of Victoria Harbour across from the Empress Hotel. By sheer luck there was enough water to get through, and to the amazement of the onlookers ashore we steamed right on out the other side.

The *Otter* was a coal-burning ship and the only way we knew to pick up a few dollars with her was to load her down with 200 tons of coal, which we picked up in Nanaimo to peddle in Bamfield, Ucluelet, Tofino and last of all Kakawis, the Catholic Indian mission in Clayoquot Sound. We paid four dollars a ton for the coal and sold it for ten dollars up the coast, but we bought it all in bulk and it had to be carried ashore in sacks to the Indian missions and lighthouse stations. Packing that coal as much as 1,000 feet up the beach was a tremendously hard way to make a dollar.

It was uneconomical to run the *Otter* as a steamboat, and we had to install new engines. We had heard of an old second-hand Bolinder engine out of the *Laura Whalen* at B.C. Cement in Victoria. It was priced as junk, about $600, and the manager said that his old boat was hardly worth discussion. But when he heard that we desperately needed the oilers and injectors for our engine, he raised the price to $800. For the $200 he made on us in that situation, he lost at least $10,000. He remembered his tightness later when we were building plants that required foundations and never purchased any cement from him.

Our crew picked up all the rusty parts around the junkyard, cleaned them up for the *Otter* and shipped them down to Ahousat in our seine boat, the *Chief Y*. There we renovated the *Otter* into a freighter, cutting off her upper deck so that she was a slick, fine ship. The operation was described by Albert Foote in his article "Saga of the S.S. *Otter:* Rebirth of a Ship" (*Vancouver Sun*, 5 April 1947):

The Otter was a steamship of 232 gross tons. At the time she changed ownership there was a semi-diesel engine lying on the docks at Victoria, in fact it had lain there for eleven years and was sold to the Gibsons at the price of junk. This machinery they carried up to Ahousat.

Astonishing things were about to happen to the former palatial passenger ship: First she underwent a major operation and had her whole insides removed. Piece by piece these pitiless mechanics yanked out her vitals until what had been her heart and lungs was now a great heap of junk piled high on the Ahousat wharf. . . .

First they sawed the upper structure, consisting of staterooms, dining saloon, smoking lounge, etc., into several sections. One by one, these great chunks of former luxury were dumped into the salt chuck. Only four staterooms, the galley and the wheelhouse were saved. The wheelhouse and the skipper's quarters were moved several feet aft.

The work went on often far into the night and by the end of June [1931] she was ready for work.

No one who ever knew the Otter in her swanky days could possibly have ever recognized her now, but the queer part of the transformation was the fact that when she had finally been all dolled up with bright paint, she had taken on lines of beauty which she never before had possessed. A trim craft she now was. Before she had always looked a bit top-heavy. Perhaps the ship was pleased with the face lifting she had undergone—let us hope so.

She had also profited by the reducing process, her 232 gross tons were now down to 140 tons. Before the ship beauticians had given her her treatments, she had many unsightly bulges, now she looked like a young girl, streamlined in the very latest fashion.

She was scheduled to make her maiden run from Victoria and Vancouver, leaving the night of June 30. One short run was made to test the engine. This was not a howling success. Several times Nick Dale came bounding up from the engine room, his face blackened from the back-fire, but Nick stuck to his task and managed to keep her moving.

Come the night of June 30; the following day was to be a holiday, Dominion Day. That afternoon, two well known government vessels dropped anchor in Matilda Creek, bent on giving their crews a holiday the following day. One was the Lighthouse Tender Estevan, the other, the S.S. Lillooet of the coast survey, Commander H. D. Parizeau in command. The officers and crews of both these ships were naturally highly interested in just what kind of performance the Otter would turn in on this, her maiden voyage since her re-birth.

Many were the wagers laid on the results; the odds seemed heavily against her. Few among those expert men of the sea believed this old ship would rise to the occasion and ever get clear of Matilda Creek under the impulse of those back-firing strange engines.

The deadline hour arrived, the entire population of the whole district was on hand, augmented by the crews of those government ships. The skipper, Gordon Gibson, barked out the command, "aboard." We leaped to the deck and were prepared for almost anything to happen.

"Bang! Bang!" she went. Nick Dale, the engineer, only smiled, he knew she was only warming up to her task; he could still feel this when her false smoke funnel began to grow red hot.

Nick was right. Matilda Creek is not very wide, mighty little sea room. And when the Maquinna or the Nora dock there, they have to back their way out. The new Otter, at that time flagship of the Gibson line, had no reverse. She was headed in the opposite direction from her course. Nick threw in the clutch, she began to move amid the vociferous cheers of the spectators. The skipper was at the wheel. He made a lovely curve and just missing the opposite bank by inches, waved his hand nonchalantly at his audience—and we were off. That night we tied up at Tofino to await the dawn which comes pretty early at that time of the year in those latitudes. The skipper gave a ham and egg party that evening to some of his Tofino friends. We saw no more ham and eggs during the entire voyage. . . .

Out we sailed the next morning at daybreak. Sparkling sunshine later, strong westerly blowing, and the old Otter seemed to love this sort of thing. I really believed she knew we had no anchor, no whistle and not too dependable lifeboat in case those diesel engines salvaged from the junkheap went on a sit-down.

All day long those engines banged their noisy tirade, but it was sweet music to me. I realized as long as those explosions were happening below decks we were safe from being piled up on the rocks. I hung around the iron ladder that led up from the engine room and every time Nick, the engineer, poked his blackened face out for a bit of fresh air, I would say to him, "how's she doing down there, Nick?"

"Swell," was his invariable answer. This was very comforting and I began to think that I had a fighting chance to see Vancouver once more.

We rounded the Swiftsure light ship early in the afternoon, that evening we docked safely in the outer harbour of Victoria. Those old shellbacks were all wrong. I tried to make myself believe that I knew all the time there was no danger, and began to lie about it all to Willy Luckovich who was entitled to tack the coveted initials A.B. back of his name. Willy had sailed around the horn so many times that this coast-wise stuff bored him.

The next day in Victoria, the skipper phoned for a junk dealer. He wished to get rid of those old steam engines. When the buyer of second hand merchandise began to haggle over the matter, the skipper said, "tell me in the fewest words you know how to use, just what this stuff is worth to you." The junkman named his first figure, thinking he would raise the ante on his next bid. "Sold," said the skipper. "Get this stuff off my ship as soon as possible."

The junkman was so astonished at this extraordinary, unorthodox method of doing business, that for once in his life he felt he should do something handsome. This he did, he returned to the ship and acted as host to a real party held in the galley.

That night we sailed for Vancouver. It was for me the end of a wonderful four months' experience. I liked those folks up on the West Coast, some remarkable characters living up there, the kind that take you at face value.

CHAPTER 8

The Otter was our second great workhorse and I felt I was in mourning for an old faithful friend when she was lost.

Our first contract with the *Otter* was to pack canned pilchards from Nootka to Vancouver and then carry back loads of herring that had been hand-brailed by Japanese fishermen in a big butterfly net. The *Otter* was the largest fish packer on the coast and we chartered her out for fifty dollars a day, which included fuel and crew. That was a bargain even in those days!

Gerry Petridge knew more than any man about the fishing business, having worked his way from a rowboat to a fish plant, Nootka Canneries, which he managed and partly owned. He could outfish any man on the coast by sheer ability and guts. Petridge chartered the *Otter* to pack fish for one dollar a ton. That was a very tough deal but we couldn't afford to turn down the work. In fact, we worked for Petridge for over a year and came to respect him tremendously.

There was a heavy run of fish in Barkley Sound on 20 December 1934. We undertook to pick up the overs and run them to the cannery at Nootka. About forty miles from Kildonan Harbour fire started to come out of one side of the forward end of the base of the two-cylinder Bolinder engine and we had to run at half speed on one cylinder. We were still making a little headway, though it was impossible to manoeuvre.

Capt. Charlie Clark, one of the finest fishermen on the coast, was waiting for the *Otter* in Rainey Bay with a set of 400 tons of fish that would have to be dumped if it were not picked up immediately. Our ship was in no condition to head back up the coast on one cylinder but we couldn't let that fine captain down. We decided to take a chance and tied the *Otter* alongside his vessel and started loading immediately.

When we hauled our engine apart that night, we found a hole in the piston head about the size of a fifty-cent piece. There were two choices: we could either dump the 400 tons of fish that would rot or we could yard out the piston and take it to Alberni to be fixed. That piston was 18 inches in diameter and weighed at least 500 pounds.

The Lord hates a coward so that night the piston was in our machine shop in Alberni. We put it in a lathe, cut out a 4-inch hole and milled down a stove lid to fit the cut snugly. All this was accomplished in twelve hours and by the next morning we were back on our ship. That night the *Otter* headed out with a full deckload of 100 tons and 300 tons in the hold—400 tons of fish which were already two days old. That meant $400 for us if they were delivered or a full load of rotten herring if we failed.

It was Christmas Eve and all the other crews were celebrating in port as we put our nose out past Amphitrite Light near Ucluelet. Not one of us had slept a wink during all the excitement of the previous night.

A tremendous southwester was blowing. One enormous wave washed away the entire deckload and 100 tons of fish returned to the sea. Our ship seemed to stay under the swell like a submarine. Water came right up around the wheelhouse; as the fish slid over the rails our burden was relieved and the *Otter* came up fast again. The loss of that 100 tons saved us because it gave the ship added buoyancy and stability.

We delivered the fish at noon on Christmas Day. Our payment for taking that chance was $300 or a dollar a ton! That is what it was like making money in those days. We were so poor we couldn't afford to turn back in that storm. But the *Otter* showed her pride as a ship and we had learned that she could venture out in conditions which would cause another vessel to flounder. News that the *Otter* had survived the storm spread quickly and from then on it was easy to obtain contracts to pack herring.

Gerry Petridge was the only man that I had ever met

who could dominate me. I admired his ambition and drive. Even at age fifty he could lick any of the young bloods up that coast.

My respect for him grew the day one of his seine boats ran into a terrible storm off Estevan Point in Clayoquot Sound. The vessel was manned by a crew of Yugoslavs who were terrified by the rough seas. Their contract was to take the fish to Petridge's Plant, but on this occasion they tried to sell their cargo to us rather than buck the westerly back to their home plant.

I telephoned Gerry and asked if we could buy the fish. He was furious when he heard that his crew had turned back and ordered the men and ship to hold fast. Petridge was so desperate to get the cargo that he started down the coast by himself in a much smaller boat. It took him eight hours to make the trip through those seas.

He threw all the skipper's effects out on the wharf and chucked every one of the crew off the ship telling them that they weren't fit to be called fishermen if they couldn't brave a few high seas. Half an hour later Petridge started the engines and took the boat back to Nootka by himself. I so admired him because he saw that it was necessary to take control of the situation and dared to stand alone against an entire crew of very tough men.

Sometime later the *Otter* was rounding Estevan bound for Nootka with a full load of herring. I was off watch and had been asleep for several hours when I awakened from a vivid dream. Although dreams seldom stay with me, this one made such an impression that I went below for some coffee.

When I went up to relieve the mate I told him that Gerry Petridge was in some kind of trouble and that we were going back to Port Alberni before we unloaded. "Gordon," he said, "you're crazy. What good could we do by going back?"

I wondered this myself, but when we docked at 4:00 A.M., the superintendent, Joe Lismus, came aboard. "Gordon we just got a telephone call that Gerry Petridge has had a heart attack in Vancouver. Mrs. Petridge is here. Gerry sent word that he wants you to turn around without unloading and take her to Port Alberni so that she can fly to Vancouver."

It was the only time in my life that a dream has meant anything special to me. That night the weather was so thick, the *Otter* was the only ship which could have made it through the seas. No airplane could fly out.

All the arrangements had been made by the time Mrs. Petridge came aboard. We headed to Alberni and she was in Vancouver with her husband before he died.

A good idea of what life was like at that time is conveyed in Albert Foote's article "My First Trip as a Deckhand on the 'Otter' " (*Vancouver Sun*, 24 June 1939).

I met Gordon Gibson here in Vancouver. Gordon was the skipper of the "Otter." I told him of my life long ambition, to make a trip as an ordinary seaman. "O.K.," he said, "If you really want to sail with me you can go as a deck hand and when I say deck hand, that is exactly what I mean."

"You're on, Skipper," I answered, "Deck hand it is, Sir."

True to the best traditions of the sea, I naturally considered it necessary to splice the main brace a few times before the good ship put to sea. I had been paired off with the cook.

Well, the fateful hour arrived. We cast loose the mooring lines and were off. Skipper Gibson made a casual inspection of his ship. He gave me only a glance but that look was enough. I began to realize that a deck hand was just that, nothing more. Well, I had asked for it and sure got it.

We steamed out through the First Narrows for Otter Bay to load herring. That cook and I were kept busy coiling up line. Just what in the world they would use all that rope for is beyond me. Then, just at this time the cook, who up until now I considered was more or less friendly to me, spoke up: "Listen flunkey, get busy there with those spuds."

I got busy. Then the cook condescended to address me once more.

"Sorry there is only about enough lemon extract to make one bit of a 'lift' for me."

The good ship "Otter" having taken on its cargo was now headed for Nootka. Nothing very romantic about a voyage of this sort, perhaps not for you, but for me it meant unusual adventure, the realization of a dream, the culmination of a hope deferred.

Yes, it was herring that filled our forward hold, over-ripe herring at that. Personally, perhaps, I should have preferred to have made my debut as a sailor before the masts in one of those stately clippers carrying proudly a cargo of Ceylon tea or pungent spices of the East.

It was not to be. I was simply a deck hand on a ship loaded with decaying fish.

Just then the voice of the "Skipper" barked out, "Go on up into the pilot house, Foote, and take your trick at the wheel."

Well, I had wanted to get some real experience as an ordinary seaman. Now I was going to get it.

I jumped to obey the order. Now I was getting somewhere.

I forgot all about those putrifying herring, forgot everything in fact but the knowledge that I was a quartermaster in sole charge of the ship; a proud moment for me.

I grasped that wheel and hung on to it like grim death. We had two hundred and fifty tons of semi-liquid fish in the forward hold. The old "Otter" groaned over the burden. . . .

The "Skipper" had pointed out the mark in the compass where I was supposed to hold her, then he walked away and left me alone.

The old "Otter" began to wobble all over the place. I became panicky. I knew that it was but a matter of moments when I should be the cause of a terrible sea disaster. Why! Oh, why, had I been so foolish as to embark on this crazy adventure? I had reached the limit of my nerves.

The "Skipper's" voice boomed, "What in the blankety-blank name of common sense are you trying to do with my ship?"

Never before nor since was the sound of a human voice so welcome. I cared not that the "Skipper's" tirade was delivered in language that fairly sizzled. My only thought, that the ship and her crew were saved.

For once words failed me. I could only murmur tremblingly, "Thanks, Captain Gibson," as I hurried aft and gazed over the stern of the ship. We had left a wake behind that looked like a snake.

Back I went into the galley convinced that a land-lubber should spend the first ten years at sea helping the cook. . . .

The next day we ran into a terrible fog. Secretly I knew this ship's crew was lost, but as I seemed to be the only one that realized our awful peril, I kept quiet about the matter. I alone, of that small ship's company was aware of our dreadful danger.

Here we were, out on the heaving open Pacific Ocean, a few

inches of planking between us and Davy's locker. Just then I overheard the "Skipper" say to the engineer "We shall make Nootka at midnight."

Make Nootka at midnight, how in the world could he feel that way about it, pitching around in a fog so thick that it was impossible to see the distance of a city block. Well, I turned in, wishing to die in my bed and with my boots off.

By some unexplainable miracle I did go to sleep. No use for me to mumble that prayer of childhood, "Now I lay me down to sleep." No question in my mind where I was going to wake up. Then it happened, the terrible event I had foreseen. There was a crunching sound, followed by the sound of men shouting to one another. I jumped into my clothes and grabbing a life preserver, made for the deck.

Great electric lights nearly blinded me. I rubbed my eyes and peered over the side. We were just tying up to a dock. I noticed a large sign over the warehouse; it read, "Nootka Packing Co., Ltd." The "Skipper" leaped ashore and was shaking the hand of Jerry Pertridge [sic], the manager of the plant.

I looked at my watch, she registered two minutes past twelve.

I listened to the conversation between Captain Gibson and Mr. Pertridge [sic], the fish cannery manager, who said, "Did you have a good trip?"

"Sure," responded the skipper. "We docked two minutes later than I had figured but we lost a bit of time on account of being short-handed."

Well, I still believe the matter was one of extraordinary luck. The night was pitch black. I turned in once more, this time to really enjoy my berth.

The cook called me at four in the morning. I had to help remove the canvas cover from the hatch that covered the hold full of liquid fish. When we raised that heavy cover there was a great rush of gas. I reeled away to the windward side. That morning I had no interest in breakfast.

The ship seemed all confusion. Clank, clank, went the endless chain of buckets as they dipped deep into the odoriferous cargo, and fed it into the hungry conveyors that waited eagerly to convert this piscatory refuse into fertilizer and by-products. When the entire cargo was swallowed up by the cannery, the hold washed down and decks cleaned I spoke to the cook about the terrible perils of the day before when we were lost in the fog.

"What are you talking about?" he said, "the 'Skipper' knew

where we were every minute. Why this here 'Otter' could have found her way through that kind of weather with no one at the wheel."

The *Otter* was later chartered out to Del Lutes, manager of Nelson Brothers Fisheries. We were carrying overs from the other packers and taking any work we could get. We were in no position to bargain.

I remember unloading 400 tons of fish from the *Otter* in six hours at the Ceepeecee plant, and falling asleep from sheer exhaustion in the pilothouse after being at the wheel for twenty-four hours.

The next morning I was awakened by Lutes, who gave me a slip showing our tonnage to be 187.5. That .5 infuriated me—I lashed out at Lutes, calling him every sort of blackguard and accusing him of being the most crooked SOB I'd ever met.

He said, "That's the law of averages, Gibson. You had better get used to it. The price of fishmeal is so low that I can't pay you any more. I have to survive, too."

In those days a man had to think fast to stay alive. We were tired when we got up in the morning and in worse condition at night. I immediately fell asleep as though dead after working fourteen to sixteen hours. In a way, we got through each day by hoping that things would be a little better on the morrow.

We were something like that big bumblebee whose wings are so small that it shouldn't be able to fly. We didn't know that we were broke or that there could be a better life. It was a case of endurance. At night we would figure that our company might make a dollar tomorrow if we had broken even today.

We would have starved to death if any of us had tried to work a forty-hour week. I thought nothing of working a hundred hours, many of them without shelter or rest.

The *Otter* was lost on 13 May 1937 in front of our logging camp at Malksope Inlet. She had been used to carry our crew into the camp and was lying at anchor. I went aboard to pump the water out of her bilges. The gasoline engine backfired causing a tremendous explosion as the gas tank blew up.

The fire drove Gibson to the deck and his rowboat, and he pulled ashore to get the tug Tofino in operation and to call help from the nearby logging camp. The Tofino was slow in starting, and Gibson rowed back to the Otter to attempt to get aboard and scuttle her but the fire had gained such headway that he could not even get on the deck. Then the Tofino came along with the loggers, but by this time the heat from the blazing ship was so fierce that they could not approach nearer than 100 feet. Explosion after explosion shook the old ship, as the fire roared on, and the flames held control until the morning of May 13. Then Gibson was able to get a line aboard and beach the smoking wreck.

(Vancouver *Daily Province*, 4 June 1937)

My brother Clarke flew up to Malksope Inlet with Capt. Fred Clarke, surveyor for the Board of Marine Underwriters of San Francisco, to inspect her remains.

CHAPTER 9

I remember when someone threatened to break us, I replied, "No one could break the Gibsons in this country because we are so used to being broke. We are in the guts of this country and if we have to go back to the beaches for clams and live on fish and deer meat you won't be able to pull us down."

We started to buy spring salmon in April 1932, selling it to American fish packers based in Seattle. We had a fish buying station at Ahousat in connection with our store, and we were also buying dressed lingcod at five cents a pound with heads off and guts out. The price of clams was fifty cents for a wooden milk box full, so at night in low tide the Indians would dig them up for a supplemental income.

When the pilchards disappeared from the coast all the fish plants closed down and good fishing vessels became a glut on the market. Most of the packing companies discontinued operations, and we were able to acquire at low prices some packers such as the *East Bay No. 1*, which had a diesel engine and packed about 50 tons.

In 1933 the American buyers stopped coming up the coast, but they encouraged us to carry our own fish to Seattle. As a result, we chartered the vessel *Roseanne* for five dollars a day, and our youngest brother Earson became responsible for running her into Seattle and selling the salmon. He paid the engineer forty dollars a month and the cook thirty dollars plus board; the *Roseanne* ran from Kyuquot to Seattle on a weekly schedule with just the three crew. The 600-mile return trip meant an incredible number of hours at work—cooking, loading and unloading the fish—and it is quite amazing that Earson was able to accomplish it all. He was extremely able, and cemented our liaison with the company Armstrong, Melcher and Dessau, who had numerous connections as far east as New York and supplied a mild cure of salmon called lox to the Jewish markets. We were paying ten cents per pound in Ahousat and getting twenty cents delivered in Seattle.

A hundred dollars nowadays would be the equivalent of a plumber's wages for one day, but a hundred dollars at that time would get you the best man in the city for two months, and he would probably be twice as productive.

The Depression was a great factor in our lives, but the coast was never like the prairies where people had to endure such hardships as snow, dust storms and drought. Everything up the coast remained the same except that the pilchards didn't come during the Depression years. We were indigenous to the economy of the West Coast and could turn our hands to anything. Whatever circumstances arose we were able to adapt to earn at least a few dollars to pay the grocery bills. We were always free men, our own bosses. In many ways that was one of our greatest difficulties as partners in business relationships. But the fact remains that we could set our own terms within economic limits. You couldn't ask a man for more money than a job was worth because in those days he had an alternative. Sheer economics kept everybody honest.

One of our strengths was that we all had different abilities and, in many instances, different friends. In this way we developed quite a network to call upon for advice or for technical skills. As far as our family was concerned there was never any quarrel about who was boss. Whichever brother was most competent in any area of our work was naturally the leader.

Once a job had been assigned there was never any clash of personalities, although I can remember some pretty heated discussions before we reached a concensus. There was nothing formal about them: we would just sit down and have a family conclave on finances or on how to get some project accomplished. In effect, every one of us was in on the process of running the business, and we therefore became very tolerant of each other. Also, we appreciated our good fortune in always having someone within our own family with whom we could discuss a problem.

Our father died in late 1933, and we brought his body down from Ahousat to Vancouver on the *Otter*. Every CPR boat slowed down and lowered its flag as we passed. Just before his death he went into some mining ventures, which were his first love. As an old-time gold miner he was able to relive his youth in these involvements.

In 1931, Ray Petrie and a group of prospectors had discovered gold at the Privateer Mine on the Zeballos River. This sparked a gold rush along the entire west coast, and the Privateer Mine became known nationally when a lot of eastern development money was poured into the Zeballos Valley.

The boom in Clayoquot Sound was relatively minor, but there were several properties up at the head of Herbert Arm which were staked by Jimmy Livesley. Dad was involved to the extent that he grubstaked several prospectors, and these stakes were registered through our store.

We had a customs broker in Vancouver who formed a gold syndicate. Dad and he went together on a mining claim that looked extremely rich, and my father registered this claim in his broker's name, giving him a ten per cent share for this service. They found one piece of rock the size of a coconut with specks of gold showing on the outside. One of the boys took an enormous hammer to fracture this chunk and it split into two like halves of a solid gold egg: a spectacular piece of rock!

I think they figured that they had found the mother lode. Dad's partner and his associates seemed to lose all sense of proportion and dealt very deviously with our father. Dad wasn't in good health at that time and became distressed. It was not so much the money that disturbed him as finding out he had a bad friend.

The rush was really on in the winter in 1933, and Jimmy Livesley and a partner were staking up one side of the Moyeha River. Billy Kermode and I were staking the other side. I guess we thought that the whole country was rich because we were staking as many as five claims a day.

On one trip Billy and I decided to stay out overnight. We started up from the old Abco Mine, which is at the 2,000-foot level, staking claims right over the top of the mountain every 1,500 feet.

We were in 5 feet of snow above the timber line. A snowstorm started to build and we had only a compass to tell us where in hell we were. By four o'clock, with darkness coming on, Billy and I found a place to make camp in the shelter of a big rock. We laid our packs down so that we could rest for a few minutes before staking a few more claims along the side of the mountain and returning to our base camp. In our packs we each had a blanket and a little food for the next day.

We left the shelter to stake two more claims, tagging any small jack pines that were sticking up to mark our trail. A storm hit, and when we turned to go back we found that the wind was blowing the snow over our tracks. We marched as fast as we could but the darkness and the storm were pressing in all around us. I began to feel that this might be my last goddamned night on earth.

Billy and I stayed close together, but we kept going round and round in a big circle. Our last bite had been a sandwich at noon. Fatigue and hunger are the greatest enemies of a man trapped in the cold.

The wind was whipping the snow in our faces and we couldn't see 10 feet ahead. It was impossible to go on so we buried ourselves in the snow right up to our necks, pulling our coats over our heads for some little protection.

We stayed in the snow until daylight, too weak to move and yelling to keep each other alive. When dawn came, neither of us had any idea where our camp was since we had lost all sense of direction. Our only hope was to get down to the river about 4,000 feet below.

The day was still so stormy that it was difficult to pick our footing, but we slithered down until we found a small creek to follow. Coming out of the snow at about the 1,500-foot level, we found ourselves in a canyon. In front of us was a bluff. It was impossible to go ahead, and just as impossible to cross the creek. We were on a steep, slimy bank covered with moss that had a 60-degree slope dropping 100 feet down to a waterfall.

I knew we had one chance in a hundred to get across the bank, and argued that we were better going back up the creek to search for another crossing. Billy was twenty years older than I was and he couldn't go much farther. He said, "Gordon, go up there if you want, but I couldn't go back up that mountain even to save my life."

So saying, he started across the slippery bank crawling on his hands and knees and grasping for something to hang on to. Quite frankly, I didn't think he had any chance of making that crossing but miraculously he succeeded. Now he was on the other side a good 50 feet away. I persuaded myself that going back up the mountain would mean another night out in zero temperatures and that I would never survive. The fact that Billy had managed to cross did not guarantee I would be so fortunate. But there was no choice, so I gambled and on my belly edged my way across to him. Billy's good sense saved my life that day.

About three o'clock that afternoon we managed to get down to the main river, and spent the night in a deserted camp which Dad had built some years before. The next morning we made our way back to our own camp and had our first meal in two days. We had acted like greenhorns on the mountain. I learned the foolishness that can get into a man's head when he has gold fever.

In those days most of the timber on the waterfront of Clayoquot Sound was owned by the Crown. If a man took out a hand-logging licence it was unofficially but generally assumed that he could take Crown trees at any spot along the hundreds of miles of coastline in the sound because the government would rather have a sawmill such as ours operating and providing employment than their having to provide relief. As a result, Jack and I would scour the steep hillsides all around the sound looking for trees that could be fallen so that they would slide into the water under their own momentum.

On one of these foraging expeditions on the west side of the main arm of Sydney Inlet, we came upon the largest and most symmetrical red cedar tree we had ever seen. It was 14 feet in diameter, 45 feet in circumference, 225 feet high; it soared 100 feet in the air before its first limb branched away from the main trunk. To our delight, it was located on a hillside, so that it could take a straight shot into the deep water of the inlet, making it possible for us to tow it to our sawmill.

Since our longest falling saw was only 6 feet we knew we must get larger equipment to fell this fabulous tree. A requisition was sent to MacLellen, McFeeley and Prior, the lumber hardware suppliers in Victoria, for the biggest falling saw they had which was 10 feet long. When the saw arrived in Ahousat, Jack and I returned to Sydney Inlet and climbed 1,000 feet up the hillside. We started to fall that great cedar at nine o'clock in the morning and worked all day. At dusk the tree groaned and began to fall, crashing through some smaller trees and snapping off its top 140 feet from the base. It seemed to pause in the air for a moment like an eagle in slow motion, before starting down the mountainside, cartwheeling end over end and disappearing into the water at a 45-degree angle. After what seemed to be a five-minute lapse, it suddenly emerged on the surface like a giant whale breaching from the depths. It was completely devoid of branches and most of its bark had been stripped away by the 1,000-foot passage over rocks and windfalls.

With one day's labour we had obtained a month's supply of cedar for our shingle mill. The same log would be worth $15,000 to $20,000 on today's market but in those days, even after sawing it into shingles, it had a gross value of $1,750, which was a major boost to our sawmill.

In all of our sixty years of logging experience in British Columbia handling billions of feet of timber, this was the most outstanding tree we have ever seen.

The *Maquinna* still called at our sawmill every ten days, and her captain, Red Thompson, advised us that the CPR was looking for a new mast for the ship and was willing to pay $100 for this special order. That was a large sum of money to us and we immediately contracted to do the job.

I knew where such a tree was standing on one of our claims: an enormous spruce tree straight, tall and perfectly symmetrical. Jack and I felled it onto smaller skid trees so that it could slide into the water under its own momentum.

This tree was 24 inches round at the base and 16 inches at the 100-foot mark. It was a perfect specimen of the type of spar that Captain Cook noted from the bridge on his ship on his first trip into Nootka Sound. He was looking for trees that would be suitable for masts for the ships of the British Navy.

We survived because we could adapt ourselves to the changing conditions of the early 1930s by falling cedar, cutting ships' spars, trading clams, salmon, seals and pelts at the store. We managed to eat very well, remain solvent and provide employment for some Indians as well as for our own families.

It was in the fall of 1933 when we were bringing Dad's body to Vancouver that we had some trouble with the Bolinder diesel engines in the *Otter*. As a result of our search for spare engine parts we heard of the famous five-masted bark *Malahat*. Little did I know then that my greatest adventure was just about to begin.

William Gibson

Gordon Gibson's birthplace: Goldbottom, Yukon

Gordon *(left)* on Grouse Mountain picnic: the end of his school career, age 12 (courtesy of Sesume Kobe)

Julia Gibson *(left)* and her four sons, Gordon, Jack, Earson and *(far right)* Clarke (courtesy of Jack Gibson)

Jack, Clarke, William, Earson and Gordon

The *Malahat*, mother ship of the Pacific rum-running fleet (courtesy of the Vancouver Maritime Museum)

The *Malahat* loading logs in the Queen Charlotte Islands, 1934

Portraits of Louise Gibson (née Redman)

Malksope Inlet: A-Frame, steam donkey, cookhouse, bunkhouse and Louise's first floating home

Pike-polers

Gordon and Gordon, Jr.

CHAPTER 10

We handled the Malahat *as though she were a tricky baby, humoured her, mastered her, made her go places in these waters. And bad waters they are, make no mistake.*

One of the great turning points in our fortunes was the purchase of the *Malahat*, a schooner built in Victoria by the Canadian Westcoast Navigation Company in 1917 from the ship's knees that my father and I had bulled out of Alberni.

The *Malahat* was a 245-foot, five-masted, baldheaded schooner, that is, a schooner rigged with no topsails, and mainsails hoisted from the deck with steam winches. She was the last of the many of her class built during World War I. She was a lucky ship, and in her years of service to us survived many perils that would surely have destroyed a less-favoured vessel. She had been in the lumber trade in 1918 and made frequent runs to Australia. After World War I she was purchased by liquor interests in the distillery business in Vancouver and became the mother ship of the rum fleet sailing up and down the United States coast from Washington to Southern California, about twelve to twenty miles offshore. In effect, she became a floating warehouse, and spent much of her time during Prohibition lying at anchor in the shallow waters thirty miles off the California coast.

Fast boats would come out from shore at night to rendezvous with the *Malahat*, which would be carrying all her lights. The runners unloaded the liquor in burlap sacks and then scattered for different beaches, sometimes travelling at 25 knots with their powerful Liberty engines.

The United States Coast Guard cutters tracked down many of the runners and boarded them within the 3-mile limit—only to find that their cargo was water. It was a difficult task patrolling the 2,000 miles of shoreline where liquor could be landed, and almost impossible to catch the smugglers when the money was actually changing hands. Sometimes the liquor was sunk in a sack and marked with a float like a crab net's so that it could be picked up by fishing boats the next morning. No law was broken unless the coast guard could catch the rumrunners carrying liquor within the 3-mile limit.

We were often propositioned by both local liquor interests and rumrunners to charter our two vessels, the *Otter* and the *Maid of Orleans*. We could have made $100,000 a year, but our father gave us sound advice which we have stuck to: "Stay out of the liquor business, boys—drink whatever you want in front of the bar, but never be sober standing behind it. I don't want our family ever to make a dollar out of the liquor business." We never have. We were too busy with our own affairs to know anything about the rum-running business, but we were fascinated by the exciting stories told to us by such fine skippers as Bill Olsen, Dan Backie, William Vosper and Bill Wright. The big boys involved in the running, those who owned either big distilleries or big ships, made a great deal of money, some amassing fortunes.

After Prohibition, the *Malahat* was sold in 1934 to a syndicate in Vancouver to carry logs. It made one trip to Prince Rupert, where the crew tried to stow the cargo, but because they were seamen rather than loggers, the weight of the logs beat them and they were unable to raise them. The ship arrived back in port with no cargo and $2,500 of crew's wages went unpaid.

When my brother Jack heard that the *Malahat* had been seized by the courts and was up for sale, he informed us immediately. At this time we were scouting for spare parts for the *Otter*, and knew that there were some stored in the engine room of the *Malahat*.

We went to a marine lawyer, Sidney Smith, hoping to buy some of the spare parts, but learned that the first certified cheque for $2,500 could buy the *Malahat;* he was not allowed to sell any parts separately.

We were stunned—figuring her worth was closer to $100,000—and asked for a couple of hours to look her over.

We got as far as the elevator doors when I said to my brothers, "That ship will be sold before we can get back. Let's buy her sight unseen." Clarke, the financier among us, went straight to the Bank of Nova Scotia and had a certified cheque made up for the full amount—almost all the money we had in the world. Within the hour we owned the *Malahat,* and had to figure out what in God's name to do with her.

The *Malahat* had cost three-quarters of a million dollars to build but when we acquired her in 1934 she was a white elephant. She was too big for a pleasure yacht and needed a crew of at least fifteen to run her; she couldn't compete on a world trade basis as a cargo ship because she was too slow, and insurance costs would have been prohibitive.

Mr. Smith told us that Richie Nelson of B.C. Packers and Capt. Barney Johnson had offered $200 or $300 under the asking price. They both came to me later and offered to buy the ship for far more than they had originally offered. It pays when you see a good bargain to buy immediately.

We went to inspect our purchase. She was lying at the Wallace Shipyards in North Vancouver. The *Malahat* had $1,000 worth of oil in the tanks; her sails were furled and could be cut up for canvas for another $1,000; her anchor chains were worth $2,000 to $3,000 apiece; her fuel tanks were full, although that wasn't worth a plug nickel unless you ran the engines.

She was a schooner in the grand old style with a coal-burning fireplace in the owner's quarters and two full-size bathtubs, one for the owner and one aft for the captain and crew. The officers' quarters were excellent, too, with heat in each stateroom which was a luxury in those days. Aft there was a stateroom for the captain and a stateroom for the mates, chief engineer and cook. This ship would become the first home for my future wife Louise and me.

The trouble was that sailors were becoming an extinct race by this time—I mean the men who could sail the really big windjammers. There were still government training ships, but the true sailors who could handle canvas were dying off.

We explored all the possibilities of coastal shipping and world trade, but the *Malahat* was too slow to be competitive. No one would charter her, not even as a cargo ship into the Arctic.

We had taken the spare parts worth $1,500 which were needed for the *Otter* and still had many left for the *Malahat*. That effectively cut the purchase price down to $1,000, but the costs of keeping the ship—wharfage, watchman and maintenance—mounted steadily.

In November 1935 when almost all hope had gone of ever making a dollar with the *Malahat*, my brother Clarke and I met Tom Kelly, a well-known logger who had contracted with the Powell River Company to supply them with logs from the Queen Charlotte Islands. He towed his logs by Davis raft in the summertime but for five months during the winter he did not venture across the Hecate Strait because of the heavy losses he had experienced. The cost by raft, even in the summertime, was running to five dollars per thousand logs. The winter delays were costly because after only six months in the water teredos would begin devouring the logs, and insurance costs were prohibitive.

We made Tom Kelly the proposition that we would sail north to Queen Charlotte Islands, load as many spruce logs as we could for five dollars a thousand, and deliver them to the Powell River booming ground in Teakerne Arm. It was a pretty rough deal but we needed the money, so we decided to take a chance and put the *Malahat* to work.

In a letter to our mother, I wrote:

Don't worry about the way we will come out on this. Kelly wants us to work with him, says he'll see we make money. I'm glad we made a success of this even if it's just to show everyone that it can be done. I really believe that the most trouble is coming from the fact that the towing company were afraid we might take away too much of their business. That's a good kind of name to get to start with. Believe me, most people in the shipping business have heard of us or will before we're through.

First we had to muster a crew. We knew it had to be a combination of loggers, longshoremen and deep-sea sailors because we had to load and stow the logs and to discharge them as well. We needed two steam donkeys, one to lift the logs aboard at the after end of the ship and another to pull them forward into piles. To accommodate all the logs we would require a 20-foot deck clearance at the highest point. Since the wheel, telegraph and engine room were all at the very after end, we decided to build a bridge that would let us look out over the top of the cargo.

Arrangements were made with Burrard Drydock Company in North Vancouver to build the bridge before we sailed, but when the shipwrights came aboard we found their plans so elaborate that we gave up all hope of being able to pull out within two weeks. Moreover, the job would cost at least $2,000. I told the supervisor, Hubie Wallace, that he was crazy to charge such a price. "We'll build it ourselves and do it for $200." His crew had started at eight in the morning. They were fired before nine, and we completed the job with our own crew in the next two days.

I'm sure that no bridge like it has ever been built in the world before or since. Four wooden posts 12 feet high and 6 inches by 6 inches were put up along each side and across the ship at 10-foot intervals. Crosspieces of 6 inches by 4 inches were nailed down on top of these with huge spikes. Beams 2 feet by 1 foot were cut in 5-foot lengths and added on top of all this. A 2-foot by 4-foot railing was put around the bridge and bolted solid to the aftermasts with no bracing for support. We were ready to sail the next day.

On the forward part of the ship, a boiler gave steam to run our winches and to raise the anchor. We bought two old donkeys cheaply because the boilers were condemned: one on the fo'c's'le head for loading and the other on the main deck just below the fo'c's'le head forward for pulling the logs into position. We were in such a hurry that these donkeys were not bolted down until we were well on our way north.

Earson and I were to make this first trip together, and we looked for a crew of at least sixteen. Our skipper, Captain Vosper, was a deep-sea captain who had twenty years experience, five years of them as master of the *Malahat* during her rum-running years. The chief engineer had been with the ship for ten years. There were a couple more old-timers but all the rest of the crew were west coast loggers whom we knew—the roughest, toughest, best workers the coast could produce.

Our first trouble came with the chief engineer, who started to lay down the law. I will grant you that he was the only one who knew how to run the engines, but he began demanding that some of his relatives be hired. We settled that quickly: he was fired before he started. That was the day we were to leave. We then called on a good friend of ours, Nick Dale, the chief engineer of the *Otter*, to join us and he agreed. We carried another engineer aboard as Nick had no ticket. The supplies were loaded, the ship was cleared, and we started out for the Queen Charlotte Islands—a place that none of us had ever set eyes on, not even Captain Vosper.

The captain had always had a tug to pull him clear of the dock and since that would have cost $100 we bucked at the cost. This was our first little rift that showed up the difference in our approach to running a ship.

I asked the licensed engineer if he knew how to handle the engines because these had no reverse gear and had to be stopped and then restarted to go backwards. Although he was unfamiliar with the engines in the *Malahat*, we decided to gamble by pulling the ship clear on our own winches. She was close to 300 feet long, lying nose tight to the dock. We took a line from our power winch on the bow and brought it outside the ship right down the dock to the stern. Letting go on our lines, we heaved in on our winch and pulled the ship out into deep water.

At 5:00 P.M. on 25 November 1935 we rang for full ahead and headed more or less for the First Narrows Bridge. No insurance company in the world would have touched us. We started up the coast under power and sail, little knowing the adventures that lay before us.

First we had to go into Nanaimo to take on coal to run our steam boiler. As we had plenty of time, the engineer practised reversing the engines on the way. We made a successful landing at the dock. After loading the coal aboard, we left Nanaimo at 10:00 on the morning of 26 November.

At daylight on the twenty-seventh we caught the tide at Cape Mudge, then ran through Seymour Narrows and down Johnstone Strait. On the twenty-eighth, my thirty-first birthday, we crossed Nahwitti Bar off Bull Harbour, where the tide runs like hell and the water is very shallow. We were a light ship with very little power.

Vosper was a fine captain, but he was a deep-sea master having very little coastal knowledge. We were opposites—he with deep-sea knowledge and Earson and I with little else but strength and driving force. Foreseeing some storage problems because of the 40-foot length of the logs, on the sly we had some of the crew cutting out the 'tween deck beams. Poor Vosper. He had no idea that his ship was being sawn up beneath his very feet!

By dark the *Malahat* crossed over the shallows of Nahwitti Bar with a strong out-running tide. All the sails were up and a strong southeaster was coming up behind, a heavy swell rolling in from the southwest. It was 120 miles to Cape St. James where we hoped to pick up a light in twenty to twenty-four hours. Our course took us out into the main roll of the Pacific Ocean.

It was a strange stormy night. I noticed the ship making a corkscrew motion because the 'tween deck beams had been taken out. Being loggers not sailors, the crew were pretty seasick. Many of them were drunks from Skid Row, and a ship rolling like a barrel does wonders to sober a man up the hard way. But my sympathy was with Captain Vosper: at two o'clock in the morning when the wind changed fast from the southeast to the southwest, half the crew were too seasick to get on deck, and unable to carry out orders even if they could. Somehow we got through that night our sails often lashing and flapping with the staccato of gunfire. Daylight finally came, and we managed to get ourselves back in order with the wind abeam. The *Malahat* was making fast time towards the Queen Charlotte Islands.

God alone knows where we were on the morning of the twenty-ninth. I was sure that the quartermaster had not been keeping on course and that we were well out to sea rather than on a straight course to Cape St. James. Our last position had been Bull Harbour at 5:00 P.M. the previous night.

The weather thickened. Captain Vosper had been accustomed to using his sextant against the stars to plot his position but we had not seen any sky for twenty-four hours. The seas were running like mountains behind us, each one carrying us forward with a tremendous thrust. The mate, Earson and I knew that we had run our time and I knew that the skipper believed so too.

By dark we were still rolling and the storm was increasing from the southeast. I knew that with the wind behind us we should have picked up the light at Cape St. James. We swung into the wind as much as we could to take the way off the ship, and packed our lead line forward. We were in about 12 fathoms of water and the heavy swell from the west had disappeared. This meant that we had to be close to shore, in the shelter of Queen Charlotte Islands north and east of Cape St. James. By midnight our speed was just 5 to 6 knots an hour. Hecate Straits are shallow so shore could have been one mile or ten miles away. Visibility was less than half a mile. Gales from the southeast were blowing 50 to 60 knots an hour. We had to do something rather than continue to plunge straight ahead. To go farther was not just dangerous, it would have been downright foolhardy.

Our sails were still set because our inexperienced crew could not take them down. The seas were steep and blacker than hell. So taking a great chance, we dropped both anchors and swung round into the wind. As the *Malahat* came sharply about the wind blew the belly out of every sail, ripping them right through the centre and blowing them into ribbons with thundering reports like cannon going off. One, two, three sails out in ten minutes! We lay there a light ship, our decks at least 15 feet above the water, the canvas flapping in disarray like a defeated pirates' galleon. Even both jibs were down in the water. The sails were never raised again as we didn't have anyone aboard who was capable of mending them.

The seas were tremendous—at least 60 feet high and so rough that as they broke over the forward deck the load of coal that we had picked up in Nanaimo was washed 200 feet aft right back against the poop deck, and the next day or two we had to wheel that goddamned stuff forward, load by load. It had been a night to remember.

It was a mad undertaking to have sailed that ship with a crew of loggers. A wise man wouldn't have done it, but I was desperate and had to make a living. The crew, too, needed their seventy-five dollars a month, for there was certainly no relief in those days.

The next morning the weather cleared by ten o'clock, the winds turning to the southwest. We had used good judgement: had we run ten to fifteen miles farther on the same course we could have been yet another ship gone down in the night with all hands. Less than ten miles ahead of our course lay a log-strewn beach. (We had anchored about four miles offshore.) As it was, all we had lost were the sails.

Again we headed north, knowing that the Queen Charlotte Islands were on our port side. None of us could recognize Sewell Inlet but the chart indicated that there was a whistling buoy and blinker light about three or four miles offshore. We sailed along until almost dusk before spotting a blinker light at what looked to be the entrance to a harbour, but because we were unsure of our position it was impossible to identify the light. Rather than get lost again we anchored for the night.

At daylight on 1 December we upped anchor and headed towards the blinker which was on a little rock. Earson and Nig McWilliams lowered the lifeboat over the side and rowed it a half a mile to the buoy. In large letters on the side of the acetylene tank which ran the flashing light was printed "Cumshewa Inlet Buoy." That's what we had been looking for. Now we knew where we were for the first time in forty-eight hours.

By two o'clock that afternoon we were at the head of Cumshewa River, which had a 20-foot differential between low and high tide. We dropped our anchor and swung around in the wind. The night was fairly calm. We felt safe. As we were in 5 fathoms of water, we used the old formula of three times the depth and put out 15 fathoms of chain.

Everyone was dead tired. We had had no real comfort for the last three days, and everyone slept except Vosper. About eleven o'clock a wind came up from the southeast and we began to drift badly inshore. The captain had taken the first watch but he didn't realize that we were drifting up the river.

Luck had been running in our favour. It was our first trip on the *Malahat* and we had survived two mishaps. The third was to come that night.

The storm was coming straight up the inlet with gusting winds up to 50 or 60 m.p.h. Our ship was light: the hull was a good 15 feet out of the water and drawing barely 8 feet at the deepest point. She had no ballast and was being driven ashore.

Before calling us on deck Vosper rushed forward to try to raise the anchor. The anchors could only be pulled up when the steam pressure was up in the boilers. The anchor chain was secured with a cat's paw, a clasp that holds the chain from running farther out and releasing its tension, so that it can be unhooked only under power. To do this could have been a fatal mistake for the steam was down and it would have taken an hour to get it back up to lift the anchors. The *Malahat* was drifting up a river of such extreme tides that she could be left settling on roots, logs and rocks. The chances were ten to one that we were finished if we didn't get out of there on the tide. We needed to let out more anchor chain to hold us, but it was too late for that also. Without power we would have to cut the cat's paw clear, sawing through two pieces of 2-inch iron with a dull hacksaw in the middle of the night. We started to steam up the boiler, but it would take an hour. The *Malahat* was being driven up the river stern first. The night was black as pitch. We got the engine started up and swung our searchlight around the shoreline. We were quarter of a mile inland at the top of a high tide at least 20 feet above low water. The branches of the trees on each side of us were not more than 30 feet away.

As at the mouth of any river, there were logs and debris that would become tangled up in the anchor chain which was still down and dragging. We had to take a chance or the *Malahat* would be left high and dry at low tide, holed by a log or keeled over on her side. The captain and I knew it was a gamble to ring for full ahead and to try to fight our way out, but we agreed that it was our only chance.

We got steam up in the boiler and rang for full ahead so that we would buck those winds and lift our anchors as we did. Luck stayed with us. There was really little hope that even under good circumstances a ship well over 200 feet long with five masts could have made its way out of a river that wasn't over 100 feet wide and goes dry at low tide. If either propeller had hit a log, stump or rock on the way out, we would have been finished.

It took us an hour to buck the ship against the winds to deep water. We dropped our anchor again, but this time in 30 fathoms. If we had lost the *Malahat*, I doubt that we would have had the nerve to go back to Vancouver. We certainly didn't have any cash to pay the wages of the crew had our venture failed. That was how uncertain the fate of our men and our ship that night in Cumshewa.

Now we had to face the challenge of loading the huge logs. We swung two heavy, 5-ton booms from the mizzenmast and lashed them together; then we set the rigging. The 'tween decks had already been cut out. The masts were only about 30 feet apart, and between them were four 12-foot by 24-foot hatches.

A boom of logs came alongside. They were choice logs and much larger than we had expected. There were about two hundred, half of them averaging 36 inches through and 40 feet long; on the other hand, some were as much as 10 feet in diameter and had been cut to 32 feet. A log which contained 1,000 board feet weighed approximately 4 tons. The smallest log here was 8 tons, and our biggest lift of 10,000 board feet would weigh about 40 tons.

One of the lighter 40-foot logs was swung on board. It would not go through the 12-foot by 24-foot hatch. A decision had to be made: change the construction of the ship or go back to Vancouver with an empty hold as the former bankrupt owners had done. We would have to take down a mizzenmast to make a 50-foot hatch accommodating logs over 40 feet long.

When I told Vosper that we had to take out that mast he blew his top and said it couldn't be done—he wouldn't allow us to try.

Captain Vosper took watch that night so that the crew could work during the day. The next morning, while the captain was asleep, I decided that one hatch had to be made 50 feet long and one mast had to go overboard. All this had to be accomplished before the skipper awakened, so we had to work quickly and quietly.

We started loosening the rigging and stays. The crew tried to cut the jumper stay right up at the top of the mast but it was shackled too tight, so I just sawed a tiny bit off the topmast and let go the mainstay. All would have been well if we could have disposed of the mast away from the ship but the noise of it going over the side wakened the old captain.

If Vosper had had a gun he would have shot me, no question about it. He was a gentleman, but his language was certainly not flattering to me. He called the crew together and told us that he would never take the ship to sea again if I carried on the way I was. Vosper was in an awkward situation. I was an owner and had to pay the bills. He certainly would have been in charge if we had actually been at sea but we were anchored. Vosper claimed that he was in charge until the ship got back to port. As far as we were concerned, Earson and I were in port now, and the man who pays the piper calls the tune. Vosper was and looked more like a real captain who had been before the mast all his life. He had a thin, weather-beaten face that made you think of the English aristocracy. He was a tough man and unmistakably a gentleman of the sea. But I doubt that he had been anything other than a ship's officer most of his life: he didn't come from the ranks. We, on the other hand, were in loggers' tin boots and mackinaw shirts and looked like workers. But I was boss, and spoke and acted like one.

Vosper claimed that our actions were mutinous, but Earson and I insisted that the ship was going to be loaded. I said, "If you're still unhappy when we're ready to sail, we'll send you back on the *Prince John*, but I don't know what in the Christ you'll use for money. We have none to pay you unless we get that load of logs to town."

We were each right and yet wrong. A captain should have plenty to say about having the masts taken out of his ship. The owner has to make money to pay the bills; if we didn't take that mast out we'd come back light and it would be a financial disaster.

About half the crew including Nig McWilliams and Nick Dale stayed with Earson and me. The rest supported the captain and would not help with the loading. They just showed up for meals. It was a fairly friendly mutiny: our troubles lay ahead of us.

We went ahead enlarging the size of the hold from 12 feet to 50 feet—four times as big. Vosper threw up his hands in horror at that.

We then had to make a boom strong enough to lift the logs aboard. We took an 80-foot spruce log, 28 inches on the butt, 18 inches at the top, and rounded the butt end as an elbow joint and set it in a round wooden socket filled with grease at the foot of the mast. It was set so it could swing inboard by gravity and centre over the hatch, the haul-back on our donkey pulling it back to the loading side of the ship. The main drum lifted on a three-to-one purchase.

We chose the largest log and put a strap on each end of a spreader bar so that it could be raised evenly. It weighed over 40 tons, and we managed to land it. We knew then that we had won that part of the game.

Three men were on the boom alongside the ship. Two of them put the straps around the logs before they were lifted aboard, and the other pike-poled the logs into place. A log was swung inboard, and using a squaw hitch around the ass end of the log, the donkey forward on the main deck stowed it in the hold. The Number One pile aft was always kept higher than the one ahead of it. The logs would then be skidded ahead and dropped into place. When we had the hold filled and before we started to put on the three piles that ran fore and aft on the deck, we picked three of the largest logs, turned them crossways on the ship, and rolled them back against the poop deck where there was about 30 feet of waste space directly over the engine room. It was these three logs that almost cost us the loss of the ship.

The deck logs were then swung aboard. We loaded logs as high as we could until the ship was so tender that putting one more log on one side or the other would cause a list of about 2 feet. A ship with a heavy cargo too low down on the keel takes broadside seas very poorly. It will roll with a sharp whipping action. A stiff ship is a dangerous ship. Ours was now a tender ship and that is a good ship, just perfect for big seas.

Vosper and his men did not help, but they certainly did not hinder us. He was as impressed as hell when he saw us lift 50-ton logs aboard, for he had no more idea of how to accomplish this than fly. He had been used to lifting 1- or 2-ton loads using ordinary seamen. Loggers were the only men who were used to handling such large loads.

Our half-assed mutiny continued during the ten days of loading and rigging the ship. Now, on 12 December, we were ready for sea. The captain with half the crew on his side declared that he could not sail. My brother and I said that he and any of the crew could go ashore and stay in Kelly's logging camp, which was closed down, until the *Prince John* came, or they could stay aboard and sail to Powell River with us. We said that we did not expect them to help with the running of the ship. Vosper made no comment nor any attempt to leave the ship. Nick Dale went down and started the engines. Earson went forward and heaved in the anchor. I rang for full ahead.

It was a quiet night when we cleared the inlet and headed for the mainland. It seemed like months since we had left Vancouver. About midnight a fair storm started from the southeast coming right abeam. The *Malahat* was rolling heavily to the swells, and before daylight the seas were high and coming directly broadside. The ship was very tender with maximum deck load.

The three great 32-foot logs each 10 feet in diameter were lying crosswise on the deck up forward of the poop and aft of the Number One pile of logs. They had been cut to 32-foot lengths because they were so damned big that trucks would have not been able to sustain their weight. We never dreamed of them moving at sea and hadn't taken the precaution of blocking them. We had forgotten that these logs had been lying in the water for about six months and that they had slimy kelp over the entire underside which made them very slippery. There was an 8-foot difference between the ship's beam and the length of the logs. When the ship started to roll heavily, they began to move—just 1 or 2 feet at first; then the full 8 feet. By the time Earson and I arrived on deck they were taking the full swing of the seas.

Before we could turn the ship's stern into the swell to stop the rolling, these three logs began to slide from side to side, like battering-rams. They crashed through the bulwark, breaking the main ribs almost down to the water line, and shot out over the lee side into the sea. You could see the sky from the engine room as tons of water poured in with each roll of the ship. The side of the ship was sprung open maybe 6 feet at the deck and the rent ran in a V down to the water line. There was no hole: the timbers gave way and were pushed out under the weight of the logs. Fortunately, our semidiesel engines kept running, but there was a limit to the amount of water that they could take shooting over them at each roll to port. Soon they would be awash.

This decided us to put our stern to the sea to protect our port quarter, which meant we could not continue to cross Queen Charlotte Sound. Instead we set our course for Dundas Island in American waters, and to keep her steady, we were forced to stay on that course for two days.

Tremendously strong southeast winds took us almost two hundred miles north of our intended crossing, from where we had to fight our way south by inland channels. With a full load it was impossible to make any running repairs.

On our trip north we had run through Seymour Narrows,

but going south I took a short cut. Instead of coming through those narrows we turned at Chatham Point and up Nodales Channel, then through Yaculta Rapids. This route cut about ten miles off the trip to Teakerne Arm. Some Union Steamship boats and fishing craft used these channels but never anything as large as the *Malahat*.

When we unloaded at Teakerne Arm, Vosper and half the crew left us, on friendly terms but intimating that we were completely crazy. The *Malahat* had 15 feet of broken bulwarks and the planking of the ship opened up to the water line. If we went to Vancouver for repairs it would cost us $50,000, so somehow we had to repair her ourselves. We did this by squaring two sides of a 60-foot log about 3 feet in diameter with saws and axes. The two other sides were left round. The new log was centred across the gash and set right into the deck and the bulwark stanchions. Then a ¾-inch cable was woven around the log just as you would lace up a shoe, out around one of the broken beams, and pulled in with a donkey, then stapled. Pretty soon all the ribs were back in place. The same thing was done at the water line to lash the ribs tight into the ship with cable. That left an ugly gash on the outside of the ship where it had been split down to the water line, and she was now far from waterproof. Some 4-inch lumber 20 feet long, with roof felting, was nailed over the repair with 10-inch spikes, the lumber coming from a local mill. This took two days, and instead of the $50,000 the shipyard would have charged, it cost us only the wages of the crew and the lumber. Before the job was half completed we were on our way back to Queen Charlotte Islands to pick up another load of logs having hired replacements for the crew that had left with Vosper. We had been away a month and had made just $2,500 for carrying half a million feet of logs. The crew of fifteen were each getting $75 a month and the captain $100 so we owed nearly $1,500 in wages—but that was all. You could feed a man in those days for less than a dollar a day. We knew that if we could make two trips a month we would make a profit.

We headed north again on 24 December with new supplies from the store at Squirrel Cove and a new crew of ten men. Only the engine room staff, chief engineer Nick Dale, mate Nig McWilliams, and head winchman Sorenson, remained of the old crew. Earson had left for Seattle because of the fish run. There were no sailors among this new bunch and it was up to McWilliams and me to make the ship run smoothly.

The *Malahat* was only making 2 to 5 knots per hour and to get anywhere we had to run twenty-four hours a day. We were like the tortoise: we couldn't afford to stop. But we had conquered the impossible.

We decided to push our luck a little further. There was a strong westerly on the first day out. The *Malahat* ventured past Green Point Rapids which were even narrower and faster than Yaculta Rapids, and out Chancellor Channel. She handled like a packer and was by far the largest ship to go through these rapids. We travelled past Alert Bay and past Port Hardy, but this time instead of cutting straight across to the Queen Charlottes, we took the inside channel up past Egg Island to Rivers Inlet, inside Calvert Island and out Milbanke Sound. Although this lengthened the trip to Cumshewa Inlet by about fifty miles, it was a much safer course.

The trip was fairly uneventful and we loaded in under three days. We headed south again to Teakerne Arm on New Year's Day. There was no conflict of authority: all our thoughts and efforts were directed towards making a dollar.

We made another three trips before running out of cargo. Clarke had arranged for us to do some charter log-carrying from Nootka Sound. The *Malahat* had made five trips and netted $12,500; our costs hadn't been more than half that. We had easily paid for the ship and had made a profit. There was no insurance on the ship or the logs—certainly none on any of us.

CHAPTER 11

We drove out to Esquimalt. I hardly knew how to give my impression of the ship which was at anchor in the bay. She was covered with a coating of ice and snow. Everything about her seemed as if it had been under a huge hammer and smashed up. She looked a perfect wreck.
Log of Malahat, 22 February 1936

We were anchored in Esquimalt Harbour near Victoria and needed someone with captain's papers so that we could clear our ship, for we had no captain, just Nig and myself, to run the *Malahat*. Victoria was the first port we had called at since leaving Vancouver 25 November.

Clarke sent us one skipper who looked our situation over and threatened to turn us in. He said that the ship could not go to sea. We had given him an advance of $100 and we had to give him another $100 to get our ship's papers back from him. Blackmail! We realized that we had to find a captain who was desperate for work.

We looked up an old friend, Pearl Fleming, who knew most people in Victoria. At 10:00 that night he put us in touch with Captain Wormald, a retired CPR captain. He agreed to take the *Malahat* out the next morning without even seeing her. He went to customs at 8:00 A.M. and met us at the wharf at 8:30; our lifeboat brought him out to the ship.

When he came aboard the snow was about 2 feet deep on the decks and everything was covered with ice, even the rigging.

I showed him over the ship and then took him to our quarters aft. Captain Wormald wanted the job, but he just couldn't believe what he saw though he had been at sea all his life. He said, "Mr. Gibson, I just cannot take this ship out." Unless I could get him to change his mind, our enterprise was finished. I answered, "If it has to be that way, at least have a hot rum." I filled him up with hot rums until two or three in the afternoon. The engines had been idling all this time. Excusing myself from the skipper, I told the mate to heave anchor and head up the coast. I then spent another three hours drinking with Wormald in the cabin.

We were well past Race Rocks, twenty miles away, by the time he realized that he had been shanghaied. He was a wild man, old and full of rum. I helped him to his cabin.

A very strong westerly hit us off Lennard Island, which is east and south of the entrance to Clayoquot Sound, and we were forced to take the inside passage. We sailed past Clayoquot. This was my home ground and all on shore knew me and had heard of the *Malahat*. Nothing like our five-masted schooner riding high out of the water had ever passed through these waters.

One of my girlfriends was teaching school there. She and all our friends were watching after the moccasin telegraph announced our arrival. The *Malahat* headed through a narrow channel by the mud flats and the old Indian village of Opitsat. The point was too sharp for us to make a turn and the tide was ebbing. We dropped our anchor and let her stern swing around, backing down to the next buoy. This caused the lifeboat at Tofino to figure that we were in trouble; but by now we were used to handling the *Malahat* and took great pride in manoeuvring her with skill.

We sailed up past Christie School, the Catholic mission, around Catfish Mountain, and then down into our old home grounds of Ahousat where we tied up to our own wharf by the sawmill and paid a visit to my mother. It was the very place that we had left a year or so ago with the *Otter*. The *Malahat* was even bigger than the *Maquinna*, and she caused great astonishment among the natives, who wondered what sort of vessel this could be. It was a great day for me.

We arrived without mishap at O'Malley's camp at Sandspit and started to load logs. In three days we were loaded, and left about 7:00 in the evening. It would be a four-hour run to Nootka Light. I took the watch from 6:00 P.M. to midnight and my brother Clarke and his mate were on from midnight to 6:00 A.M.

All went well until about 10:00 P.M. when we were ten miles south of the Nootka Light. The Estevan Lighthouse lay about ten miles ahead. A storm started building from the southeast.

I turned the watch over to Clarke and the mate, and said, "The light ahead is Estevan. When you get there in a couple of hours, change your course to east by south." Until this time we had been travelling straight south. Clarke and Nig McWilliams were both very fine seamen so the ship was in good hands. Being very tired, I slept through till 6:00 A.M.

When my watch started the storm had increased to a full gale of 60 m.p.h. I decided it was no use to try to buck that weather and headed back to Nootka Sound. When daylight came at about 7:30 I found there was nothing but breakers ahead and we were far west of the Nootka entrance. Instead of making progress to the south and east, we had been blown—while going full ahead—ten miles to the west and north. I plotted our position quickly: we were lying behind Bajo Reef and had a tremendous wind on our beam. An underpowered ship like the *Malahat* is simply a victim of drift in these circumstances. To anchor would be impossible in such high seas. There was a billowy sort of cloud and I knew that the winds would be hitting 70 m.p.h. and could possibly reach hurricane force before long.

Bajo Reef is really a group of uncharted reefs. Everyone leaves them inshore and goes around, except crab fishermen and the Indians on a quiet day. It was impossible for us to go around them because we did not have the power to buck out of our present position.

Our decision was to take a chance and run between the reefs where no ship our size had ventured. It was high tide—thank Christ—and that gave us an extra 12 feet. Every rock that was 10 or 15 feet underwater was breaking in those seas, and we could look straight down on huge beds of kelp. I went forward to the bow of the ship and stood up on the logs, waving hard to starboard or to port to help Clarke avoid the kelp and rocks. I'm sure that our chances of getting through there were about one in a hundred.

We were drawing 24 feet of water, in a place where even

shallow draft boats of 5 feet did not dare to go. We were running before the wind making about 8 knots with a tremendous storm behind us. Our only hope was to swing into Nuchatlitz Inlet which lies behind an extremely sharp point of land. This meant swinging from a westerly course to north by east and making about a mile run through ragged, dangerous, uncharted rocks. Only our momentum carried us around that point, but we got in the lee and half a mile farther on dropped both anchors. Even with both anchors down, for the next twelve hours we had to use both engines full ahead to hold us in position, because the wind had reached gale force.

We had been reported as having cleared Nootka Light. Our last position seen by Nootka Lighthouse was in behind Bajo Reef, and Captain Henderson of the *Givenchy*, the government patrol ship on the coast, was instructed to find us. The skipper, however, said there was no use losing two ships for we were undoubtedly lost, and he had the good sense not to try to track us down.

No one dreamed that we would survive the storm. It was a case of sheer luck, not good management. We played our cards as best we could and they turned out to be good enough to save us.

Two days later when the storm abated, we picked up our anchors, circled behind Nootka Island, and arrived three days after in Victoria. The *Malahat* swung into Inner Harbour and tied up to some booms for unloading just opposite the old Bapco Paintworks.

We had been away many weeks, during which no pleasure, comfort or love entered our lives: just hard work and accomplishment. I wanted off the ship for a good hot bath and company with someone for whom I could feel respect and affection.

We all went ashore the first night; I phoned up a girlfriend who was a lovely person. She was getting serious, but God knows, marriage was farthest from my mind. We went out for dinner and then I talked her into coming back with me to the Empress Hotel where I had taken a room for the night. I was dressed fairly well and my clothes didn't smell of fish. Loggers smell of timber and that smells good.

I remember walking around the lounges with her after dinner; it just wasn't customary for a girl to go up to your room in those days and you couldn't exactly suggest that she should sleep with you.

The Empress Hotel is like a rabbit warren, a maze of endless corridors, and I must have taken a wrong turn. We passed a security guard who asked us where we were going. I gave him the room number, and he asked me why we had not been shown to our room. I told him that we had registered and gone straight into the dining room for dinner.

I'm sure he thought we didn't look married because not more than half an hour later he knocked on our door and told us that overnight guests were not allowed. I tried to stall him by telling him that it was none of his business and that we were going out again. About half an hour later he came back again, and now I had to make him wait a little while I put on part of my clothing.

We had been only talking and dreaming as young lovers do. In those days a man had more respect for a woman and didn't have the quick rapist style that takes all the romance away from lovemaking, or treat it like some kids do as casually as having another cigarette. So I put on my coat and tie, stepped into the corridor and said, "You leave me alone, this is none of your goddamned business." He got a little upset and shouted, "Get that woman out of your room."

Now I resented this very much because she was a lady, the type of girl a man would love to marry. To scare the jesus out of him so he wouldn't bother me again that night, I grabbed him, opened the exit door in the hall and held him over the fire escape. I didn't actually hang him by his feet; I just picked him up and said, "You son of a bitch, you mind your own business and leave us alone or you're liable to bounce on that pavement down below there." It was about five storeys up.

I hoped I had put such a scare into the security guard

that he wouldn't bother us again. My girl and I got a little farther along, and had just got into bed when the guard came back; this time he had the police with him. They threw us both out of the hotel and threatened to arrest me. We took a taxi to her house. Until now it had not been a satisfying or successful night, but in the next three hours I was able to make up for lost time.

At 8:00 the next morning I was back on the job, and by 8:05 we had dropped our tongs on the first log. As soon as the cable tightened you jumped from one log to the next pile of logs, an easy leap of about 8 feet.

I hadn't had any sleep for at least twenty-six hours, and I had drunk a fair amount of whiskey; I had been with a girl as many times as disturbances would allow. As a rule I was damned good at jumping, but this time I missed and dropped 30 feet to the very bottom of the ship, hitting about ten logs on my way down—bing, bang, bong.

Everyone thought I was dead. The crew put a rope around me under my arms and it took three of them to pull me back up to the deck. The crew wanted to rush me to hospital but I asked them to leave me alone for an hour or two, so that they would get on with unloading the logs. I knew what had caused me to fall, and felt that it was somehow a payment for my sins. I didn't feel too bad and thought that if sex cost only that much, I was certainly willing to pay the price.

The crew had taken off my clothing and sized up the bruises all over my body. They lit a fire in the heater in my cabin, and I laid down on the bed with a few stiff belts of rum to cut the pain. All hands were sent back to work. At noon, four hours after my fall, there was a knock at my door. As I got up to answer it with the glass of rum still in my hand, I fell flat on my face on the carpet. Luckily I had my shorts on, because looking down at me was a man I had been trying to impress at the bank the day before. On our arrival I had gone up to see our banker and asked him if he'd cash our cheques. He said that he would but he'd like to see whether we really had any logs aboard. I therefore invited him down to the ship for lunch. His name was Bill

Mulholland and he later became president of the Bank of Montreal, but at that time he was a branch manager. He had with him his assistant manager.

The whole room must have smelled of rum. I looked up at him and said, "Jesus Christ, what a show. You're apt to think I'm drunk!" I thought I had wrecked our chances of getting any money, which worried me more than all my bruises.

But when he saw that I had kept the ship working even after my accident, he felt we were a good risk. Instead of hurting our credit it must have improved it a thousand times because from that day on he was a great supporter of my brothers and me.

Since nothing had been broken in my fall I was in fair shape a day or two later.

The steamship inspector who had tried to condemn the *Otter* arrived with orders to condemn the *Malahat*. That would have meant the end of our business. He was the same character that Clarke and I had threatened to choke in the engine room of the old *Otter:* he had certainly not forgotten us.

"It's been reported to me, Mr. Gibson, that there is a hole right through the side of your ship under that patchwork."

I denied it, explaining that the patchwork was to protect the side of the *Malahat* while the logs were being lifted aboard. I was half wrong and half right (as the patchwork did help keep the ship dry) but he decided that everything looked safe enough and this time the *Malahat* passed inspection. Just as he was leaving I questioned him about the source of his information.

"Mr. Gibson," he said, "you have a rat aboard your ship. One of your crew reported the repairs several weeks ago to our department. I can't tell you who it was, but be well warned that he is a trouble-maker."

There was only one man aboard who had been in Vancouver at the time the report was made. I had brought him down as my guest on the trip from Powell River. In spite of all my bruises, I was so furious that I rowed with him later that evening after we had left port.

Every man on the ship, including myself, had to make a living, and I felt that it was unforgivable of him to come back on board and accept my money after betraying all of us. If he had felt so strongly about the manner in which I was running the *Malahat* he should have quit.

I was pretty strong in those days and I gave him an awful licking—kicked the jesus out of him would be a better way of putting it—and threw him out on deck, warning him that I would chuck him overboard if he ever went down aft. He could sleep in the fo'c's'le if he wanted. Jobs were so scarce that all the men hated his guts for putting our living in jeopardy. They needed a job as badly as I did.

I kicked him off the ship when we arrived back in port. There was a rumour that he went up to the Arctic, but I made damn sure that he didn't have much of a chance on this coast; he was a no-good bastard who lacked both sense and esprit de corps. I guess it was something like the old Captain Bligh days, but that was the only way things could be run.

I was still having a lot of pain from the fall. We had about an hour's unloading left to do so I sent my skipper to get our clearance. He was half an hour ahead of orders from the Steamship Department to cancel our clearance. We pulled out of Esquimalt Harbour and started for Queen Charlotte Islands with no supplies aboard. I figured that the last place the Steamship Department would expect us to head for was the port of Nanaimo, and therefore the next day we docked in her harbour and loaded coal, oil and groceries. I knew we had to be away before daylight just in case any government inspectors were checking for the *Malahat*. At 4:00 A.M. I suddenly realized that ninety per cent of the crew were missing.

I called a taxi and, as it happened, the driver was a woman. I told her she couldn't possibly take me where I wanted to go as I had to venture into the red light district to get my crew. She said, "You have the right driver, sir. That's where I got my start and I can show you around."

There were about ten houses on the street and somehow the word got around that I was on the search. Each time I went to a house, the madam said that the crew had just left, but by 6:00 A.M. I was back aboard the ship with the entire crew. We set out once again for the Queen Charlotte Islands.

The government had put out a search warrant for us. I travelled by different routes on each trip and refused to pick up telegrams that I was certain were waiting in Sewell Inlet.

We made two more trips into Teakerne Arm, each one grossing us $2,500, and it was on the third trip that the government ship caught up with us. The boat, *Adversus*, could make up to 15 knots and our best was 5 knots. They came alongside demanding us to "stand by in the name of the King." Then a boarding party came on the *Malahat* and forced us to anchor in Alert Bay.

We were ordered into Admiralty Court in front of a judge who wore a big white curly wig and long robes. I'd feel lucky if I got out of there with my head still on my shoulders and not rolling away by itself.

I was charged with running a ship after it had been condemned, and running a ship without a master having captain's papers. I had never had the time to get any papers, Christ, no. You can run fish boats, fighting ships and yachts without papers—but not freighters. The *Malahat* was a kind of bastard, which hadn't been classified as a freight ship and didn't have enough power for deep sea. It was the only ship of its kind in the world, and our company tried to claim that it was a log-carrying power barge.

I was accused of risking lives, getting in the road of other ships and chancing a severe marine mishap because I had no papers. At last I had my opportunity to speak.

"Your Honour, I've been at sea for many years, and the *Malahat* is a boat that will never sink. There has been no risk. She will float under any conditions since she is constructed of wood and is carrying a cargo of logs. There are boats being allowed to run up and down this coast that are made of steel and are so rusty that you can kick the bow in. They would sink in a second if they hit a log. As far as her being dangerous, why those boys are safer on the *Malahat* than they would be in the town. Even my own mother has been aboard and made trips with us. As for this lawyer stating that I have no papers, he's absolutely wrong. I have papers that I am very proud of."

The whole court fell silent. Even those who knew me looked astonished. The judge eyed the prosecutor wondering if there were some remote chance that an error had been made.

"Mr. Gibson, do I understand you are claiming you have papers and papers that you are proud of, sufficient to run this vessel? What kind of papers are they, may I ask?"

"Your Honour, I have papers that very few captains possess. A diploma for two years of regularity and punctuality at Sunday School."

The tension in the courtroom was broken. The judge banged his gavel and dismissed the case.

"You will make the necessary repairs, and you will certainly not make any trips without a captain having proper papers: no more Sunday School certificates will be allowed."

CHAPTER 12

My years on the Malahat *taught me that hard work, ambition and nerve will mostly beat brains and ability.*

By 1936 we had a wonderful young skipper with us by the name of Dan Backie, one of the finest seamen I have ever met on the coast. We also had Wormald on board in order to avoid any trouble with the inspection department. Backie was a Scot. Only 5 feet 8 inches and stockily built, he could lick most men 3 inches taller because of his agility and tremendous determination. He was the kind of captain who was down in the hold working as hard as any of the crew loading logs, so that as the last log was swung aboard the ship, the anchors would be in, engines running, and the full ahead signal clanging. The load would be lashed down during the next two hours before we hit rough water.

Dan was very productive and had fine character and judgement—a man I could depend on and in whose hands I increasingly left the ship. A natural seaman. He wasn't as adventuresome as I was, but that was perhaps very good since he had much more respect for the impossible than I.

Early in 1937 Clarke, Dan and I were heading across Hecate Strait in the Queen Charlotte Islands. On this trip the *Malahat* was fully loaded and feeling hard a southeaster that had strengthened on our starboard side. We were running for cover off Laredo Channel when only half an hour away from the passage we realized that we weren't making any headway at all. We tried to get back into open water. But for every mile we made ahead, we drifted two sideways.

About 4:00 P.M. we swung around again to port and tried to run for the open waters north, with the sea astern. Although it was still daylight, the storm had reached a full gale of 50 to 60 m.p.h. with tremendous seas running. We knew that if we went on we would crash on the rocks in the night, as land was just two miles off our starboard side. Checking the chart, we saw what appeared to be a reef about a quarter of a mile offshore. We figured that our anchors might just hold on the jagged rocks if we could clear that reef by only a little and drop our mud hooks in its lee.

The anchors caught; the ship swung round, our engines going full ahead. We had about half an hour to decide whether to abandon ship and put ashore while there was still daylight, or take a chance and ride out the night.

All that night the seas got bigger, and by the next morning the storm had if anything increased. By 4:00 P.M. the winds were almost hurricane force and even the water behind the breaker was coming up over our forward deck. We were heavily loaded, and under all this strain one of our anchor chains suddenly parted. We heard it snap. That left us not more than two ships' lengths off an almost vertical coastline, with only one anchor to secure us. After calling the whole crew aft we made the decision to try to make it to shore in the lifeboats before dark; we believed there was no chance that the single anchor could hold all through the night.

Orders were given to provision the lifeboats with axes and every man with a tightly sealed bottle containing matches and a little kerosene, so that if any of us reached shore, he would not perish from exposure.

It was late in the afternoon. The decision to abandon ship had been made without reference to Wormald because although he was a fine skipper he was not a coast man. What we needed now was a real pike-pole skipper.

Both lifeboats were ready to be launched; I figured our chances were about even that we could make the shore. The seas were running the whole length of the ship and it was all our pumps could do to keep the water from getting round the engine.

Everyone was aft when we started to lower the boats. I went below with Clarke. The old captain was lying in his bunk. "Well, boys, you go on now. I'm nearly seventy and I could never make shore. Here with my ship at least there'll be some chance. The rest of you go on if you want to but I'm too old. I can't climb those hills, nor can I stand the exposure. I'll die anyway. Thank you, good-bye."

We argued that the anchor couldn't possibly hold, and that we would be killed if the deckload of logs ever got loose. Dan and Clarke and I felt we just couldn't leave the old captain but we didn't know what in God's name to do with him. All this took time, and by now we realized that it was too late to find shore in the fading daylight. It was now impossible to row against those seas, and so all we could do was hope that we could last out till morning.

That was the third time we should all have been lost at sea. The chances of us holding there were one in a million, especially with all that strain on our anchor. It just shows the good judgement of the old captain, for we would all most certainly have been drowned in those high seas had we abandoned ship.

It's hard to describe what it's like seeing all that white water flying around and the cliffs looming astern with the darkness coming on. It's a funny thing; you would think you'd be scared, but you go below and have your coffee and do everything you normally would. You're calm, you're cool and collected. You don't exactly do any praying but you sure as hell do a lot of wishing.

The storm continued that day until noon. Then it started to abate, and within an hour it had died down completely. But soon the wind swung to the southwest gusting up to 20 m.p.h. A southwester could have thrown us back on the rocks. The *Malahat* had to get out. We could not last out in that position for more than an hour.

We could not pick up our anchor because it was on the other side of the reef, so the chain had to be severed with a hacksaw, and we had to chance our power getting us out. The *Malahat* was going full ahead on her engines when our chain dropped into the sea. There was a half hour of nip and tuck: it took us ten minutes to make way 100 feet, then another gust put us right back where we had started.

Fortunately the ship was fully loaded. Had she been light the wind would have tossed us back on the rocks. After another half hour the *Malahat* gained enough to clear the reef, and once more we were in deep water and darkness was upon us.

We headed for the open sea, gaining perhaps a half-mile an hour. If the storm increased we would be carried back on the shore without our anchors to save us. Someone must have been on our side, for the *Malahat* was the luckiest ship I've ever known—not once but a hundred times. No one will ever know where we were that night. She just plugged ahead, and at daylight the next morning the weather was so thick that none of us, including the captain, had any idea what our position was. Since we had no sounding gear or navigational aids of any kind except a compass, we carried our lead line along the side of the ship clean up the fo'c's'le. The mate threw it overboard from the fo'c's'le head and by the time the ship had moved we had our soundings off the poop deck. By this means we knew that we were in over 40 fathoms of water and fairly well offshore.

The storm abated that afternoon and we went down the coast to Powell River to unload. There we bought two new anchors and anchor chain costing more than the original $2,500 we had paid for the *Malahat*.

This was not the end of the mischief, however. Our contract to carry logs with Tom Kelly paid us five dollars a thousand; his company decided that we were making too much money and cut our price. As a consequence, we had to work even harder and make more frequent trips. All this came about because of my foolish pride.

While in Powell River we were invited to attend a banquet with officials of the Powell River Company including the head man of their logging division. Tom Kelly got to his feet and made a speech about how successful our log-carrying venture had been, taking full credit for the idea of carrying logs rather than towing them across the straits.

I should have kept my mouth closed, but it was difficult to forget that on the first trip we had woefully needed another $1,000 to meet our payroll and had been refused a loan by this same man. Yet there was Kelly claiming that he had had full confidence in the venture and had known it would be a great success.

My pride was touched by his speech and I jumped to my

feet. "Tom here had not enough faith to lend us $1,000 and we almost went broke for the need of it. It has been our own labour and our lives that have been up front."

My rebuttal was foolhardy and certainly poor tactics psychologically, because the next day Kelly called me in and cut the price to four dollars a thousand.

A month or two later in the middle of winter we were making a routine trip down the coast, going ahead when the weather would permit, anchoring in shelter when the wind was too strong to proceed. For two frustrating days we had been driven back five miles on our course, then gone ahead five miles trying to pass Egg Island which lies outside Rivers Inlet and halfway across Queen Charlotte Sound. After fighting the winds for forty-eight hours we returned to Rivers Inlet. That midnight, after twelve hours' rest, the sky suddenly cleared. There was still a tremendous sea running but the wind swung round to the north. The northeaster was pretty well behind us when we decided to up anchor and cross Queen Charlotte Sound for the shelter of Vancouver Island.

Because of the southwest storm over the last two days driving the water into Rivers Inlet, the sudden change of wind and a strong ebb tide, we made good time of 6 or 7 knots when we swung out at midnight. Dan Backie turned in. I was on watch with the mate. The logs were piled so high on deck that despite the 12-foot-high bridge running the full width of the ship, you could only see from the wings. All was well and about 1:00 A.M. I went below for a while. It was a bitter cold night and the natural thing was to leave the bridge for a spell and go down into the warmth of the wheelhouse. Maybe it was some sort of an intuition, but after half an hour I felt nervous and looked out the porthole. There was a lot of heavy foam, which is always associated with conditions not too far from land. Our course should have cleared the nearest offshore rocks by two miles, but I went back to the bridge feeling uneasy. Nothing showed in the pitch black but the water breaking on the sides of the ship.

Just as a precaution I jumped down off the bridge to the wheelhouse and said to the quartermaster, "Put her a couple of points to starboard." I said to the mate, "Let's go up and look things over." We both went to the bridge. I still did not like the look of the storm and ordered a full course change of a few more points to starboard.

Two minutes later I saw, like a flash in the sky, a huge breaker at least 50 feet high in front of us about one point off the port bow. I knew then where we were. That was Paddle Rock, and there was just one chance in a thousand that we might clear it.

I ran to the wheelhouse and yelled to the mate to put the helm hard to starboard. We had less than two ships' lengths to go before we hit. I knew it was too late to call the engineer to reverse the engine. Running down the 30 feet of steps I reversed the starboard engine myself to help swing us. The rock was just abeam our bows. Up on deck again I saw that our stern was swinging towards the rocks. I again ran below, put the starboard engine full ahead and yelled to the quartermaster to throw the helm hard aport.

There were twelve men aboard. Six men sleeping in the fo'c's'le all sure to be drowned if we hit that rock! The logs would be adrift a minute later, making it impossible to lower the lifeboats. Paddle Rock has a tremendously deep water hole off one side, and by the grace of God, it was on this face that the sea tossed the side of our ship. Another great wave boosted us up and we could have jumped right onto the rock, but we touched and slipped down the side with the kiss of a mermaid. It seemed that the seas caressed us and washed us away. But I was certain we were through if another wave took us down on that rock. Again our poop deck was thrown up even with the top of the rock, and the *Malahat* slipped down its side a second time.

I ran below decks calling to everyone, for there was no possibility of going forward to call the men there. Running into the captain's room, I shook him on the shoulder, "Dan, I've lost your ship." He jumped up in his underwear and came on deck just as the next big wave washed us clear. I'm sure it was as close as any ship has ever come to Paddle Rock and disaster!

Knowing that we had to keep out from shore, we headed

out to sea with the prayer that the *Malahat* had not sprung a leak. The strain on all of us had been intense. I went below and took a good swig of rum—I'm not sure if it was one full glass or two bottles. It simply had no effect whatsoever. The boys in the fo'c's'le had slept right through the whole episode, little knowing that for a couple of minutes the chance of their living was one in a thousand. I still feel to this day that nothing but the luck of that great ship *Malahat* saved us that night.

We made more scheduled trips on the *Malahat*; and we also made a deal to buy timber in Nootka Sound so that we could greatly expand our operations in that area. Dan Backie was running a steam towboat for us called the *James Carruthers*, and Nig McWilliams had been skippering the *Malahat*.

In 1937 I was in Malksope Inlet when I received a telegram from Clarke saying that the *Malahat* had been forced into Bamfield Harbour in Barkley Sound because of a broken tail shaft, which left us with just one 150-horsepower engine. Bill Olsen, the skipper on this trip, was waiting for a tow into Victoria so that the necessary repairs could be made.

At that time I was on the *Joan G*, a ship with a 135-horsepower engine, and I immediately made the sixteen-hour run down the coast. My crew consisted of a twenty-year-old engineer and an Indian mate. We had no gear aboard except 800 feet of ¾-inch cable but no tow winch.

I knew that this would be the last trip for the *Malahat* under power because we were experiencing increasing pressure from the government.

The cost of replacing the tail shaft and the propeller that had just been lost would run between $3,000 and $4,000. The Steamship Department had such a list of complaints about repairs needed to the *Malahat* that I knew she would not pass the next steamship inspection.

I agreed to tow the ship into Victoria with the aid of the one remaining engine on the *Malahat*, but I neglected to mention to Bill that first we were going 200 miles up the coast to pick up $15,000 worth of logs waiting for us in Malksope Inlet. Then we would set out for Victoria.

I headed west after clearing Cape Beale. Bill thought I would be going east and tooted his whistle a few times to attract my attention. I had fastened my towline on his anchor chain, 20 feet underwater so that he couldn't cut it free even if he had wanted to. We had no communications at all, and were too far apart to holler to each other because I had at least 1,000 feet of line out. Bill was furious and put his one engine in reverse while I kept the *Joan G*'s engines in forward. He had no steerage way. For a half hour the *Joan G* and the *Malahat* had a tug-of-war. Bill and I were two strong and determined characters.

How could I fire a man who was on another ship 1,000 feet away, and anyway, even an owner can't fire a captain while at sea. With just one engine Bill had almost no manoeuvrability, and soon the *Joan G* began to make a little headway.

Of course he was as angry as hell, but he could see that we all needed the money from the cargo waiting for us.

After the logs were loaded at Malksope we slipped out to sea, the *Joan G* ahead, the *Malahat* behind. Because the *Joan G* wasn't a licensed towboat, we let go of the *Malahat* off Race Rocks, and I transferred from the *Joan G* as I didn't want Bill to be in any more trouble in an already difficult situation.

This time we had to unload in Victoria Harbour. We dropped anchor and tried to swing round to port to make a starboard landing on the far side of the harbour. The tide was falling and I found that I could go neither ahead nor astern. We were fully loaded, drawing about 24 feet of water and our bow and stern settled down into the mud. There was nothing to do but wait for the tide.

About 7:30 the next morning the CPR night passenger ship from Vancouver found us square across the channel. There was no way in Christ's world for her to get past us, and her captain came to the bow and told me to get our old freighter out of there; I told him to go to hell, that we had as much right to be there as he did. I told him that we were stuck on the bottom and he would have to wait until the tide came up just like anyone else. The *Malahat* took up the full 250 feet of the centre of the channel.

I wasn't very popular with the ferry passengers who were delayed for at least three hours. Even the big tugboats couldn't grab our stern and swing us around because we were stuck so fast. With the incoming tide, our stern swung around and we were able to make our landing.

That was the last trip for the *Malahat* under her own power. She couldn't pass her inspection and we certainly couldn't afford her repairs. As a consequence we decided to remove the two engines from the *Malahat* and turn her into a barge to be towed by the *James Carruthers*. She joined our fleet of log-carrying barges: the *Forest Pride, Tolmie* and *K.V. Kruse*.

The *Malahat* was lost at sea, as reported in the *Vancouver Sun* on 23 March 1944:

Schooner Malahat, famous old rum-runner, which foiled coast guarders more often than they were successful, is now reported a "constructive total loss" by surveyors, who flew last week to Green Bay, Barkley Sound, to inspect the log-carrying barge. She has been pounded to pieces by Pacific waves and B.C. logs.

Coastguarders report regretted the departure of their old enemy.

Caught in a west coast gale the Malahat started to flounder late last week. Her crew was taken off, and she was towed to shelter. It was believed her strong wooden hull had stood up under the battering, but inspection has shown her log cargo awash in her long hull, broke free like stampeding corralled buffalo. Driven by the surging seas, they thrust their thousands of tons of weight against the bulwarks and carried them away. They thumped the hull and started timbers everywhere. All escaped, floating up from the lower hold, as top layers broke free through the bulwarks, crashing and smashing ribs and planks and staunchions.

The *Malahat* had been the only self-powered, self-loading and -unloading barge, until MacMillan Bloedel built the *Haida Brave* in 1978 at a cost of $15 million. It cost six thousand times as much as the *Malahat* and carries only four times as much cargo at twice the speed.

CHAPTER 13

There are some things that a man finds out only with time. It is like buying a pair of shoes and finding that you enjoy them more after you've worn them a month than you did when you first put them on. It's somewhat the same with a wife: you have to get used to her and learn to know her before you can really appreciate her. Louise was the woman of my dreams because she had lots of brains as well as beauty. I've always admired intelligence in a woman.

The first time I met Louise Redman was in 1935 when I was taking a load of fish on the *Sunrise Ranger* into Seattle. Because there had been a lot of fog on this trip I was forced to keep my head out of the window all the way down the coast and as a result I caught a bad cold. We should have landed Monday morning about six o'clock but the weather was so thick that I missed Seattle completely and went three or four miles past the wharf. We couldn't afford to be late: our cargo of fish was worth $10,000 but if it didn't get to market until the next day, it would be graded #2 fish. Instead of making a little profit we would lose a few thousand dollars.

After we had unloaded and weighed the fish I went to see Herman Breeze at the elaborate offices of Armstrong, Melcher and Dessau who were purveyors of mild-cured salmon to the New York market and the major purchasing agent for our cargo. Herman buzzed for his secretary to come in and make out the cheque. That's the first time I saw Louise. I noticed that she was very beautiful and had a lovely figure. When she walked out the door the cheeks of her backside moved up and down. I jokingly commented to Herman that here were two more places to hang my hat. She was petite and attractive—the exact opposite of me.

Louise couldn't have been as taken with my appearance because when I called her that evening to ask her to dinner or a dance, she turned me down flat.

Since we weren't leaving until the next morning and I had no company except two Indian boys, I decided that I would meet some women and have a little fun. I put on my store clothes and went to one of those dance halls where you buy a roll of tickets and give one to a girl for a dance. Four tickets cost a dollar and I bought a roll just to be on the safe side. There were about fifty women sitting around the wall. Being a little cautious, I waited awhile before asking for a dance. Up the coast we were good dancers. In Tofino and even at Ahousat, we danced better than most people dance now. We would dance all night when there was a fiddle and enough light. Eventually, I asked a young lady for a dance and was turned down, so I thanked her and asked another girl. She refused me, too. I thought I'd ask another girl farther on down the row. I went all around one side of the room but didn't have any takers for the first dance. I went to the back of the room and sat with a bunch of men—and wondered what was wrong with me. I felt really rejected and lonely.

Later on I went to another group of women and asked each of them to dance. I had no luck that time either. At last I decided that if respectable women wouldn't dance with me then I would try elsewhere. I called a taxicab and found a sporting house where there was dancing and drinking.

I found out later from Louise why no one wanted to dance with me. I smelled like rotten fish, because my suit had been hanging in the ship. I was completely unaware of the bad odour, probably because of my cold. No wonder none of the girls had wanted to dance with me. I must have smelled like hell when I met Louise fresh off the boat.

I didn't meet Louise Redman again until Earson and I were in San Francisco on a business trip. Earson had already met her since he had been skipper on most of the fish-packing trips to Seattle. He discovered that she had become the secretary to the vice-president of the Union Pacific Railway in San Francisco. Earson telephoned her when we arrived and asked her to get a date for me so we could make a foursome. That night Louise and I were picked as the two best waltzers in a dance competition. I was very flattered to be her partner and that night I asked her if she would marry me. She told me not to be so foolish, that she would no more marry a fisherman than a fly. Why on the earth would she go north to that wilderness? She laughed at my proposal.

Earson and I continued south, and on our way back we picked up one of Louise's friends and gave her a ride to San Francisco. Everything would have been fine and I would have got along faster with Louise if I hadn't tried to make a little proposition to her friend during the trip. She told Louise about my advances. I wrote several letters to Louise after that episode, but there wasn't much enthusiasm in her replies. But I was still very keen on her, as this letter to my mother indicates.

20 March 1936
Squirrel Cove, B.C.

Mother, I want you to meet Louise Redman sometime this spring, she's a lovely girl, she has the kind of qualities I want and I'm sure I can tell real quality when I see it. She's the kind of girl that our family needs. I know you'll like her, Mother—she's all alive, even in the head. Beautiful but not dumb. . . .

One day I telephoned Louise from Powell River; I told her that I could have three days in San Francisco and asked her to go out with me. When she agreed I chartered a plane and flew to Vancouver, then caught a flight south.

I met an interesting character on the plane. He asked me to give him two tens for a twenty-dollar bill and then he offered one of the tens to the air hostess as a tip. When she turned it down, he put it in the envelope and left it on the seat ahead.

By chance we took the same bus from the airport to the St. Francis Hotel. After we had registered he asked me to join him in the bar. When I excused myself to phone Louise he suggested that she get a friend and that all of us join him for the evening. The party was arranged. I thought he was a little forward but he seemed a nice enough fellow.

It turned out to be a very embarrassing evening for me because we went to the first nightclub that I had ever been in. It was a private club having a fancy brass elevator. I saw him give the elevator operator a ten-dollar bill. I began to feel a little uneasy.

We went up to the bar and he ordered a special bottle of champagne. I threw out a ten-dollar bill to buy the next one. I thought that was big money. He insisted that we were his guests and told me to give the money to the bartender as a tip. I said, "I'll take the goddamned money back. If you're going to do the paying, you can damned well do the tipping too." Later in the men's room I demanded, "Have you counterfeit money? How in the hell did you get so much?"

"That's none of your damn business, Gibson," he said. "I've had a lot of money left to me by my dad and I'm going down to Santa Anita to run my racehorses. I imposed on you by inviting myself for the evening so I would like to pay the bill." That was the first and last time I was ever impressed by a big spender.

Louise thought I was a cheapskate because I let another man pay for all the drinks and then took back my tip. She told me that evening almost ruined our relationship. The next morning I met her again and tried to persuade her to marry me. I felt at home on the waterfront so we went for a walk along the docks and looked out over the harbour. A three-masted ship about 80 feet long was anchored in the bay. Louise explained that it belonged to John Barrymore and that the people of San Francisco were very proud to have it in their harbour. Suddenly I had an inspiration.

I pulled out a picture of the *Malahat* as a virgin ship on her way to Australia in her lumbering days with all her sails swirled out, and told her that this could be her honeymoon ship. "That little thing out there is a toy compared to my schooner."

She had been writing to me care of the *Malahat* so she knew that I owned the ship, but she had no idea that the masts had been cut down and the 'tween decks were out. I pressed my advantage. "You are the only girl I've ever met that I wanted to marry—and I'm going to. It doesn't matter to me that you say you won't. We'll arrange all that later."

We were married in a civil ceremony in Seattle on 11

May 1936. I was a bit nervous and had several drinks to steady me. I asked the parson how long the ceremony would take and when he said twenty minutes, I offered to double his fee if he would cut the time in half! After we were married I gave him $100 instead of the $50 I had planned, which ran me a little short of cash. On the way to the airport I made the mistake of borrowing $50 from my new wife. She was a little startled that I didn't have any money, and probably wondered what kind of situation she had got herself into. I have paid her back ten thousand times but it seems to me that I always owed her the principal. She claimed that she was my first financial backer. I think it would have been better to have made a deal with the taxi driver instead.

My family took rooms on three floors of the Devonshire Hotel in Vancouver for the reception. It was quite a party. All the respectable people were on the top floor having tea and cakes with my mother and Louise. No one drank in front of Mother. The next floor down was for our semi-respectable business associates to whom we probably owed money. The bottom floor was for the people we had spent our lives with—the loggers and fishermen.

As the evening wore on the respectable people from the top floor went home, as did most of the people on the second floor. I got down to the third floor and Earson, who was my best man, had quite a time getting me up to my room. I was an hour late on my wedding night!

Galt Brothers, one of the wholesale dry goods companies who supplied our camps, gave us a honeymoon trip to Harrison Hot Springs. It was five years before I found out that the hotel was built on a large lake. I had missed it entirely on my first trip. We stayed for two days and then went back to see our friends in Vancouver. A honeymoon is much better after you have been married ten years because you've had time to appreciate one another and don't feel those uncomfortable lags in the conversation.

I guess the greatest surprise of Louise's life came the day she climbed the Jacob's ladder to the deck of the old *Malahat*. The men were tougher looking than on any other freighter I've been on. The only comfortable part of the ship was our private lounge in the owner's quarters which had a bathtub and flush toilet, a bedroom, sitting room and a real coal fireplace. That's where Louise had to spend most of the next six months or so; although she was often up on the poop deck because she was so desperately seasick when we were in open waters. The *Malahat* rolled like a barrel.

At times the storms were bad enough to scare even the most experienced sailor. Many of the toughest men I've worked with couldn't have stood being aboard that wreck. I'll never understand how Louise endured those months. I'm sure she was terrified most of the time, but we both had the kind of pioneer parents who became closer and stronger in hardship or poverty, and so did we. Louise sailed with me until I decided that she should stay ashore with my mother for a while because we were expecting our first child.

I don't know why Louise stayed with me. I think that it was out of a determination to make our relationship work. Louise was the one to make all the changes and I am sorry to admit that I was unbending and my life went on as before. I can't speak highly enough of her resilience and character. It was she who made our marriage work out.

CHAPTER 14

The reason we were able to start so many camps in such a short time was that I moved on to another project as soon as I found a man as capable as I was of running the camp. I always knew how to pick good workers.

My brothers and I were determined to diversify as a result of the trouble we had with the Kelly Spruce Company when they cut the price paid us for carrying their logs from five dollars a thousand down to four dollars, then ultimately three dollars. At that rate we would be losing money, so we ended the deal and did a little customs work in the fall of 1936 carrying logs for O'Malley Lumber Company on the side and picking up a few charters into Vancouver.

That spring Jack and I had cruised for timber on the west coast of Vancouver Island hoping we could establish a business not only cutting but also carrying our own logs to market in the *Malahat*. We found a timber limit in the shelter of Cape Cook in Malksope Inlet and made preparations for camp.

Although we had made close to $100,000 in the last two years with the *Malahat*, a large part of the money had been invested in a gold mine at the head of Herbert Arm. This venture turned out to be a losing proposition, and our bankers suggested that we stick to fishing and logging and forget about making a fortune in mineral speculations.

Once again, we were starting from scratch, because we had to both fell the timber and find our own markets. Earson went up to Malksope ahead of us on the *East Bay No. 1* with a crew to fall some timber, while Clarke purchased a donkey and the necessary rigging. They were loaded on board the *Malahat*, and with a crew of twenty men we left Vancouver knowing that we had to come back with a full load of logs to make ends meet.

Louise had come back aboard with our son Gordon, who was born 23 August 1937. She was looking forward to living in our first home—a floating house on a log raft that I had bought from the Indians for seventy-five dollars. A bride's dream!

The trip up the coast was rough: we hit strong westerlies and had to anchor twice on the way, rolling steadily. All the loggers were seasick, which did wonders to sober them up for the hard work that lay ahead. Many of the reefs up by Malksope were uncharted and we had to pick our way in between them with extreme caution as the *Malahat* was drawing 12 feet of water when light and 24 feet when fully loaded coming back out of the inlet.

Malksope was to be the first big camp we owned aside from the little shingle bolt camps of the 1920s. Our first task was to cut large logs for a float and then construct a combination cookhouse and bunkhouse out of lumber that we had brought from Vancouver.

This float was built with twenty spruce logs, 120 feet long and 8 feet on the butt, lashed together with the butt ends lying forward. On top of these we laid four logs crossways, which were lashed down to make a floating foundation for the steam donkey and the bunkhouse-cookhouse.

At the front of the float we raised a 100-foot A-frame, and held the entire rig offshore with a stiff-leg. All our timber was felled within 1,000 feet of the shoreline and the logs were pulled into the water by the steam donkey.

Three weeks later Louise, young Gordon and I moved into the little Indian shack. The float and the bunkhouses had been constructed; over 500,000 feet of logs had been hauled to the water's edge and loaded on the *Malahat*, which was headed for Vancouver with Capt. Dan Backie. Earson returned to fish packing. In a month from the time we left Vancouver to come up the coast to Malksope we had yarded over a million feet of logs out of the wilderness. These logs were worth $15,000 on the market and we were to make at least two trips every month.

When we were loading the *Malahat* for her third trip to town, a tremendous storm blew up. The A-frame was secured to the beach with 1¼-inch cables, and tied alongside it was our entire cargo of a half a million feet of logs. Our little house was lashed to the boom.

I was back up the hill about 800 feet when a twister blowing up to 100 or 120 m.p.h. broke our house loose from its mooring, and it started to float up the bay. At the same time one of the boom chains broke, and the logs burst out all over hell—$15,000 worth!

My wife and child were adrift, but I knew that the house was safe enough since it would settle on the mud flats half a mile away. Unfortunately, Louise didn't know this and she was absolutely terrified that she might be heading straight to Japan as there was nothing between the mud flats and the open sea.

I had to make a quick decision. The half hour that it would take to catch the house would cost us our entire load of logs—everything we had in the world—because they would scatter in every direction at the head of the inlet. The worst that could happen to the shack was that it got stuck on the flats. The floating home was worth $75 and the boom was worth $15,000.

I decided to save the logs first. I had to untie the boom sticks and run round the farthest logs, then tie one end to the shore and make a purse so that the logs would not be driven up onto the gumbo at the river mouth. The next three hours were spent saving the logs, and by the time I caught up with Louise she was a very scared and unhappy girl. It was difficult to explain how those logs could be more important than she was. They were our bread and butter. Louise did once remark, years later, "Well, Gordon, I will say that you've been a good provider. But your job always came first!"

In January of 1938 we made a deal with an outfit in Seattle to purchase timber in Muchalat Arm as we had run out of timber in Malksope. This new camp was fifty miles of outside waters and another fifty miles of inside waters from our present camp. We had a few days of work left in Malksope Inlet, but it was important to take advantage of any of the rare clear days at the first of the year to tow our complete camp. Otherwise we might have to wait several months for fair weather and calm seas. I arrived back in camp one fine afternoon and knew that the tow had to be made immediately, even though we had no insurance.

That night, after booming the logs and untying everything from the shore, we hooked up the float with the A-frame, the cookhouse and bunkhouses, our own little house, and about fifty boom sticks to the towline of the *Joan G.* The Pacific Ocean was as calm as a millpond so we had a fair chance of success. The crew were all asleep in their bunks and had no idea that they were headed for a real adventure. About daylight the next morning we were making 2½ m.p.h. in open waters with forty miles to go before reaching the protection of inside waters. All was well until three o'clock that afternoon when the westerly that had been helping us along so nicely started to freshen. The seas came up so rough that the swells rushed through the bunkhouses, and our logging crew got so excited that we had to lower the lifeboat and bring them aboard the *Joan G.* The little house which we had bought from the Indians completely disintegrated. The logs washed out from under her, the walls crumbled and finally the peak of the roof disappeared under the swells. That was the sad end of our first home. All the floorboards in the bunkhouses were washed away.

About midnight, thirty hours after we had left Malksope Inlet, we were in inside waters once more. It had been a wonderful trip considering the little we had lost. At dark the next night we were at our new site where we were to spend the next two years making our greatest start in the lumber business. We were ready to begin work almost immediately and lost only three days for the tow and site preparation.

This time I built Louise a lovely floating home and beached it in a little bay where large fir trees came down to the shore.

That fine old workhorse, *the Malahat*, was still carrying our logs to Vancouver, but we bought other hulls: the *Forest Pride*, which had been a wooden sailing ship similar to the *Malahat*; the *K.V. Kruse*, and the *Tolmie*. We converted them into log barges, and to tow them we acquired a North Sea tug, the *James Carruthers*. We were able to juggle things so that when one barge was in tow, another was being loaded and the third discharging her cargo.

The barges were kept working full time though we only had one caterpillar and a donkey. I was mainly working ashore while Dan Backie and Bill Olsen, the first mate, ran the towboat, *James Carruthers*. After the purchase of the barges our logging increased to about two million feet a month.

The *Joan G* had been purchased by Clarke in 1936, while she was still on the rocks north of Prince Rupert. She was called the *Maid of Orleans* then, and had been built as a black-birder and later been in the Arctic with Capt. Christian Klengenberg. She was sheathed in hardwood and could stand any winter without being damaged by the ice. Although she had a shallow draft, she ran aground outside Prince Rupert. Earson went north to salvage her, changing her name to the *Joan G* after Clarke's oldest daughter.

As was the case with the *Malahat*, we were unsure what to do with her. Again luck turned our way: American ships plying north from Seattle were hit by a seamen's strike. As a result, mine operators in Juneau couldn't get blasting powder and we found that we could get one dollar for each case we delivered. So we loaded up at James Bay just outside Victoria and headed north with 5,000 cases. When we came back, the strike was still on and the mines needed another load; we delivered 10,000 cases for $10,000. Because the *Joan G* had cost us only $5,000 landed in Vancouver, we had made more than enough to pay for the ship in the first three months.

This ship was our workhorse for many years and towed many a Gibson raft. She packed loads of herring and pilchards into our plants. During World War II when we needed more power for towing and engines were hard to come by, we took the engines out of the *Malahat* after her hull was condemned and put them in the *Joan G*. This more than doubled her horsepower.

She was a great work boat and would still be running had not a careless and seasick engineer forgot to put lubricating oil in the drip system. Those rugged old engines, two-cylinder Bolinders which turned about 300 revolutions, nevertheless kept running for hours after all lubrication had stopped. On examining the engines we decided that the cost of repairs would have been greater than the cost of brand new engines.

By 1939 we were operating four camps in the Nootka Sound area, and one of our best purchases was the O'Malley camp at Chamiss Bay. The complete camp was offered for sale at an auction in Nanaimo for $5,000. For that amount our company acquired a large floating camp, cookhouse, bunkhouses, gasoline tug, blankets and supplies, four steam donkeys and a complete set of cables. But the finest part of the deal was the timber: half a million feet cold-decked (that is, felled and in piles of about a thousand logs, ready to be pulled into the water), two million feet fallen and bucked, and five million feet standing. It was a big step forward; now it was possible to build a really substantial camp.

The fact that we acquired this camp so reasonably shows the tremendous difficulty that most logging companies on the west coast were experiencing, primarily because they weren't able to get their logs to market without losing a great many on the way.

Our having grown up in the area was a considerable asset because we were familiar with local customs and conditions. Many companies that had failed were run by absentee owners, most of whose supervisory staff were imported. There were other factors in our favour: we had now established good markets of our own, and had developed a strong deep-sea raft so that our losses at sea would not be so great.

The Davis rafts, which were being used by most outfits, were unsuitable in heavy seas, and therefore caused many delays during bad weather. Yet the crews still had to be paid. Because the *Malahat* had been converted into a self-powered barge we were not delayed by the weather to the same extent.

It was at this time that some associates and I developed the Gibson raft. It was stronger and less expensive than the Davis raft, and later the patent netted me royalties from other loggers in Canada and the United States. This description of the raft from the *British Columbia Lumberman* of July 1948 summed up its success:

After three years of service under the most severe conditions to be encountered off the West Coast of Vancouver Island, the Gibson raft, designed by J. G. Gibson, production manager of Gibson Bros. Ltd., . . . is pronounced by its inventor 100 per cent satisfactory.

Developed by Mr. Gibson for deep sea towing after the manner of the familiar Davis raft, the new Gibson raft is, he reports, much less expensive and simpler to build and to break down, building cost averaging out at about 75 cents and breakdown at about 25 cents.

Recognition of the stability of the Gibson raft is seen in the fact that the company has been quoted a greatly reduced insurance rate. So far, however, they have been so successful in towing through all weathers and all seasons that not a single loss has been incurred. On one occasion a Gibson raft broke away in a storm off Cape Scott and was five days adrift in heavy seas before being picked up intact. . . .

Most significant feature of the Gibson raft, and the point on which it differs most widely from the Davis raft, is in the use of a separate mat, in two sections, on which the raft is made up and which is then cast adrift ready for the immediate re-use at the booming ground. Mr. Gibson's original mat is still being used, as is most other original gear, such as blocks and tackle. The Davis raft, on the other hand, relies on a mat which becomes an integral part of the finished structure, to be towed to its final destination and broken up, with the result that a new mat or "floor" must be built for each raft. . . .

Each of the two sections of the mat, is made up of logs floated side by side and connected by a number of wire ropes preferably laid alternately over and under adjoining logs, across each section and back to the starting point where the free ends of the ropes are clamped together leaving a free length lying in the water to be used later for hauling the section to which it is attached from under the finished raft.

In 1940 after our barges had been taken over by other towboat companies and then lost at sea, we relied almost exclusively on the Gibson raft to get our logs to market.

Later that year we took over another large timber tract

in Nootka Sound at Sandspit. For about $15,000 we purchased one of the North Vancouver ferries that had been condemned: we put in a machine shop, filing room, electric light plant, dining room and washrooms on the main deck; every man had an individual stateroom on the upper deck and had the use of well-appointed reading rooms to relax in. It was probably the most comfortable portable camp on the West Coast. This was towed from False Creek to our new site at Tahsis on the west coast of Vancouver Island.

Our insurance company was dickering over the rate they would charge for insuring the ferry. We had the timber felled and the donkey up the hill, though no logs were in the water yet. About two weeks after the converted ferry arrived, something happened to the oil-burning system in the dry room, where the wet clothing was hoisted to the ceiling, and our palatial portable camp caught fire. I was about ten miles away at the head of Tahsis Inlet, and by the time I arrived at Sandspit it was almost dark and the ferry was a total loss. It was a terrible sight to see that ferry burning.

The men had formed a bucket brigade because we didn't have proper fire hoses and had tried so hard to put out the fire that they forgot about the equipment. Nothing was saved: all the saws, axes, bales and even kitchen utensils were burned. We lost almost all our tools, for the men had just brought in their saws and axes for sharpening. The fire had been impossible to put out because it had travelled between the double walls of the ferry. However, some of the men managed to save their bedding and a few of their personal belongings.

Sixty men were sitting on the beach; not one of them had more than a few dollars. We had paid their fare to come up and they hadn't been working for more than a week. Our foreman and I went that night to a camp which we knew was for sale by the Olsen Logging Company. There was a watchman on duty, and knowing that we didn't have time to argue I simply told him that we had already bought the camp, though in fact we were still negotiating with Bill Olsen a few days later.

Because we were well known the watchman didn't doubt our word, and that night we towed the camp to Sandspit. It was a complete floating outfit with accommodation for a hundred men, some tools and blankets. We were ready to work first thing Monday.

We wired Vancouver and got a complete set of tools flown in the next morning. By Tuesday we were back in full swing. There was no choice but to keep on. We had lost $50,000 worth of camp and tools and had no insurance, but we built other camps ashore and our logging increased by leaps and bounds.

When luck goes against you, often it comes back some other way. The purchase of the Olsen Logging Camp was good for us since we acquired not only the floating camp but also a very powerful Vivian diesel engine on a skidder-type logging machine, several donkeys, and a large amount of timber already felled.

CHAPTER 15

Between 1936 and 1938, Zeballos boasted a population of approximately 1,000 inhabitants. The community had a 20-bed hospital operated by the Red Cross Society, a school, a bakery, a laundry and several general supply stores—plus a well-staffed "goat ranch"—the name given to bawdy houses in those days.

Nootka Sound, April 1976

In 1939 we had a camp near Zeballos, and Earson and I became quite involved in the life of the town. In almost the centre of the square mile that we were logging was an oasis of free enterprise built by a French madam named Audrey.

Audrey had run up against some hard luck when her first house was flooded out. Every spring afterwards when the rivers freshened and the water caused a lot of damage to her property, her girls would get a little excited. Perhaps Audrey had taken to reading her Bible because she came up with the idea that she should build a kind of Noah's Ark. Since we had some spare culled logs, we put skids under her house and moved it onto the logs. That was how we met; and although in some towns her house would not have been considered the social centre, in Zeballos it certainly was.

One good deed deserves another. It was wartime and I was on a committee to raise money for the Zeballos Hospital. We organized a Klondike Night, and with the co-operation of the police had an open bar with all profits going to the Red Cross. All the ladies of the district dressed up in old-fashioned costumes and sold their dances for a dollar apiece. We used bogus "Klondike dollars" which were exchanged at the rate of ten for every real one-dollar bill, so that the guests felt they were getting a lot of fun for their money.

Some of the women in the town had a very narrow-minded view of morality and fought to keep Audrey's girls away from the dance, but we wouldn't hear of it for they were our best attraction. As the liquor consumption increased even respectable married men paid dollar after dollar to dance with these charming young girls. A lot of so-called respectable women got very few dances and their noses were out of joint for weeks afterwards.

When the party came to an end about three in the morning, I had $500 in Klondike money. I was going to throw it away since I didn't want to collect on it, but one of the young ladies asked me to give it to her, proposing that I take it out in trade!

The evening was a great success and we raised over $5,000. If anyone lost money that night it was the girls from Audrey's who gave their time and talent to the Red Cross, carrying on in about the same manner as they would during their normal night's business.

One day I picked up Audrey on my way to town and offered her a cigarette. She replied, "No thanks, Mr. Gibson, I never smoke. In fact, I don't let any of my girls smoke. It's very unladylike, don't you think?"

The town got a lot of business from the men working in the mines up the valley and from our logging camp, but it seemed to me that Audrey had the best little gold mine in the area with the least capital investment.

When Zeballos closed down after the mines had been worked out, Audrey stopped off in Tahsis and made me a very fair proposition. "Mr. Gibson, if you have a house here that I could rent, I'll bring a couple of my girls down and save you all the trouble of having your men go to town all the time. You can have half the profits." I wouldn't have known how to set it up in our books and so turned down one of the best business deals I've ever been offered: a guaranteed profit with no investment.

In 1939 I was flying down to Vancouver at least once a week on Ginger Coote Airways, which was the only airline servicing the west coast of the island. On one trip I learned that Ginger owed so much money to his creditors for gas that he figured this to be his last flight. I told him to charge his gas to Gibson Brothers and to credit that account whenever he carried passengers for us.

Our arrangement had continued for about six months when Canadian Airways Limited came to the coast with twin-engine equipment. Ginger's aircraft were single-engine and maybe not as safe, but we stayed with him because we were so financially involved. Moreover, Ginger and his pilots would fly under the most difficult conditions, and therefore were more adaptable to our needs—providing we had sufficient courage to fly with them. Ginger Coote never flew very high so there was more chance of flying into a fish boat mast or a lighthouse than into a mountain when we flew back from Vancouver via Victoria following the shoreline all the way up the coast. We also began to carry our men from Vancouver to camp by seaplane, and then to co-ordinate schedules with our camp tender, *Machigonne*, running out of Port Alberni between our Muchalat, Sandspit and Zeballos camps.

Ginger's airline equipment needed constant overhauling so in the fall of 1939 we arranged more financing. As we were the single biggest creditor by far, the control of Ginger Coote Airways was turned over to us as shares in settlement of their debt to us. We paid off all their creditors and resumed business.

We must have been flying hazardously because in one stormy weekend four of our five planes had landing accidents. No lives were lost but our planes were out of commission for a while. One caught fire in Nanaimo because the pilot forgot that the fire extinguisher was under the seat, earning himself headlines for heroic efforts in rescuing his passengers, though, in fact, he jumped out of the plane and ran 100 feet before remembering to open the door of the aircraft!

With so many planes damaged we had to decide whether to go out of business or buy more. Clarke and our general manager went down to Los Angeles to negotiate for a Ford tri-motored float plane that would give us capacity to carry three times as many passengers: twenty rather than seven. Our other planes were Norsemans and Wacos.

Our competitors, Canadian Airways Limited, saw a

chance to step in. They sent their manager from Vancouver on a special flight to see me at the camp, and then flew me back to the city. We met in the Vancouver Club on Saturday night and no man was ever treated more royally, or filled with as much whiskey. I made a deal subject to my brothers' approval to sell the airline for $80,000 cash. We were to retain our wrecked equipment and claim the insurance. I phoned Clarke and we agreed that our auditor and I would travel to Winnipeg on Monday to sign the deal.

I arrived home about four o'clock that morning, parking my car on the boulevard in front of my home in Point Grey. Fortunately, my wife insisted that I take a cab to the airport and I managed to sleep for a while on the airplane. But I was still feeling so rough from partying the night before that I rushed to find a washroom during a short stopover in Lethbridge, Alberta. In my haste, I slipped and fell on the icy tarmac. The plane was scheduled to stop for only ten minutes but my condition was such that relief could not be got in so short a time.

The manager knocked loudly on the toilet door, threatening that the plane would take off without me. "You'll lose your goddamned job if that plane takes off," I yelled. "I can't move out of here because of the fall I've taken on that slippery walk: you don't have brains enough to throw some salt out for your passengers. To hell with you." The entire conversation was conducted through the locked washroom door. I may add that we arrived as scheduled in Winnipeg that evening.

Our auditor, Bill Cotter, and I were the guests of Canadian Airways, so we turned down the waiting bus, fully certain that we would be met. After half an hour we called a taxi. My temper was definitely not improved by finding that our reservation had been made at a hotel several miles away. We had already drunk up all the whiskey we had with us and since it was a Sunday evening we had to buy bootlegged liquor to tide us over.

At 10:00 the next morning Canadian Airways phoned and asked us to meet them. "You'll have to come to us—we're not going to deal with people who are this ungentlemanly. We are your guests. You used me royally until I consented, and it puts me in mind of the man who will help a girl out of her clothes but won't help her put them on again. To hell with you. Just keep on waiting over there—in fact, forget the whole deal altogether." There were great apologies and they came over to our hotel. But I still felt very offended.

When they arrived, I said, "Gentlemen, I'm going to teach you to be nice to your guests in future and the lesson will cost you another $10,000 on the purchase price. That is what I consider my feelings to be worth over the last twenty-four hours!" They looked at each other wondering which of them could have been at fault—but they paid the extra money. I since jokingly refer to that incident as my $10,000 taxi ride.

Since 1936 when we left the Kelly Spruce Company to go into our own business, we had started five large camps and had acquired some good equipment. We figured we had some of the finest camps up the coast, but not everyone felt as we did, as indicated by this nice piece from the *B.C. Lumber Worker* dated 26 November 1927, entitled "Haywire and More Haywire at Gibson Brothers Camp":

Gibson's Bros. Camp,
Nootka, B.C.

Editor:

Talk about haywire, this camp takes the cake for anything I've seen in my fifteen years logging on the coast.

For the first there is no bathhouse, no dry house, no bull cook, and no life outside at night. There is a two by four sidewalk in front of the bunkhouse. One bunkhouse is on the same float as the A-frame and when the wind blows we often get water on the floor, and enough to keep a deaf man awake. Another bunkhouse is on the shore as well as the office, and when we go for our meal, we have to walk about three hundred to four hundred feet on the shore. If the tide is in we walk through the brush and then on a stiff leg, and another two hundred feet, and then climb over rubbish on the slope which is littered with wire and other things. So it is both dangerous and miserable to get to and from. Often we have to cut our own wood, split it and carry it in. The only thing that is alright is the cook. He is pretty good. A little more variety of food would not hurt.

The cookhouse is tied up alongside the A-frame, but it seems that they are short of haywire, because sometimes there is five to six feet between the two; so you have to jump to get across. The warm water is heated in a washtub in one of the bunkhouses, so you know how much hot water we are getting. For light we have coal oil lamps and it often happens we have no coal oil; but we get lots of promises of improvement from our big boss but we have not seen any yet.

The work on the rigging is not highball so the boys tell me. Falling is by contract, 70¢ M. and the ground not too bad, but lately it seems impossible to suit our boss. We kicked on the scale one time, and he promised to come out and do the scaling himself but so far we haven't seen him do any scaling. However, our kick had some effect, for the scale has been better to date. There is only one set of fallers left here. The filing shed is behind the cookhouse with only three walls; no skylight, no heat. Board is $1.35 a day; fare up here about $15.00.

It sure would be a good thing if the union could come up here for a visit. I don't know if there is many union members here or not but it sure would be a good place to get some. There are about thirty men employed here now. They are working one side cold-decking and then they skyline it out. As you know, we have to make our own beds. I have had a change of sheets twice in two months. One of the boys said, the only consolation was that he could lay in bed and spit through a knothole in the floor. The floor is one inch shiplap (single floor) so there are lots of holes and cracks. Wages have been increased lately since the new hooker or foreman came up, thanks to him.

Wages so far as I can find out are:

Rigging slinger, $6.00; one choker man, $4.50; other choker man, $4.80; fireman, $4.00; wood bucker, $4.00; chaser, $50.00 per month. The new chaser who came up on the last boat gets $5.50. The fireman has been working for $50.00 a month until this last month.

There is no stretcher in the camp and no first aid kit out in the woods. Sometimes there is no boat in camp for four or five days. We've been lucky for no accidents have happened here for a long time.

K. M.

There was a day when every man who worked in a logging camp or sawmill knew his boss. A crewman often stayed with the same operation for many years, and could present his grievances with expectation of a fair hearing. That time has past.

I feel that unions are very necessary because companies are now much larger and therefore impersonal: the men must have someone to negotiate for them. This works to everyone's advantage because the union takes some of the burden of responsibility for fair treatment of the workers off the boss or owner, and even diminishes his financial obligations towards his crew. If a man was loyal to the same small outfit for a considerable length of time, he had the right to expect that he would be given special consideration in the future. Now the union helps him demand maximum benefits on a daily basis—sometimes, of course, without due regard for the future welfare of the company or the people who are dependent upon it.

I am against the big international unions because conditions differ from country to country, and a settlement that is excellent in one set of circumstances may well be detrimental in another. Poor management of an international union, like an international company, can have a long-range effect on the economy of an entire country. Any monopoly, either by management or union, scares the hell out of me.

CHAPTER 16

I'd be no damned good in the army unless they gave me a job to do all by myself. I'd hate like hell to have some young fellow of higher rank but junior experience tell me I was going to charge the enemy if I thought that my chances were nil.

When World War II came along I was thirty-six years old with two children. I was much more capable of taking out airplane spruce and building airports than of being a soldier. Besides, my hearing was never good, especially when it came to hearing orders!

I was in our Muchalat camp on 7 December 1941 when word came to us that the Japanese had bombed Pearl Harbor. It was feared that the Pacific coast of North America would be vulnerable to a further Japanese thrust and so the authorities decided that airports would have to be constructed on the West Coast to provide one defence against possible attack.

Because we were known to be operating large camps on the Pacific coast, it was natural for the Department of Transport to involve our company in clearing ground at Tofino as fast as possible as the first step in the construction of a defence base for Canada's aircraft.

During a spell of cold, clear weather in January 1942 I towed all the floating logging camps and equipment that we had in the Nootka Sound area behind the old *Joan G* through forty miles of outside waters into Clayoquot Sound and up to the Tofino airport site. But the floating houses took such a beating rounding Estevan Point that they disintegrated, and though we saved our machinery, our bunkhouses were a total write-off. Consequently, we decided to build bunkhouses ashore for our men.

Prior to the bombing of Pearl Harbor, Coast Construction Company had contracted to clear the land for the airport, but they had tried to clear the ground with caterpillars and were constantly bogged down in the mud. When we took over the contract we changed the whole procedure. We divided the area into 200 sections, each 400 feet square. Between the sections we put in roads, and set up spar trees, so that our donkeys could yard out the logs. The stumps were gathered into piles every 800 feet and burned; the residue was refed into the fire until there was nothing left of the overgrowth but ashes.

We built a wharf for unloading our barges and brought in thousands of yards of gravel. Then, after our contract came to an end, Coast Construction levelled the ground and built the airport.

Coast Construction's contract was awarded on a cost-plus basis, that is, ten to fifteen per cent above cost. The more the project cost, the more profit to the company. There was no incentive for the contractor to perform efficiently because the profit realized was in direct ratio to the amount spent by the contractor on the project. For instance, when we first went to Ucluelet, fuel oil and gas were being dragged on a stoneboat by a cat which was costing $300 a day, until we pointed out that the fuel could be brought in by barge via Tofino and over the mud flats at one-twentieth the cost.

War creates this sort of inefficiency. The sensible way to tender government contracts would be on a cost-minus basis, setting a cost figure and rewarding the contractor with the difference. My brothers and I never accepted a cost-plus contract. I don't remember ever receiving a personal pay cheque from anyone. All we knew was that we had to work like hell, and we were appalled that there was no incentive for others to save time or money. Cost-plus contracts favour the inefficient and lazy.

The men working on the wharf had lacked esprit de corps until the Japanese attacked Pearl Harbor. Suddenly, their production jumped a hundred per cent, and we increased the number of piles being driven from twenty to forty per day, which indicates the kind of performance men can give in an emergency.

There were about 200 men employed in building the airport, some of whom lived in Tofino. The road to the airport was really just a cow trail, so bad that even our crummy would bog down in the ruts and potholes. Jack suggested that every time our trucks travelled to Tofino we load them with gravel to spread on the road, and that we chop a hole in the platform of the trucks and shovel the gravel through it into the ruts instead of all over the road. The government engineer decided he wouldn't allow this practice because it had not been specified in the contract. I told him, "Mac, that's the way I'm bringing in our liquor, and I'll have to cut you off your bottle a day if we don't keep the road open." The engineer had an immediate change of heart and that road is still travelled today.

The potholes did not enhance what little social life we had. One of the young commissioned officers asked me to make up a foursome with him and a couple of WACS. The officer wasn't allowed to use an army truck, and when I picked him up in my own vehicle I found that he had come equipped with a mattress and some blankets figuring on a little lovemaking on the way. That made me a little envious. I drove down that damned road like a man possessed, knowing full well that the couple in the back were flying all over the mattress. Every few miles I slammed on the brakes—and solicitously inquired how they were making out!

The Tofino airport was a completely wasteful project, since the fighter planes could have taken off along Long Beach itself. But we loaded our pile driver on the back of an old truck and drove piles every 500 feet from high water down to low water so that the Japanese bombers could not land while we were building the airport. I am proud to say that many of these piles are still sticking up today. We also assisted the regiment in building machine gun redoubts along the beach, which we made using huge drift logs bulldozed over with sand as cover.

Demolition experts laid charges across the runway in trenches every 500 feet so that it could be blown up in the event of a Japanese attack. Although some felt that millions of dollars had been wasted on an elaborate airport from which not one aircraft ever departed on a fighting mission, had the Japanese attacked the West Coast, this site would have been vital.

We started work on the Tofino airport three weeks after Pearl Harbor and the threat of attack was so real that the military authorities insisted a box of groceries be kept in every home in case it became necessary to evacuate the women and children. I carried a gun in my car at all times as did many others.

A large number of Japanese fishermen suffered considerable hardships during the war. These men were not particularly politically motivated: they were of peasant stock with a strong work ethic.

A little tension had grown between the Japanese and white fishermen—understandably so, because the Japanese worked harder and delivered better fish than did the average white or Indian. They ran a tightly knit organization and were extremely competitive, but they did not always have the spirit of co-operation under duress that was necessary in that wilderness area. Perhaps they were not always as politic as they might have been, and this caused some resentment in the villages, but the Japanese were certainly prospering until Pearl Harbor.

They had formed their own co-operative fishing societies and sold all their fish themselves, running their own packers into Vancouver and Seattle. Each society was dominated by a secretary, a well-educated Japanese who spoke fluent English and was both boss and bookkeeper. Some people believed that because these secretaries were so obviously not of the fisherman class, they might be agents for the Japanese government.

After Pearl Harbor and the invasion of the Aleutians, the military authorities in Canada decided that there was too large an alien population on the coast having an excellent knowledge of the Pacific waters and a high mobility in the form of their boats. So all Japanese fishing craft were impounded and taken to the Fraser River estuary. The government was faced with the problem of how to maintain a thousand small boats and decided instead to sell them rather than let them disintegrate to the point of worthlessness for want of individual care.

The value of property had already declined dramatically for both white and Japanese because no one was certain whether or not there would be a fishing industry the following year. Now there was a sudden glut of boats on the market. A boat that had been worth $10,000 in peacetime was suddenly worth only $2,500. The whole economy had taken a nosedive under the threat of invasion and there were few potential purchasers for anything.

In 1942, when our contract at Tofino ended, Bob Filberg of the Canadian Western Lumber Company was placed in charge of spruce production required in the manufacture of Mosquito fighter bombers, and we were given authority to take spruce from any location on the west coast of Vancouver Island no matter who owned the rights to the timber. It seems quite a coincidence that we should have been pioneers in the aircraft spruce industry in both the First and Second World Wars. We had far more sophisticated methods of logging in 1942, however, and didn't have to use old bulls for pulling out logs as we did when I was a boy. We started production at Zeballos, Tahsis, Bowden Bay, Trout River and Ucluelet. Only the best straight-grained trees were logged. Our cost of production was $400 per thousand feet, compared to the average of $1,000 per thousand feet at the government camps in the Queen Charlottes. The spruce camps were simply tacked onto our other timber camps since they were what are known as tractor operations, that is, the logs were pulled out with a tractor and logging arch.

After we had completed the Tofino airport site, we were asked by the government to put through a telephone line connecting the Tofino airport to Alberni and other points. Sometimes naval and army personnel were sent to help with the construction of the line and I found myself, a civilian, in charge of military personnel. This caused me some difficulties.

The soldiers were being taken by truck to and from the work site and our camp at McLean Point, a trip of two hours each way. So much time was being spent in travel, and so little in getting any work done, that I told their commanding officer we were moving camp and the soldiers would live in tents close to the work area. Our work schedule had them on the job for five days and then off two days.

A soldier may not expect to fall timber and put up telephone poles but we were fighting a war after all, and I truly believe that 10 civilians trained in the woods would have accomplished a lot more than those 200 men. The second problem was the resentment of the senior army personnel towards civilian supervision. For the first few weeks I was not allowed to go into the officers' mess though most of the soldiers who were working on the construction gave me their full co-operation. That insult made me so angry that I made a telephone call to a Mr. Magee in Ottawa, who was in charge of co-ordinating the project. Word came back that I was to be treated as an officer, and I entered that damned place just once to establish my right to be there. But I never bothered to go back. They had their responsibilities and I had mine.

In 1943, the American and Canadian governments decided that more airports were needed for defence. Having established that we could clear land efficiently, we were asked to start work on an airport at Cassidy, near Ladysmith, on Vancouver Island. Because it was an emergency situation, no tenders were called for the project; we were simply telephoned and asked to begin immediately. When we inquired about the financial arrangements, we were told, "Just start and send the bills to us. Get the kind of men you need, regardless of the wages you have to pay them. The project must be completed as quickly as possible. Arrangements have been made with the Bank of Montreal so that you can issue your own cheques immediately."

Ladysmith was a suitable site for an airport since it had been logged off once, though there was a second growth of about 20 inches in the stumpage. I had been shown where the airport was to be, and I vowed that this time the job would be done efficiently.

There was some dispute about who owned various parts of the site but this was all arbitrated later. I went to the farmers in the area and told them where we would start and that it might be necessary to go through their ground or to move their houses. A few people complained about our operating this way, but no one ever said we couldn't.

Our greatest problem was manpower. Almost every able-bodied man between the ages of eighteen and thirty was overseas. We had a mandate to pay any amount to seduce men from the nearby logging camps. The Comox Logging Company, managed by Jimmy Sheasgreen, was the first on my list. I told Jimmy that we needed a hundred men, ten donkeys and ten caterpillars immediately, and that we were willing to pay twice his wages. Jimmy saw the sense of the offer, for we could have wrecked his logging camp by stealing away all his men, so he co-operated by sending his good men and equipment.

Our plan was to keep all equipment on rubber wheels so that we would not repeat the mistake made in Tofino of allowing machinery to constantly bog down. A gravel road was put through the centre; every 600 feet a spur road went 600 feet in either direction, so that the whole area was divided into 600-foot squares. It meant that no piece of equipment was ever more than 300 feet from a roadway.

In each of these huge squares we hooked out all the salable timber and burned poor timber and stumps in a great bonfire. That way all logs and stumps were disposed of at one time. The only bug in the pail was that an official from the Forestry Department came from Victoria to order us to stop burning those enormous piles. I took pleasure in telling the B.C. Forestry Department to go to hell, because we were working for the Department of Transport in the interest of national security.

With the co-operation of the Comox Logging Company and other small contractors, we built the airport for less than half the approved cost and twice as quickly as was expected given the manpower shortages.

After the Cassidy airport was completed, we built a ten-mile road from Port Hardy to the nearby airport. It was another "to-be-finished-yesterday" job. Men and equipment were even harder to get than before. There wasn't a man under sixty working on this project; we had men who had been rejected by the army and couldn't get a job anywhere else. If a man could turn the steering wheel and press the brake in a truck, he was hired.

We had to cross very soft, boggy, gumbolike ground, or as we called it, loonshit. When a stump was yarded out, a 6-foot-deep pit of mud would appear. The contract specifications called for us to remove the gumbo and replace it with gravel. Whoever had drawn up those plans had absolutely no idea what that meant. The situation put me in mind of a verse by Lewis Carroll in *Through the Looking Glass*:

> "If seven maids with seven mops
> Swept it for half a year,
> Do you suppose," the Walrus said
> "That they could get it clear?"
> "I doubt it," said the Carpenter,
> And shed a bitter tear.

I decided to use the corduroy road type of construction. We cut all the trees to within one foot of the ground and left all the small timber and stumps from a foot down in the roadbed. Taking the largest logs, from 24 inches up, we laid them end to end about 30 feet apart along either side, making a border down each side of the roadbed. Then a continuous stream of trucks dumped their loads of gravel in the centre which was spread to a depth of 4 feet over the top of the stumps and rubbish wood that we had previously packed down. This gave us a road with proper drainage, 4 feet higher than the land on either side. Because the surrounding land was swampy, I'm sure that the buried roadbed will last hundreds of years since it takes that long for wood to rot when it is kept wet and away from the air. I am proud to say that we managed to build the thirty-three miles of road and put up telephone poles in less than three months.

One day an air force amphibious plane brought eight officials to inspect our work and ensure the road was being built to specification. I met them at the wharf, put them in a crummy and took them to see the road which was then two-thirds built.

They spent half an hour at the end of the road, just lounging around and watching our men yarding the timber that would form the roadbed, some of them idly talking to the cab driver or to men in the crew. My patience ran out completely. The trucks couldn't move past them to dump the gravel; the whole project had ground to a halt.

I walked up to the only civilian in the group and asked him what particular phase of the work interested him the most. His face lighted up, and he took out an identification badge which stated that he was "expediter" of airport construction in Western Canada. As I had never heard the term before, I said, "Expediter. That sounds to me as if it's a man who speeds up the goddamned job, is that right?" He nodded. "Well," I said, "I'll tell you what we'd better do: just tell the whole goddamned bunch to get back in the crummy and I'll pour a drink down your throats, because all we're doing here is slowing things down instead of speeding them up!" My offer was the first thing they showed any real interest in.

Even before this project was completed, we were instructed to build an airport on an island three or four miles outside Prince Rupert. I was told by a Mr. Chilcott, of the Department of Transport, to arrange clearing operations immediately, to purchase the necessary equipment and to build the camps, because the Japanese were expected to attack the coast.

I had a look at the site and knew that we were going to run into tremendous difficulties. Although there were good approaches by sea from both directions, the site itself was entirely unsuitable. Walking over the ground, armed with 16-foot rods to measure the depth of the gumbo, we were amazed to find that in some places the loonshit was deeper than the rods; in other spots the rock outcroppings stuck 10 feet above the surface.

This was a major construction job, and if the threat of attack was imminent, as I was led to believe, time was very precious. I sized up the situation as being at least four times as difficult as Port Hardy or Tofino. Moreover, manpower was scarcer in Prince Rupert than on Vancouver

Island. The only men we could have hired were derelicts, and this job called for highly skilled labourers—men who were expert at blasting. Yet we needed a force of 500 men. And it would all take time, something that no amount of money could buy.

When I was carrying logs in the *Malahat* from the Queen Charlotte Islands, I had seen a marvellous beach at Sandspit in the Queen Charlottes that would be excellent as an airstrip for fighter planes. These islands were forty miles farther into the Pacific, and therefore closer for unloading our transport ships. The sand was packed so hard and level that it would have made a fine racetrack. I phoned Ottawa and told them about the beach at Sandspit. A meeting of Canadian and American military personnel was subsequently held in Vancouver where I described this and other sites as being far more suitable for the proposed air base.

One American official insisted that the island off Prince Rupert was the proper spot, regardless of the cost in manpower. It was obvious that they were trying to save face. Not one of the whole goddamned bunch had ever seen the area. It seemed so foolish to me that I threatened, "I'll take this to the highest courts in the land and raise such a stink that you will all be embarrassed. You will be building a monument to the inefficiency of numbskulls in the Armed Forces."

A week later they reversed their decision. At no time was the financial angle ever discussed. War is never efficient, for it is only the result that counts. I suppose the Germans and Japanese must have been less efficient than we were, even at our worst.

CHAPTER 17

A man had lived in one of our camp houses for married couples from the time Jeune Landing started, and his children grew up there. Proctor was the man's name, and he ran our biggest truck because of his seniority. Proctor's son, being about six years old, said, "Look at my father's new truck," and his little friend said, "That's not your father's truck, that truck belongs to Mr. Gibson." The little kid hung his head kind of ashamed and said, "Gee, does Mr. Gibson or does God own everything?" That's what you think in a little camp. Mother said God owns this and God owns the timber, and the kid thought that his father owned the truck. His dad washed it, rubbed it, nursed it—it was a new one, the best we had.

In 1943 after completing most of our airport projects, we contracted with B.C. Pulp and Paper to log off an area of ten square miles in Quatsino Sound. B.C. Pulp and Paper were unable to meet their logging requirements themselves because there was an enormous demand for pulp yet men and equipment were scarce. We were the natural choice to run a tight logging operation. B.C. Pulp and Paper agreed to buy the timber which was owned by the Crown; we would repurchase it from them with the understanding that they would buy logs from us at an average price of one dollar per thousand under the Vancouver price. Any production over 150 million feet would belong to us. The job was started with only one caterpillar to haul in the logs, an A-frame and two small floating camps, since equipment was impossible to buy.

Because of the war and the remote location of the camp, I knew that we would have to build the best camp possible to attract good loggers. Before we built the new camp at Jeune Landing, men in logging camps lived in a central bunkhouse having beds spaced around the wall, but I had lived out of town long enough to know that a man needed a clean room to himself.

We built the best bunkhouses on the coast. Each cabin was 28 feet square with seven bedrooms and a bathroom. A 16-foot living room was in the centre of the structure with a stove and reading facilities. Every man had a private room with curtains on the windows and a carpet on the floor. In the laundry and dry room everyone had his own locker numbered to correspond with his room number. He had to leave his work clothes in the locker and change into clean shirt and trousers before dinner. The men co-operated and no caulk boots were ever worn in the living quarters. This was such a big step forward in logging camp conditions in British Columbia that the giant logging operations figured we would spoil our men.

But such treatment gave us a choice of men. In fact, I remember one IWA union representative, Mr. Pritchett, saying that if all the companies treated their men as well as we did at Jeune Landing there would never have been a need for the union. We also built about fifteen lovely little houses for families which rented for twenty dollars a month, a school and a recreation hall. The extra expense required to create good living conditions paid off, for we never had labour trouble in that camp over the next fifteen years.

This project went ahead under several different managers, but the one who deserves the greatest credit, Bill Becker, was in charge for the last eight years: as hard-working and as forceful a man as I have ever met.

One of our six-man logging crews seemed to be getting bone lazy. When one day they piled only sixty logs in a spot where the timber was thick, Bill decided to show them up. He went out with the crew and told them to sit on a log and do absolutely nothing. Bill went into the woods where they had been logging and worked by himself. He set the chokers, blew his own whistle, and by the end of the day Becker had logged a hundred logs on his own. At five o'clock that evening he met with the loggers and said, "Boys, you're fired. I don't mind your taking it easy, but if I can do ten times as much as the lot of you, then you are certainly rubbing it in." Those men left the camp without squawking to their union. They realized they were working for a man who was really a man.

It's incredible how lazy a person can be. Late one afternoon at our Tahsis operation I wanted to see my foreman but he had just left camp in his pickup truck. He could not have been too far away so I jumped into my car and floored the engine in an effort to catch up with him. Just as I entered a curve I saw something lying in the centre of the road. It was a 12-inch by 18-inch chunk of wood which obviously had fallen off the back of the wood truck. We were logging about five miles up a valley and the men would bring back chunks of wood from the mill to steam our donkey boilers.

The tire tracks of my foreman's truck clearly showed that he had swerved around this huge piece of log. He had no idea I was following him, and probably figured that a piece of wood in the road wasn't his responsibility. It made me so damned mad to think that he wouldn't take a minute to stop his truck and throw the wood off the road that when he arrived back in camp in the evening I was waiting for him. As soon as he walked through the door of my office I shouted, "Ted, why did you go around that 12-by-18?"

"What 12-by-18?" he asked.

"The goddamned 12-by-18 block in the middle of our logging road. Who in hell did you think was going to move it? You bastard, you know that a fully loaded truck on a downhill grade would have no chance to stop in time and would be wrecked. It would have taken you just one minute to throw that chunk of wood off the road. You're fired!"

Everyone thought I was very cruel since the man had been with us for five years, but he had proved to me that he was irresponsible and goddamned lazy and I didn't want him in my operation one second longer. It may seem as though I was unfair to him but in the long run it was for the best. Sooner or later he would make another careless mistake, one that could cost someone's life.

A definition that I picked up in a Catholic tract brought this point home to me: "The thought in an act must be good and kind. The act itself must be good and kind. Above all else the result of the action must be good." I might think that giving a bum a dollar to buy more whiskey is kindly and humane, but I believe I would be in part responsible if the whiskey bought with that dollar killed the man. So although my intentions might be kind, the result of my action would have been harmful. Sometimes the kindest thing a man can do is to look down to the far end of the road and see what the result is going to be.

I planned to be at Jeune Landing for a few years, so I built a lovely home for Louise. At this time we were still running logging camps down the coast and towing logs into Vancouver. No sooner had I finished our home and brought my family up to Jeune Landing than the decision was made to build a mill at Tahsis. I had to move down the coast again. It had been like that since we first married: two or three months together and then our plans would change. Louise decided to move to Vancouver permanently so as to provide a stable home base for our family.

Our daughter, Louanne, was born 14 March 1939. Louise drove herself to the hospital. Although I was delighted to have two children I saw very little of them until they had finished school and married.

One of the regrets of my life is that I never experienced a childhood. We were expected to work and help our family. Mother gave us a belief in honesty and hard work by her own example. She did everything for us but provide the pay cheque, and our father never interfered with her decisions about our well-being, nor did he ever undermine her discipline. Mother was boss at home: she looked after the house, taught us manners, cut our hair, took us to church and held the family together under very difficult circumstances. Father was often away from home for long periods of time so the burden of bringing up four youths fell on her shoulders.

When I worked up the coast driving a team of horses for my father I was treated as a man rather than the boy I was. For this reason, when I became an adult I keenly felt the responsibility for feeding and educating my children. I believed that the finest goal a father can achieve is respect for providing adequately for his family, finer than being a gracious husband or loving parent.

That philosophy made Louanne and Gordon grow up faster than most children, with the ability to make intelligent decisions. If they wanted to learn how to fish they had to do it on their own because I didn't have the time. I also got a wife who could think for herself, and knew how to handle her own money. This made her feel independent and proud of her abilities because she never had to come to me for consent. I always delegated when I had confidence; moreover, I had learned never to rein in a willing horse.

I believed that a man should pick a wife with as much care and common sense as he would choose the captain of his finest ship, looking for a capable and intelligent companion rather than allowing infatuation, sex or the passion of love to command his reason. No man is a unit unto himself, and I knew that I had to marry someone who had the abilities and sensitivities that I lacked myself. The fact that Gordon and Louanne became the fine people they are is a reflection of the character and genuiness of their mother.

Louise was a girl who accepted facts for facts. Logging was my life. I didn't want to do anything else, and she adapted marvellously. I had given her the little house that had drifted up Malkscope Inlet and another at Muchalat, so the house at Jeune Landing was our third. When she moved to Vancouver she started to make her money work for her. I had given her about $200 a month all the time she was living up the coast, but she hadn't spent much of the allowance and invested it in a house on Keith Road in North Vancouver. She sold that $5,000 house in 1940 for $9,000 and bought another house for about $11,000, selling it two years later for $22,000. We then built our next home on Marpole Avenue for $25,000 and it was sold for $55,000. In 1950 we bought Spuraway—30 acres, swimming pool, badminton court, stables and paddock—for $75,000. By the time it was sold it was worth $450,000. All this was Louise's doing and I must say she was certainly a great businesswoman.

I was too busy to allow myself the luxury of missing anyone. A soldier can't sit in the trench thinking about his wife. He should think of how to win the war. I couldn't allow myself to wish I was at home. I just hoped to Christ that I would be successful enough to go home feeling that I had done my part as a good provider. I had no major interest in my life at that time other than accomplishment. We worked up to eighteen hours a day, seven days a week.

I was in Jeune Landing when the *James Carruthers* and a tow were caught in a bad storm that had come up from the southeast. She had been heading west from Quatsino Sound in favourable conditions until she rounded Cape Scott into the full force of the storm. The skipper contacted me by radio telephone and I decided to go to her aid as she was slowly being driven out to sea. The only ship available was the *Joan G*, a good ship but without much power.

Six hours later we reached Cape Scott and were able to put a towline on the *James Carruthers*. In twenty-four hours the *Joan G* and her charge were back in the comparative shelter of Cape Scott. The southeast storm abated but a southwesterly came up and forced us to anchor. We were lying about a quarter of a mile offshore with 1,000 feet of line between the *Joan G* and the *James Carruthers* and 1,000 feet of line between her and her raft. Between the boats and shore were reefs. When the wind moved southwest, the raft swung around towards the reefs and I could see that it would be on the rocks unless we moved quickly. It would take at least ten minutes to heave in our anchors, so instead we ran the chain right out leaving it clear of the *Joan G*, and then steamed full ahead out to sea.

The southeaster became so violent that we lost all interest in the raft. The skipper of the *James Carruthers* and I figured our best chance was to run to Port Hardy for safety. We let the raft go: it was a case of saving the ships and the men aboard.

When the storm abated a couple of days later and the sun came out for the first time, we returned to the spot where we had last seen the raft, and fortunately we found her intact. She was still in deep water and we were faced with the problem of picking up her dragging cable. Our solution was to tie our stern towlines together, and then pay out between 200 and 300 feet of line, moving the ships down on either side of the raft. The bridle formed by our lines slipped underneath the raft quite easily and we were able to pick up our towline on the first pass. The line from the raft was fastened to the winch of the *James Carruthers* for the long, tedious tow back to Port Hardy and then on to Vancouver.

Our saving that raft, which was not insured, was great luck. Moreover, we remembered where we had dropped the anchor which had been cut adrift from the *Joan G* and it too was recovered. Just how much good luck is indicated by the fact that the raft was worth $50,000, the towline $3,000, and the anchor gear $3,000.

One of my friends, an official with the CPR coast service, had been on holiday with me at Jeune Landing when I went after the *James Carruthers*. He had asked to come with me, thinking that we would be away twenty-four hours, not five days. Not only was he seasick the whole time, but he was scared to death. When it came time for him to leave the ship, he said, "Gordon, I have always thought I would like to be in the logging, towing or fishing businesses instead of the dull routine of CPR cargo freighters, but after these last few days I have decided that no one but an overly ambitious fool would go into a pioneer industry in a pioneer's country."

Two months later the *James Carruthers* made exactly the same trip from Quatsino round Cape Scott to Vancouver. She was towing a raft of a million feet worth $40,000 to $50,000 and uninsured. This time the captain was Bill Olsen, a man with thirty years experience in the fishing and towing industry. He later became one of the best-known pilots on the British Columbia coast.

The run around Cape Scott from Quatsino Sound takes about sixteen hours under tow. All was well when Olsen left. The sea had been fairly smooth, but the wind came up from the west when the *James Carruthers* had about five miles to go before rounding Cape Scott. The wind increased, blowing the ship and tow back towards the shore. Bill figured he would lose any headway he had made if he pulled straight into the wind. He telephoned me as conditions worsened and we kept in touch every half hour.

As the westerly strengthened the ship would gain three miles ahead only to be driven back closer to the shore than before. Olsen lost the raft after battling the winds and seas for twelve hours. It started to break up on the rocks as he tried to pull it out to sea. When the *James Carruthers* itself was being driven into the breakers, Olsen wisely decided to drop his towline and run for safety.

Bill phoned me and said, "Gordon, I've lost a towline and a $50,000 raft. Let's just pack it in." I radioed, "No, come back here. I have another raft ready and an old skyline will do for the towline. You can't go into Vancouver before we get another raft to town to pay our bills." A skyline is a logging cable 1½ inches in diameter and 1,500 feet long. Bill put this on his winch and started out with the next raft. No one can survive if luck is forever against him, but our next twenty rafts got through and we recouped our $50,000.

It was necessary to make these kinds of decisions quickly, almost instinctively—to take chances, or our enterprise would fail. Throughout the period when we were towing logs between the west coast of Vancouver Island and the mainland there were at least ten times when it would have been disastrous if any of our crew, our company or our bankers had faltered or slackened their efforts. It might have taken years before anyone else gambled on opening up those remote parts of the country. After each major setback we had a little grace given to us so that we were able to recoup our losses.

It was the uncertainty—the "ifs," the "ands," the possibility of making a little money here, gambling again and losing it there, as well as the trouble we had selling our logs in Vancouver—that encouraged us to consider building a mill on the west coast of Vancouver Island. We wanted to attract large ships of 10,000 tons or more to come in and pick up lumber for foreign markets. Above all, we knew that we had to find some way to reduce the ever-increasing cost of towing.

About this time the great controversy about Forest Management Licences began. These licences were grants of public forests by the Province of British Columbia to large lumber companies allowing them cutting rights in perpetuity. In return, the recipients were supposed to replant, so that the amount of timber would remain constant after reforestation and annual growth. In the view of the Bennett government the purses of the provinces and private enterprise benefited from Forest Management Licences, because the government charged a stumpage fee and the companies were assured a steady supply of timber for their operations. In my opinion, the small independent logging companies would be wiped out or become subcontractors because under this arrangement the contractors would be just hewers of wood subject to the whims of those companies which held the Forest Management Licences.

B.C. Pulp and Paper applied for a licence, and made a deal with Alaska Pine that if the licence were granted, Alaska Pine would sell out. Alaska Pine didn't think that there was a chance in the world of the licence being granted and unfortunately we were too busy to oppose the idea very vigorously. The next thing we knew we had tree farm licences all around us. Our days were numbered: we had five or six years at best before an independent logging company such as ours would be forced out of business because it could not secure sufficient cutting rights to maintain its camps and make a profit.

The government granted this Forest Management Licence to B.C Pulp and Paper because the company claimed that there were only 19,000 feet per acre instead of the 60,000 feet per acre that was the average yield in our logging operation. That gave them three times more timber than they were entitled to have. I never dreamed then that I would spend years of my life fighting this issue.

But Forest Management Licences were not the only problem. In the logging industry, fire is one of the greatest hazards. In the fall of 1943, during the night, one started at Jeune Landing high up in the woods. We had a limited amount of hose and old-fashioned fire pumps. The crew worked all night trying to contain the fire, and in the morning I flew to Vancouver to try to get more pumps and hose from the Forestry Department. They refused, saying that they had no extra equipment. Consequently, we lost a day of fire fighting and I had to borrow fire-fighting equipment from other truck loggers in the area.

The fire was contained to 4 or 5 acres, but our closest

water was at the 500-foot level and we had to pump the water in stages with about 200 feet elevation between each pump. It was damned hard work to keep four or five of those old-fashioned engines running at the same time. The fire gradually got the best of us though we fought it for three weeks. However, we managed to keep it away from our cold decks and fallen and bucked timber, because the wind changed direction and blew the fire back over the burned-off ground.

Our company asked permission of the Forestry Department to stop fighting the fire long enough to save our cold-decked logs, because if the wind switched again and the fire doubled back it would destroy them. Permission was refused. At that time we had about 7 million feet of timber felled and cold-decked.

I decided it was absolutely necessary to save that timber and against the department's orders we took out a couple of million feet. It was lucky we did, for after sixty days of fighting the fire the wind changed to the opposite direction. It turned into a dry southeaster: a hell of a lot of wind but no rain. Five million feet of timber were destroyed and three donkeys written off. We lost about half a million dollars in burnt-up timber. Our insurance was inadequate and so we had to replace the equipment and start all over again. But it was an efficient camp and we could stand such a terrible blow. We were back in production in a very few months.

The last six months were a sad time. By 1955 we were coming to the end of the timber. It had been fifteen years since we first started at Jeune Landing but now the Forest Management Licence holders had sold out again to the Rayonier Company and our contracts were not going to be renewed. We were cutting about 6 million feet a month and our camps were running like clockwork. Our company tried to renew its contract, not only with Rayonier but with every other major company. Everyone talked glibly of opportunity for all in the Crown forests, but there was not a contract to be had. Out of desperation we sold our equipment to the Rayonier Company. I am not saying that they did not pay us a fair price but all our loyal employees who had been with us for many years had no choice but to work for another company or leave. Only a small percentage of the men stayed with Rayonier.

Construction of the mill at Tahsis, 1945

The mill destroyed by fire, 1948

Tahsis, showing booming ground and family housing

"Gibson raft"

Head millwright *(right)* and assistant

"Eccentric Canadian"

"One to say 'here he comes' and one to say 'there he goes.'"

PRESERVE YOUR FORESTS

"... bit tough ... But Good."

RE-ELECT GORDON GIBSON

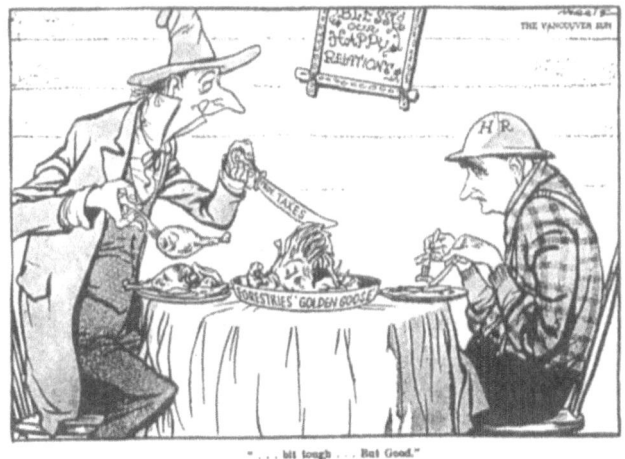

The 1955 provincial campaign

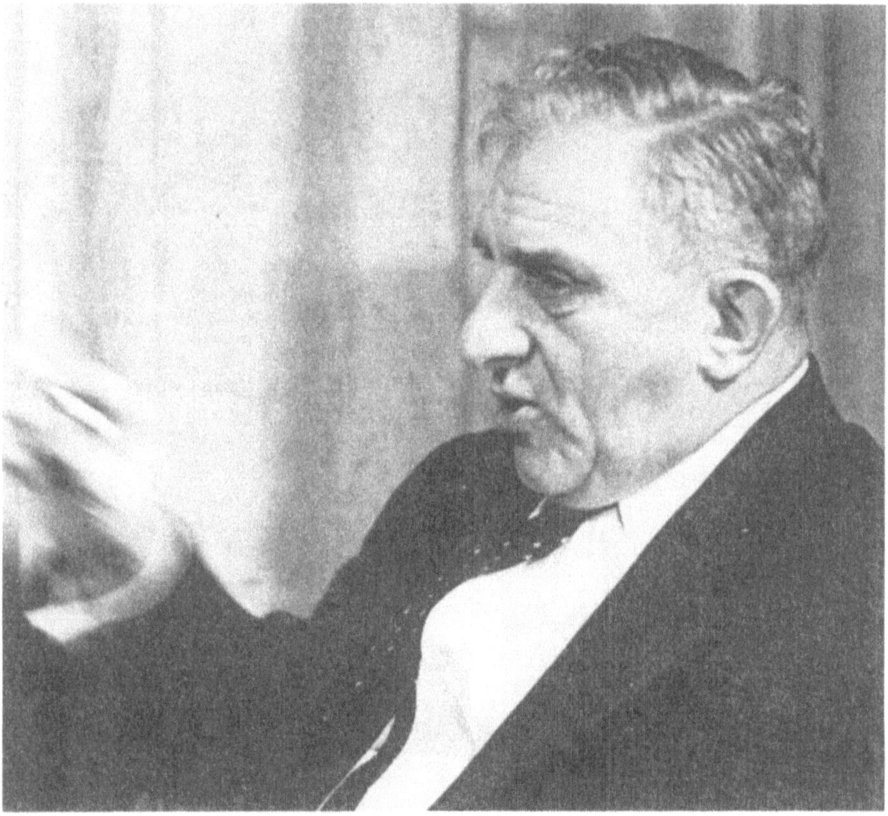

(Courtesy of the *Vancouver Sun*)

Gertrude Gibson (née Schneider)

The *Norsal*

CHAPTER 18

I remember that first big ship coming into Tahsis. I was standing in my caulk boots and tin pants tying the lines to stumps to secure the ship. I yelled, "Everything is first class," and I looked up to see this big Negro staring down at me from the deck. He says, "You boss here, mister?" I nodded and he said, "One thing about this place is that a man can't be put in jail."

I asked him what he meant by this remark and he answered, "You's all in jail and you don't know it." He just looked down the inlet—we were at the end of hell as far as he was concerned.

Today's thriving community of Tahsis grew out of our belief that it was possible for deep-sea ships to come to the west coast of Vancouver Island to pick up lumber for worldwide export. It is located in Nootka Sound, twenty miles from Friendly Cove where Captain Vancouver first landed on the hunting grounds of old Chief Maquinna. Our conception of this mill was from the beginning far bigger than any of our other ventures. We knew we would have to produce a shipload of lumber at least every two weeks to guarantee continuity of supply.

Other companies far larger than ours, Nootka Wood Products for one, had gone broke on this coast because they had built either too soon or in the wrong location. One mill had been built in an inlet where little sunshine ever penetrated and the freshly cut lumber mouldered within a month while waiting to be shipped. It was difficult to convince any banker that we could succeed in building a profitable operation where so many others had failed. H. R. MacMillan predicted that without access to a railway we would have little chance of success because the area was extremely isolated, and so our operation had to be large enough to warrant ships calling on us.

We did consider as an alternative to building at Tahsis

taking over the Robert Dollars mill at Dollarton, which was being dismantled, and continuing to send our logs to Vancouver, but we were having problems finding a market for our lumber in Vancouver, so we settled on Tahsis and bid for the Dollarton mill machinery. Although the surrounding land was mountainous, building at Tahsis had several advantages: there was a level plateau at the head of the inlet with easy deep-sea access for ocean-going vessels; the site faced southeast getting maximum sunlight. And our logs would need to be handled only once instead of being towed to Vancouver at considerable expense. Even using the Gibson raft, we had been losing one out of twenty tows, and when we sent a raft of 1,200 logs to Vancouver it would invariably arrive 50 to 60 logs short. One per cent of our logs were peelers, used for making veneer because they were free from knots. These were worth about three times as much as ordinary logs, selling for about $35 a thousand feet. Since some of them were as much as 3,000 cubic feet, each log stolen or lost at sea was $100 never recovered.

Jack had reported that there was an exceptionally fine stand of timber along the Tahsis River, which meant that a sawmill could be run for about a year on logs felled near the river and floated right into our booming ground.

For our first year, the logs were dumped at the mouth of the Tahsis River just a quarter of a mile from the mill's jack ladder—a revolving chain with cleats that carries the logs from the water to the upper deck of the mill. Over the next six months many a log went through our mill and into a ship's hold, on its way to other parts of the world within a week of the time it had been felled. This economy of handling was one of the reasons that we were successful.

Charlie Broadbent, a construction designer, was hired to plan the mill, which we wanted running in six months. I ran the project at Tahsis while Earson and Clarke were in Vancouver working on the plans and looking after our other business interests, some of which were whaling, canneries and Giant Mascot Mines.

We bought the old Olsen camp and towed their floating bunkhouses and cookhouses to the millsite so that we would have accommodation for our crew: time was of the essence.

Herman Steinoff, the best cat operator who ever worked for us, was hired to clear the millsite, while my crew and I started the four-day job of building a pile driver. We still had no plans for the mill: they wouldn't arrive until a month later. Our machinery, boilers and steam engine had already been loaded on a barge at Dollarton.

The mill was built contrary to all rules of good construction. We started our 16-foot-wide log slip first, driving all the piles from high water to low water on a 35-degree slope. We then started driving piles for the main part of the mill. It was built high off the ground with an 18-foot clearance. The mill was to have five rows of piles set crosswise on 10-foot centres with an 8-foot span between each row of piles. We put in one bent, or 10-foot by 40-foot section, every day, capped it, then moved ahead to the next row. If this was accomplished in eight hours, we called it a day; if not, we continued working until it was finished.

Those construction men were the greatest crew we ever had. There was a real esprit de corps among us, and if we were short of pilings, the crew would go out after supper with our towboat, the *Temiscouta*, and between seven and eight o'clock pull in twenty piles that had been felled along the shore. Sometimes they took a bottle of rye or a couple of cases of beer and had a singsong on the way back to camp. On Saturday night most of the crew took off for the beer parlour in Esperanza, and didn't get home until the early hours of Sunday morning. Ten men a week were added to the crew as the project grew.

To ship milled lumber from Vancouver was prohibitive, so we used 12-inch to 16-inch logs for piles, which cost us nothing. Half the piles we drove were deadheads and almost worthless to the sawmill. If a log is sunk by the butt it will stand longer than a milled timber because it has four times as much wood for the teredos to devour: they honeycomb through the entire butt without ever crossing paths diminishing by half the strength of a big timber.

We had started with a dream and $100,000. On 21 February 1945, Gibson Mills Ltd. entered into an agreement with East Asiatic Company (B.C.): East Asiatic would advance $75,000 on the understanding that they would get fifty per cent of the total production of Gibson Mills at competitive world prices. East Asiatic had no equity in Gibson Mills, but wanted an option on our lumber production to guarantee their export market. It was Clarke's friendship with Chris Busch, manager of East Asiatic, that led us into the arrangement which would eventually become a great partnership.

By the end of February our crew was up to fifty men and we needed more bunkhouses, so we bought any old camps in Nootka Sound that were still afloat and towed in the rest of the Olsen camp. Three 16-foot bunkhouses were built in Vancouver on open-deck fish scows 20 feet wide by 40 feet long. Each bunkhouse had two decks with living accommodation for twenty men. We towed them to Tahsis to house our crews.

The machinery for the mill arrived at the end of February. Somehow we managed to pull the edger, roll cases, carriage and tracks with a temporary winch up the slope of the jack ladder.

The mill was 40 feet wide, 18 feet high and 200 feet long. The roof was partially completed by the time Charlie Broadbent and my brother arrived with the first set of plans. They also brought along a civil engineer to lay out the millsite. Broadbent's plans called for square timbers set on top of concrete pilings underneath the main deck of the mill. I had used hemlock and fir piles figuring that although these timbers would rot out in five years, we would either be able to replace them by that time or have gone broke. I had to use what materials were at hand because we were short of time and money. Broadbent had designed a Cadillac whereas we needed a secondhand Ford.

The designer's first remark after setting up his transit and reviewing our work was that the floor of the mill ran downhill about 6 inches. I told him we had built it that way intentionally so as to have gravity favouring the roll of the lumber as it left the mill. Charlie Broadbent just shook his head, and we finished the mill without referring to his plans.

Time was precious. On one occasion I had to go to Vancouver on business and left the engineer-in-charge with the job of moving two boilers about 100 feet off a scow into position in the mill. When I arrived back at Tahsis two days later, only one of the boilers had been moved halfway off the scow. The crew had spent hours jacking and reefing it and had made little progress. At that rate it would have taken two weeks to get the boilers in place.

I called in Herman Steinoff, and we lashed a 24-foot log 16 inches in diameter over a logging arch attached to the cat, and hoisted it about 20 feet. We put slings around the boilers, picking them up like big logs, and moved them 200 yards into position. With the help of three men, we had the boiler in place by dark that night. I guess we were a little rough because one of the boilers was dented and our engineer had to report it to the boiler inspector. It caused us a little trouble with the men from the boiler inspection department but at least there was no delay: we couldn't depart from our schedule even by a week.

By the first of May our crew had grown to about eighty men. A man with a great record as a sawmill superintendent was hired and we turned over part of the management to him. He had been used to building sawmills around urban areas and found it tough to cope with our haywire operation. He was very knowledgeable about mill construction, but he saw so many problems that it was almost impossible to overcome his inertia and he became very despondent.

On one occasion when I was away, he overloaded a scow at low tide with sand and gravel needed for the base of our steam engines and power plant. The scow was so heavy that when the tide came in it stayed on the bottom. The water pressure sprung all the caulking and we had to get another scow.

Something seemed to happen to the vital drive of the camp. He didn't know that the impossible, with the right superintendent, only takes a little longer to accomplish. The job was just too much for him. He was sent back to town, and I once again took charge while we searched for another superintendent.

As construction progressed we built a big cookhouse that

could feed a hundred men at a time. We still had part of the wharf to build, and so much lumber was needed for construction that the little mill in Zeballos owned by the Darville brothers could no longer supply us. All our logs had been sent to Vancouver, and to get lumber we had to get our mill running.

Providing houses for married couples turned out to be one of the best innovations in our camps, and Tahsis was a good example of what can be done to promote community spirit in an isolated area. With a crew of six carpenters we built houses about 20 feet apart along the bank of the river, the easiest place to clear. The houses were 24 feet by 32 feet, each consisting of two bedrooms with a bathroom in between, a living room in the front and a kitchen. Our crew turned out a house every four days: just a crude affair with a floor covered in heavy tarpaper, a shingled roof and a privy at the back. There was no running water. That would come later. We sold the houses at cost, charging from $200 to $400 depending on the size and location. A man was allowed to improve his house as long as he occupied it, and he could sell it back to the company or to any other employee. Some men made a profit of $2,000 to $3,000 after living in one of these homes for a few years. We built about fifty houses and tried to improve them so that the men would be more comfortable. We felt that any man who invested time in his own home would be more likely to remain loyal to us and would be much happier when his wife and family came to join him. To add incentive I promised to have a school ready by the next term.

It felt great to have accomplished so much, especially when I remembered that only twelve months before I had sat by the Tahsis River with Bruce Haggart, a freight manager for the CPR, and, over a bottle of whiskey, confided, "Bruce, you won't believe it, but within a year I'm going to talk my brothers into building a sawmill here. We'll build a town where ships from all over the world will come to take away lumber. We'll build homes right along this river where you and I are sitting. We'll put in a church where people will go to Sunday School and get married. We'll put in a school." And I remember him saying, "Gordon, you'd better take another drink, I've never heard you this drunk before."

The first log went through our mill on the first of August 1945. Within a few months we had to be ready to load a ship with 2 million feet of lumber. For a few days every week the crew operated the mill to cut lumber. There were still houses to be built, a wharf to be finished and a boat service to be established so that we could bring in our work crews. We needed sawyers, an engineer, edgermen, agents from the Public Lumber Inspection Bureau (PLIB), greenchain contractors to pile the lumber and three crews of eight longshoremen. All this had to be organized so that we would be ready to load a ship in November. From then on ships requiring from 1 to 2 million feet of lumber cargo were scheduled to arrive every two weeks. Although everyone was working to capacity, it seemed impossible that the project could finish on schedule. By the end of October we started a night shift to stockpile enough lumber to load the first ship, the *Tipperary Park*.

When the mill was started up we used whatever lumber was available to fill the first order, which was for the East Asiatic Company, and any sizes that were rejected went into building houses and finishing the wharf. Two weeks before the arrival of the first ship we had only half the cargo cut and our wharf was still unfinished. It seemed an unreasonable task to cut a million more feet of wood with an absolutely green crew and a mill that was not yet running efficiently. We had to guarantee to load 2 million feet on the first ship or pay the freight on an empty hold, because Tahsis was the ship's last port of call in British Columbia before heading out to sea.

The 10,000-ton *Tipperary Park*, arriving in November 1945, was the first ship to come into the port of Tahsis. Our jetty was 40 feet wide and 300 feet from shore. The captain and pilot were concerned that our dock wouldn't hold if an offshore wind came up, so we secured the ship with an extra line to a stump on shore. To load the after hatch we had to move the ship forward at high tide and hoist aboard what lumber we could before pulling the ship out on the ebb tide.

When the *Tipperary Park* arrived we were still 300,000 feet short of our complete load, and the last order was pulled off the head saw two hours before the ship left port. It had taken four days to load her. The captain was very proud that he had brought the first ship into our harbour, and had helped start an enterprise which would load many thousands of ships. Had any of us faltered during the six months prior to loading, ours would have been like the other mills built in the area that had broken both men and dreams.

As it was, one of our superintendents told me that the mill would break up and we would go broke. The unfortunate man was so troubled that after leaving Tahsis he slashed his wrists with a razor and was found face down in the water of Vancouver's English Bay. He was a very fine man, but he thought we were doing the impossible because he hadn't been used to working under such adverse conditions.

November 1945 was the turning point in the history of Tahsis; from that time on we never looked back.

After sex, food is closest to the hearts of most loggers. When the night shift started we had to enlarge our cookhouse to 150-meal capacity, hiring male cooks and fifteen waitresses who lived in a nearby dormitory. I would never take the responsibility for what happened in that dormitory. The waitresses were certainly happy-go-lucky girls and I am sure that waiting on tables was just a sideline.

One of the waitresses who had been at Tahsis for about three months came to me one morning and said, "Mr. Gibson, my sister is going to have a baby." I replied, "Don't let that worry you too much. We'll help you all we can and send her down on the next boat."

"Mr. Gibson, I think that will be too late!" With that she took me up to the dormitory and explained that the baby was expected any moment. After my wife had sized up the situation we gambled by flying the young woman in our own seaplane to the hospital at Zeballos. Somehow she managed to walk down to the dock. Before boarding the seaplane on the morning that her baby was born she had carried out all her usual duties as a waitress, serving breakfast and cleaning tables.

Thanks to the local Catholic priest, a man I admired for his ability in solving delicate matters, I had the pleasure of being a guest at the wedding one month later. It was a big day in town, the only interruption to the party occurring when the bride had to slip away to nurse her baby.

Two new waitresses came to live in the girls' dormitory. They must have drunk too much beer on their first Saturday night in camp because they spent most of the evening going from one room to another in the men's bunkhouses. Apparently the night watchman couldn't get them under control as they were wild with liquor. By daylight they had passed out on the floor and I was called to pick them up.

I tried to tell them as kindly as possible that they had to leave the next day, but they were still terribly drunk and defiant and said they wouldn't go. Their language was the worst I have ever heard. We finally came to the understanding that I would take them down to Vancouver that afternoon in our plane. They wanted to go back to work but it couldn't be allowed. They slept right through the two-and-a-half-hour trip to Vancouver, and when we landed at the dock they were still belligerent: "What the hell are you going to do with us now? Turn us over to the police?" I told them I would be glad to drop them downtown or anywhere else they wanted. I think they could hardly believe my offer was real and not a proposition.

My home was on Marpole Avenue just off Granville and I stopped the taxi in front of our house, hoping my wife wouldn't see me with these two godawful-looking girls. I paid the driver and gave each one of them ten dollars. That was the best twenty dollars I ever spent in my life.

The next day when I was ready to go back to Tahsis I called a taxi to take me to the airplane. The taxi was from the same company as the day before though the driver was different. But he had heard the whole story and told me that the two girls had said I was the first man who had ever used them like ladies and given them ten dollars apiece for nothing. They just couldn't understand it.

Most of our crew were not regular church-goers. In the fall of 1946 we built a church for the Shantymen, a Pentecostal denomination that had a good local following. Dr. McLean had built a hospital about ten miles from our mill beside the beer parlour, the cannery and the church. He travelled up and down the coast in a little gasoline-powered boat, dedicated to his medicine and his missionary work. Dr. McLean took charge of the little church we built, which could seat about eighty people, but his congregation started to fall off, finally getting down to five or six attending on a Sunday morning.

I called him in and said, "Doctor, you have to get some more people in that church, or I will let the contract out to someone else." The good doctor replied, "Gordon, if you would just help me I know we can get that congregation." I promised that I would help him for only one Sunday because, as I told him, there was no use two of us taking on the same job. I promised to keep the crew working six days a week and pay the bills, but he had to make that church go on Sundays.

We put up a notice on the bulletin boards saying that I would take everyone down to the beer parlour in our boat on Saturday and bring them back at 2:00 in the morning if they would promise to be at church by 11:30 on Sunday. We had an overflow crowd—we couldn't get them all in!

This was the only time I ever preached a sermon in my life; I thought back to my old Sunday School days and gave them a good roar about what I thought religion meant. Dr. McLean let me pick some of the songs that the boys knew. It was a very successful day and from then on many of the crew who were feeling tough on a Sunday morning from the revels of the night before would go to church to find a little consolation.

The head waitress usually acted as my housekeeper. One day I was stuck in bad weather and didn't get back to camp until dusk. Louise had arrived in Tahsis ahead of me for a visit and found a young lady sitting in a chair reading a book. "What do you do here, dear?" asked my wife. The girl replied, "Oh, I'm Mr. Gibson's housekeeper. He's just such a lovely person. I have never been so fascinated by any man in my life."

She was more or less fired by Louise, and I slipped her a few dollars extra to heal her wounded pride. Louise announced that when she got back to town she would send me a suitable housekeeper. She did: a tiny Oriental man by the name of Toy Yick who couldn't have been more than 4 feet 8 inches tall.

John Millar, our chief accountant who retired in 1977 after forty years' service with Gibson Brothers, sent me the following account of Toy's arrival.

Toy Yick presented himself to Tom Christie who was in charge of our Port Alberni office, and who made all the arrangements on our passenger service boat from Port Alberni to our camps at Ucluelet, Tofino, Nootka, Tahsis and Zeballos.

Toy was a very apt name for this delicate little man. Mr. Yick seemed to fill all the qualifications for cook and housekeeper and bought a pass on our camp boat, stipulating that he would go up to Tahsis if we would guarantee that his passage would be relatively trouble free. Evidently Toy Yick was not a sailor. Mr. Christie reassured him that he would enjoy his trip saying, "Even if it does blow a little bit out there, you will enjoy the heave of the mighty Pacific." Toy boarded the *M.V. Machigonne* with several other passengers and they proceeded forty miles along the inside passage in the Port Alberni Canal, but when they got off Long Beach the seas became very rough.

This tiny man had such a difficult time in the heavy seas that the crew had to lash him to the deck railings and keep an eye on him during the entire five hours to Tahsis. Evidently he spent most of his time "heaving up" in the mighty Pacific!

By the time he arrived on the wharf, Gordon's new cook crawled off the ship on his hands and knees completely covered in vomit. He was so weak he had to be carried up to the hotel in a wheelbarrow. Gordon was absolutely bewildered and his first comment was, "What kind of a creature is this? That little fellow doesn't look big enough to carry a frying pan." Toy Yick vowed that he would stay at Tahsis forever if there wasn't any alternative to that terrible journey and claimed that if he ever did get out he would tell that son-of-a-bitch, Tom Christie, about the heaving mighty Pacific!"

I decided to take pity on Toy; instead of sending him on the *Machigonne* again he was flown to Vancouver in our private seaplane. When Louise asked me what had happened, I replied, "Louise, just a little family pride, dear. It wasn't too bad when everyone was insinuating that I was sleeping with my housekeeper, a good-looking girl, but when they said I was sleeping with a Chinaman I just had to let him go."

One of the hardest things about starting a venture of this magnitude is that it is almost impossible to avoid the occasional accident. In one of our camps at Muchalat a young man was riding on top of a trailer loaded on the platform of a logging truck, and when the truck took a curve in the road the trailer fell off, crushing the boy's right leg at the thigh. He was hurt so badly that he went into shock and didn't seem to feel any pain. The weather was too thick and dirty for a seaplane to come and pick him up, so my first-aid man, John Millar, my wife and I started out by boat on the twenty-mile trip to the hospital in Zeballos. The boy was quite cheerful and fully conscious all the way. Unfortunately, we had no morphine on hand.

When we arrived at the hospital the doctor examined the boy's injuries and told us that his leg had to be amputated at the thigh. The kid threw his arms around my neck and cried, "Will I live? Please don't leave me alone." I tried to reassure him. He pleaded not to be given any sedation. "If you put me to sleep, Doctor, I will die." He died within half an hour.

I have regretted that boy's death all my life. Unavoidable tragedy is sometimes the price of progress.

There seemed to be a steady supply of liquor coming into the Tahsis camp and it took me a couple of months to find the culprit. We caught our head plumber, who was making $1,000 a month over and above his salary by bootlegging.

I called him in and said, "Joe, there is no use denying it as we have all the evidence. We have to fire you; we just can't tolerate bootlegging here."

"Gordon, I think you're very foolish," he said. "If I don't bootleg there will be somebody else who will. How about me splitting with you?" I remembered the promise to my father about staying out of the liquor business, and I let him go, though you could always buy a bottle of liquor somewhere in that camp. I have to admit that I did my fair share of drinking. Hardy Tarves, our sawmill accountant in 1945, tells this story about me:

I first met Gordon Gibson on 20 November, 1945 while they were trying to get the ship loaded before that first Christmas. To tell the truth, I was very nervous as I had heard of his reputation as a rough, tough son-of-a-bitch, but I soon came to understand his ways. He was the best fellow I ever knew to put figures into words and pictures that a simple man could understand, translating three million dollars into carloads of wheat or shiploads of logs.

Gordon used to describe himself as a moderate drinker, that is, never more than a bottle and a half a day! I remember one horrible stormy night, a Sunday, Gordon was sitting by the fire wishing to hell that there was a drink around, when suddenly the door flew open and there appeared a soaking-wet figure with a gunny sack over his back.

"Where do you want this stuff, Mr. Gibson?"

"Oh, just put it in the back room" Gordon replied. The little man dropped the sack and we heard the welcome clink of bottles. "Do I owe you anything Mac?" says Gordon, without asking what was in the sack or why the man was there.

"No, it's all been taken care of Mr. Gibson. Goodbye." Out he went with no word of explanation. It all seemed rather strange to me but I helped him finish off those bottles and said nothing.

The next morning, in comes Earson, who was then sales manager. He says, "Say Gordon, by any chance has a chap come up from the ship with some liquor that I paid for?"

Gordon was the most natural born lucky man I ever met.

Fire is one of the greatest hazards faced by a logging camp and we had our share. After the *Tipperary Park* had been loaded, a forest fire started up the valley. We fought it for two or three days; the wind was blowing away from the camp and the fire was two miles distant, so we were not overly concerned. It hit the great timbers and almost burned itself out, but during the fourth night the wind changed and started to blow down the valley towards the mill. It moved about a mile towards us the next day putting our camp in jeopardy. With the wind propelling it through our burnt-over slash it came within 50 feet of our lumber piles.

The fire circled around the mill and up through the homes we had built along the shoreline. It took us at least three days to get that fire under control and we learned our first real lesson about being properly prepared. We had to run overtime and double up with the same crew because production for our next shipload had been set back three days.

There was nothing to forewarn us that the next great fire would be such a disaster that it would change the course of our lives.

CHAPTER 19

I remember Gordon pounding his desk—"Every man-Jack thinks he has no job. They have to know that nothing is going to stop us: the mill will be rebuilt!" So saying Gordon dug out the old pile driver, and twelve hours after the fire had started on the afternoon of July 6th he started to drive piles for the new mill with a crew of oldtimers. For my money they had some kind of guts.

Jock Munroe

I don't suppose that there is a more horrifying sight to any lumberman than a huge mill on fire. Our operations had been closed down for a week to allow us to tie in a large addition to the mill and to renovate the greenchain and rebuild the bull-edger. Clarke and I were in Vancouver overseeing our whaling operation on 5 July 1948 when we were told by telephone at two o'clock in the morning that the mill was a raging inferno: "The whole shiteree has gone."

Jock Munroe, our chief accountant in camp, reported that the welder had been putting the finishing touches on the bull-edger late at night when a spark from his torch went through the conveyor belt into the sawdust below, and within five minutes the mill was like the inside of a red-hot furnace with flames consuming the roof and machinery. The workmen had to fight their way out, and it was all the fireman on watch could do to tie down the whistle cord and run for his life, because the fire spread almost instantaneously from the conveyor belt to the boiler room.

A fire in a sawmill explodes three times as the particles of sawdust in suspension move out from each other expanding in the heat of the blaze. Each explosion triggers another and on the third blast the whole area blows.

We had no sprinkler system in the mill and although the sawdust under the conveyor belt was dampened down constantly, once the first spark hit the ground there was no hope that the mill could be saved. These conditions were not limited to our mill: in those days there was simply no money for extra safety precautions. But even the greatest sprinkler system could not have controlled that fire after the first puff.

Clarke and I left Vancouver at daylight in a small plane. It was an unusually clear morning, and as we were passing over Alberni we spied a small sawmill not far from the H. R. MacMillan site. After a three-minute discussion Clarke and I decided we would fly back next day and buy the little mill at any price. We could not afford any delay in our business and it would be far easier to tow our logs to Alberni than to Vancouver, our only other alternative.

When we arrived at Tahsis the mill was a complete loss. The wharves had survived, along with a few piles of lumber and our houses, but our power plant had burned up and would have to be reconditioned or scrapped.

The crew was still fighting the fire with the few hoses we had, to try to cool it down. We knew that the spirit of the camp would be broken if we waited to work out plans, so instead we started operations immediately. At one o'clock in the afternoon of 5 July, while the fire was still burning, the pile drivers started pounding in piles beside the site where the mill had been lost. We had forty families dependent on us, and we knew that our orders must be filled immediately or we would go broke. The ships were coming to load our lumber and if we were unable to meet our contract we would lose credibility with our financial backers.

After leaving the Tahsis operation in the hands of our fine superintendent, Alan Ramsey, Clarke and I flew to Alberni and negotiated for the Strumbach mill. The asking price was $10,000 more than our offer, but by the next morning the mill was ours. We were now faced with the problem of starting up a second operation and getting our logs to the Alberni site. We put on two shifts of sawyers and cut about half our Tahsis production, achieving 50,000 board feet a shift. The rest of the lumber for the shipload was negotiated for locally, and I am proud to say that when the first ship came into Alberni we were ready with a full cargo.

The welder who had started the fire went to pieces and

wanted to quit, but I wouldn't let him, stressing that the fire had been an unavoidable accident, and that for the sake of his family and his own self-respect he must stay with the job.

Then the financial rebuilding started. We had bought insurance on a straight-cost basis rather than on the replacement value of the mill and operations. We seemed to have momentarily run out of luck and borrowing power.

The East Asiatic Company, with whom we had dealt in the past, had acquired a lot of timber in Nootka Sound, and had used our operation to mill some lumber. When our mill burned down, East Asiatic considered building one of their own. We knew then that we had to make a deal, because two big mills could never compete in that area.

East Asiatic proposed that we build a much bigger and better mill on a partnership basis. They were so powerful and had control of so much timber in the area that unless we went in as partners they would build their own mill in competition with us. East Asiatic's proposition was fair and gentlemanly since they could have gone on without us. It really meant that if $100 million were necessary at some later date, East Asiatic could find it without our having to cosign the loans.

To complete our agreement, Clarke flew to Copenhagen with Chris Busch, manager of the Vancouver office of East Asiatic. After his meeting with the board, Clarke sent a telegram to our office in Vancouver to the effect that EAC would supply all required funds and referring to an agreement about future expansion. The telegraph operator felt that some mistake had been made in the transmission and added the letter H to form "EACH"—which addition significantly changed the meaning of the message.

Our office cabled back "NO DEAL" and Clarke informed the board of the East Asiatic Company in Copenhagen that we had said no. He felt that we should have gone ahead, but flew back to Vancouver; it wasn't until we all sat down together a few days later that the mistake was discovered.

Clarke had been put in a pretty embarrassing position with East Asiatic's directors, who undoubtedly thought they were dealing with a very eccentric family. Nonetheless, we managed to iron out our problems, and on 22 January 1949 we formed a new company, Tahsis Company Ltd., with East Asiatic holding fifty-one per cent and Gibson Brothers holding forty-nine per cent of the total shares. The operations and management control of Tahsis was vested in Gibsons for ten years, during which time two employees of East Asiatic would be trained by us. East Asiatic Company was exclusive selling agent for all lumber produced at Tahsis. Gibson Mills assigned all its timber licences to the Tahsis Company while the East Asiatic Company advanced money to rebuild the new mill at Tahsis.

Two weeks after the federal election had been called in the spring of 1949, a seaplane arrived at Tahsis and put off two passengers at our dock. I was on the wharf that day teaching a young fellow how to drive 8-inch spikes with a sledge hammer when I saw these chaps making their way towards the office. Just from their appearance I knew that work was the last thing on their minds and I wondered what in the hell they might be up to.

Out of curiosity I sent Robbie Robertson, our superintendent, to find out who they were, and he reported that one was the CCF candidate and the other was his manager. My brother Jack was the Independent Member for Comox-Alberni, and thinking I would have a little fun with these two deadheads, I shook their hands and made a great fuss over them.

"Make yourself at home, boys. I'll send one of my men to get your bags. You're going to be guests in my house. You might be representing this district sometime and I'd like to get to know you." The bastards were floored: they hadn't expected this kind of reception in a Gibson camp. I took them up to the house and poured them a few drinks—not one or two, but half a dozen—and arranged a big political meeting for eight o'clock that night. I asked my foreman to round up a good crowd, and after a few more drinks I said to my guests, "Would you boys like to have a little sleep before the meeting tonight? Generally, I'm chairman, but I want the candidate to have the honour, because although my brother is the local Member of Parliament I want you fellows to get a really fair shake. I'm a labour man myself." They couldn't have swallowed my story better.

When they woke up I offered them a drink and we sat in front of my big bay window overlooking the millsite. One of them asked, "Mr. Gibson, how did you get started in life?" and I said, "Well, boys, our family believes in individual opportunity. I started to work at twelve years old and our whole family worked together. We built a sawmill from nothing. To be very frank, I haven't joined the CCF because I like being my own boss, hiring men and having them work for me. With the brains you two fellows have I can't understand why you don't want to be your own bosses. I'll be honest with you, I need men as bright as you fellows are." I could see they were getting interested so I played my hand very carefully, not too much, not too little, giving them a drink whenever they seemed receptive. We got into a long discussion of government control versus private enterprise. I led them on, telling them I was desperate for men of their calibre. They were so gullible that they seemed to believe every word. After a few more drinks, I suggested several times that we go in to dinner but they preferred liquor and a little more flattery. When a delegation from the meeting came to remind them that everyone was waiting for their speech, they didn't seem much interested.

They were fairly comfortable by now and had changed their views on life. The manager said, "We're not doing any talking here. I can see that we've been of the wrong spirit for years. We're going to become capitalists like Gibson." The CCF candidate said, "I'm taking a job for Gordon. I've never been used as well as I have this afternoon. There will be no speech—just tell those fellows how lucky they are to work for Gibson." There was no speech.

My guests drank until 11:00 P.M. and I helped them to bed. I guess they felt ashamed the next morning, because they sneaked out of camp. That was the end of socialism in Tahsis for the next five years. I wondered what might have happened if a man like that candidate had been elected and sent to Ottawa to represent the district. At the first sign of comfort would he have thrown over socialism and joined private enterprise? I have never schemed so hard to win a girl's favour as I did to convert those two fellows to capitalism.

The mill was running pretty smoothly now. We had built two berths for ships, and our cargos were usually ready a week or two ahead of time, but we still had a few problems because we had constructed the mill so haphazardly.

Clarke and Jack arranged for an efficiency expert in the sawmill business to come to Tahsis and give me some advice about costs. We were losing $10,000 every month feeding our crew so I sent this so-called efficiency expert to the cookhouse to find out how to reduce this cost. He took charge and things immediately went from bad to worse. He changed cooks three times and got into trouble with the union. After a month I called him in and said, "Things are getting worse instead of better. How about giving me your efficiency report." He said he would be ready in two weeks, and I told him that would be two weeks too late and I wanted the report immediately.

According to him everything was wrong: no wooden sidewalks between the houses, no woodsheds, no recreation hall. All these problems were real, but he carried his tirade a little further: "Mr Gibson, you might be all right as a foreman, but you are the wrong man to be manager of a place like this. A person just has to look around your office to see how badly this operation is run. There are no filing cabinets, no books of reference—"

That was when I lost control of my temper. "Young fellow, if there are ever going to be any books on the walls of this goddamned office, I will write them. It's too late for me to start reading what other fellows are doing. I was considering firing you before, but you are definitely fired now. There is too great a difference between your theories and the practical workings of this situation."

That was the end of our efficiency expert—he had lasted just six weeks. Efficiency experts and do-gooders who give advice to others about how to make a success of themselves are a pain in the ass. I doubt their ability to run a wheelbarrow around the corner without a map.

CHAPTER 20

Prince Axel asked me to call him by his first name and I replied, "I know lots of Axels out there in those woods, but you're the only goddamned prince I ever met."

In 1949 Clarke and I went to Copenhagen to put together our financial policy with East Asiatic. We had entertained the chairman of the board, Prince Axel, on the West Coast several years previously. Prince Axel was the cousin of the King of Denmark and much the elder statesman, playing somewhat the same role as Lord Mountbatten. The Prince and I understood and liked each other immediately. He was a very big man, at least an inch taller than I. He was an airplane pilot and a great polo player, and he was one of the few men I have met who could drink as much liquor as I could and still look like a gentleman. He never appeared drunk unless judged by a very sober man, and I don't think there were ever many of those around him since he was usually the soberest of the lot, probably because of his years of training as a public figure.

Prince Axel was most gracious to us during our visit to Copenhagen. When Clarke and I first arrived at his massive, grey head office with one of his directors, a man called Jensen, we were stopped by a doorman who objected to my lighted cigar. Evidently the man who started East Asiatic Company, a very domineering character, thoroughly disapproved of smoking and had left orders that there would never be any tobacco in their head office.

The doorman said, "Sir, you're not allowed to smoke here," and I replied, "It's goddamned strange that you fellows came and smoked all you wanted at my house. I'm not an employee of this bloody company, I'm a partner."

I kept on smoking deliberately in the boardroom as if to say that they were not going to change my way of life at all, and that perhaps I was not so sure we wanted to do business with them. We would have to come to a mutual understanding, and it was going to be decided right then with my cigar. Clarke was pretty angry with my rudeness. He didn't say anything in front of them but I could see that he wanted me to get rid of that goddamned cigar. It was obvious that I was the odd man out.

I was used to smoking White Owls and it would have been another story if they had complained about the cheapness of the cigar. I could have forgiven that, but I always figured that if I started to enjoy a dollar cigar I would never be happy again with a five-cent one.

We talked for a while and I continued puffing on my cigar. At last Prince Axel said, "Gentlemen, I'd like to smoke also. Let's all join Mr. Gibson and make him feel welcome." They all started smoking.

I thought it amusing to see those men who had control over the disbursement of millions of dollars acting like schoolboys because twenty years before the founder of their company had objected to smoking. The founder must have enjoyed his liquor: after our business meeting the wine flowed freely.

We were in Copenhagen for four days and were treated most graciously as honoured guests at two dinners after we had completed the details of our partnership with East Asiatic. At these dinners we were seated according to protocol next to Prince Axel, the chairman. We were partners and the rest of the table consisted of employees and shareholders. Clarke and I were the only members of the group who actually owned some assets: even Axel was a shareholder. It was like the head of the CPR meeting a man who owns a little railroad.

(I have never accepted the position of chairman of any board that could fire me because I wouldn't last two hours. So I'm afraid to play that game. When it was suggested that I be invited to join the board of MacMillan Bloedel, H. R. MacMillan said, "Gordon is too hard to handle." I believe that all a man has control of is himself from his toes to the hair on the top of his head, and if he's not in charge of that he's not in charge of so much.)

On another occasion Clarke and I had dinner with Prince Axel and Princess Marguerite and a few members of the

Royal Family. I will admit that we were both at a loss for a few moments but soon we felt absolutely at home and held our own conversationally. Later that night Clarke and I went out on the town, pub crawling. It was hard to believe that two or three hours before we had been dining with royalty. Had we been born and worked in Europe it would have taken ten generations for backwoods boys such as ourselves to have made that step.

Before we left Copenhagen the East Asiatic Company gave us a choice of a dozen different presents to take home as a souvenir and I picked a tiny Royal Copenhagen elephant. I told them that to me it was a symbol of the places where East Asiatic had made the most money, of countries like Siam where elephants are used, just as a little fishing boat might remind them of the West Coast. I still have it in my house.

When our business was finished in Copenhagen we flew to London and stayed in the Savoy Hotel. We were given a beautiful suite, attended by a maid and a valet. I remember being impressed by the size of the bathroom. The bathtub was so large that on a foggy morning there would be trouble getting back to shore. I had never seen a bidet before and when I pressed the button, water squirted right in my face: the butler knew I was a real hick from the country.

The day before we were to leave I put a call through to Louise, saying that we would be home in a few days. She was a girl with a lot of good sense, and asked if we had been to Paris. When I replied that we hadn't she said, "Well I want you to go over there and get all your darned foolishness about women out of your head."

I wasn't taken in by my Parisian experience because I do like to have a little conversation with sex. I'm not like that William Hart, a big silent type, who didn't need a woman and just rode away into the west.

One night Clarke and I went to the Lido Club. We thought we would be big shots and tip the maitre d' five dollars. The man looked at the bill and didn't even say thank you; he put us at the back of the hall.

Whatever may be said for the charm of French women, I realized how wise my wife had been to send us to Paris. It did nothing more for me than to make me appreciate what a fine home I had. Clarke and I left for Canada in a Stratacruiser which stopped at Prestwick to take on more fuel. It was dusk and I could see the lights of the airstrip as we came in. We were in a position to land, flying like a mallard duck coming in on water with its feet ahead. About 50 feet from the ground I felt the nose dip. Before the engines could lift the plane we hit the ground, smashing the nose gear right off.

We skidded 300 yards, nose down, tail up. The pilot reversed the propellers. The blacktop and gravel cut through the gas tanks and the whole aircraft burst into flames. Within minutes the fire engine that had been running alongside us doused the plane with chemical foam. It took about ten minutes to put the fire out.

There was complete silence inside the airplane. A hundred and fifty passengers sat like a bunch of dead animals, with no sound or sign of panic. I made the first move and tried to open the exit door off the bar, which was downstairs in the belly of the aircraft, but it opened outward and all the baggage had been flung against it jamming it from the far side. I later raised hell with the Boeing Aircraft Company, for all doors should swing inward from any main cabin so that they can be opened easily in an emergency.

We had to climb down a ladder that seemed like a couple of hundred feet off the runway and as I began to walk around the plane, I was stopped by a fireman. I was so emotional I said, "Get out of my road or I'll hit you," feeling that we had been used badly enough without anyone giving me orders.

After a long wait in the airport I shouted, "For Christ sake, haven't you got anything to drink around here? We all need one badly." The airport manager came out with a tray of one-ounce drinks. Five minutes later I said, "Look here, don't save your liquor, bring out the whole goddamned bottle and a few more besides; we need a bottle apiece. We're in no mood to take drinks one ounce at a time."

If any of us had had any brains at all we would have said that after such a close call we were just too terrified of air travel to go any farther. But like fools, we continued home on the next plane.

By March 1949, the new mill was in operation. It was much bigger and more efficient, with a 10-foot bandsaw, a modern carriage and better machinery. We operated two shifts with most of the men who had been present on the day of the fire. Now the mill had an efficient sprinkler system: we didn't want to lose our mill a second time.

About this time a young apprentice from the East Asiatic Company who had been trained in Denmark joined our firm. He was half as strong as I but he had energy galore, and I have never seen a young man put such effort into his work. He was to learn everything about the lumber industry and worked side by side with me. He was put on every job from cookhouse to yard foreman in the mill. I don't remember ever asking Jack Christensen to do anything that he didn't do with full enthusiasm and intelligence, and he rapidly moved up through the ranks. I am proud to say that today he is president of Tahsis Company in Vancouver and a close friend. I admire that type of young man, although if everyone worked as hard to get ahead as Jack did, it would make it even more difficult to get to the top.

Tahsis now had a strong financial basis. We built good homes for our employees and put in more roads and blacktop. I made a deal with the government to build houses: they would pay eighty per cent of the cost and we would give preference to returned veterans.

The idea seemed fine but it got bogged down in red tape. I found these houses were going to cost five times as much as the houses we had already built. We had to hire a surveyor to say exactly where every house could be placed, and put them on cement foundations. Moreover, we had to use first quality building material which was the same lumber we were selling, instead of using reject lumber which was unsalable. The plans called for a front and back door with an alcove, and a specified number of windows in each room. Our men weren't allowed to do their own plumbing and wiring. In the past we had operated on a barter system—I'll do your electricity if you dig my cesspool. I soon realized that the cost of these houses would escalate from two thousand dollars to four thousand. One morning when I saw three civil servants being paid to stand around and watch three of my carpenters work, I got so fed up that I scrapped the government project completely. The government's way of working just made no sense to me at all.

By this time flush toilets and running water had been put into all the homes. We had a first-class school with three rooms, and a large recreation hall for dancing and social affairs. We put in a small restaurant that ran twenty-four hours a day for the off-shift crews and their families.

There were many setbacks and disappointments. One of our main logging camps in the Tahsis Canal had a woods fire which we fought for a couple of months, and I learned something that I had never known about fires: they run downhill faster than uphill. This fire started at the 1,500-foot level from the friction of a cable running over a dry log. Unfortunately, there was not water nearby. It did not look very dangerous for the first few hours, and was contained within an acre of ground. The foremen and I put all our efforts into cutting the fire off on the uphill side and managed to control it there. In fact, we thought we had it beaten. Although the fire was well controlled, on the second day the stumps started to burn out, rolling downhill and starting new fires. By the time that day was over we had a fire burning out of control from the beach right to the top of the steep hillside. A fire like that costs a lot of money, since it took seventy-five men out of the regular shifts to fight it for over two months.

One of our finest men, Frank Grobb, wrote of this period:

In early 1951 things were not going as well as expected at the mill and we needed extra financial backing. Gordon would fly up a group of prominent bankers in his plane and march them around the sawmill and then treat them to a palatial dinner and of course, plenty of drinks! Many bottles of V.O. and great stories of the west coast would go on till three or four o'clock in the morning. But at six o'clock the next day the weary green-faced bankers would be awakened by the smell of eggs frying in half an inch of grease. He gave them all a big breakfast which they could hardly refuse without losing face, and hurried them out of the camp, explaining that the work must go on and that he was very busy etc. On the plane home the bankers would express their great admiration at his drive and pace, and his ability to consume vast amounts of liquor without apparent consequences. By this time Gordon was in bed—sound asleep!

The new mill never had the same appeal for us. We were not interfered with in any way and we had a good ten-year management contract but small frictions began to creep in. There were times when it would pay East Asiatic to load a deckload of lumber on one of their own ships already bound for some foreign port where they could carry it at no extra cost.

We had logged out the Tahsis area by this time and had planted a new crop of young fir trees. That was our first try at reforestation. The philosophy of reforestation sounds good but 99.9 per cent of all trees replant themselves, because seeds lying dormant in the ground will germinate in the sunshine and warmth. Natural regrowth is almost as fast as reforestation. Also, it costs close to $200 an acre to replant and when this is amortized over a hundred years at 10 per cent, it will be found that planting trees is extremely costly. The places our company logged off when I was a youth grew back into lovely stands of new trees. There are some who believe that the cut-out and get-out logger is absolutely wrong, but the first requisite of proper reforestation is to cut out the old crop and allow nature to replant.

You can compare a forest to a herd of cattle. Beef is at the zenith of its weight and value in three to four years but if it is allowed to mature to sixteen or eighteen years, it loses worth on account of its age. Unless you reap a crop of timber at least every hundred years you will be left with a decaying forest half filled with old dead trees. The new growth can't begin because the sun can't get down that far. If a natural catastrophe had taken one per cent of our forests every year we would now have twice the timber we have because we'd be in a cycle of the new coming up and replacing the old.

After 100 years of lumbering, sixty per cent of our forests are still virgin and the trees are rotting. Seventy-five per cent of the forests of B.C. are overmature and although they are possibly uneconomic to log, they should still be cut back even at a loss so that new timber will come back. After 100 years only the hardy trees get bigger and their increase is much less. A stand of timber 500 years old has less wood in it than if it had been harvested at 100 years. We could sustain a cut of 15 billion feet a year instead of the 10 billion now being cut. Twenty years ago, at the first Sloan hearing to determine the inventory of British Columbia timber, the people of the province were told that we had one-quarter of the timber we now know exists today. It was at that time that the government became so worried about the future of our forests that it started allocating timber by tree farm licences to a favoured few who got them through lobbying the politicians. Many times I suspected that underhanded means were used to acquire these licences.

It was about the time when Forest Management Licences started to become popular that our company was offered cutting rights to a tremendous volume of timber from Estevan Point to Cape Cook. Our family considered it wrong to accept a policy that was so detrimental to the province. Between East Asiatic and our company we had twenty-five years' timber, which was all we felt necessary to amortize our capital. But East Asiatic felt differently: they liked the idea of having forestry rights in perpetuity. It became apparent that a new deal had to be made. We thought it best to start negotiating for East Asiatic to eventually buy us out. These negotiations took the better part of the year.

I was also having some personal problems with one of East Asiatic's employees. In fact, I once caught him snooping among my employees, asking how much I was drinking and what I was doing, so I took him out for a ride in my boat the next day and dropped the hint that if I had any more trouble with him, he had better be a goddamned good swimmer or he would drown on his way to shore. He had high ambitions to get rid of me but my brothers and I had an excellent arrangement with East Asiatic and there was no chance that he could oust me.

We decided to sell out finally because East Asiatic was considering building a pulp mill which would cost close to $100 million and would take twenty years to show a profit. We could have held shares in the company but we would have had a forty-nine per cent interest and would have owed about $40 million. The operations were becoming more complex and my brothers and I were not really capable of running such large plants. Moreover, we were getting a little tired by now. It seemed better that the Gibsons step aside from a partnership that had been very satisfactory.

In 1952 I took Prince Axel on a trip up the west coast in our yacht, the *Norsal*. We had been doing a little hunting and fishing at Campbell River, and as we came around Cape Cook about five miles offshore on a beautiful clear day, I figured that now was the time to sell my idea.

"Axel," I said, "we own from here to Cape Cook clean down to Estevan, an area far larger than your whole country of Denmark. There are enough trees for your company to run on forever. We'll help you all we can but we might only be good for another ten to twenty years. We would rather turn it over now to a company like yours that will go on forever."

When we got back to the mill that night he said, "Gordon, how would we run this operation without your family?" I replied, "Prince, I've only had five years of schooling. I was never trained to run a large operation. This concern is getting too big for us now. You have trained men who are experts, and if you pick a man like Jack Christensen, within a year you'll be running five dollars a thousand cheaper than we are now and producing twice as efficiently. We're just starter-uppers. I'd put Jack in charge right now."

Christensen was put in charge of the whole operation though he was a very young man. Clarke flew to Copenhagen and brought back cheques that made each one of us a millionaire in his own right.

It was twenty years before I went back to Tahsis. I had

left clothing and a pair of shoes in every camp and I guess they were gradually used by the Indians and workmen. Even my workboots disappeared.

East Asiatic couldn't have been kinder to us. In fact, I was asked to be a director for the next year, but I never went back. It would have been like a man looking up a woman whom he has truly loved. It would have broken my heart.

CHAPTER 21

Any man who is master of his own little boat can go anywhere at will and is far more fortunate than the man who must hire another to be his captain, even if he can afford the finest stateroom on the **Queen** *Elizabeth. It all boils down to being in charge of the situation, be it challenging the sea or destiny itself.*

Boats have always been my second love. In 1946 we bought a 110-foot submarine chaser, the *Machigonne*, from the Canadian War Assets Disposal. Many of these ships were put up for sale after the war ended because they had been specially designed for their war work and were virtually useless as cargo or pleasure craft. They had been costly to build and the federal government was criticized for selling them cheaply, though almost everyone who bought one soon regretted the purchase since they had huge gasoline engines that were expensive to run, or to convert to diesel.

The *Maquinna* still called in at Tahsis every Sunday, but we were expanding so fast that she couldn't handle our freight; we needed machine parts and supplies brought in as well as passage for our crews. We decided to run the *Machigonne* out of Port Alberni as a passenger and cargo ship calling at Ucluelet, Tofino, Tahsis and Zeballos.

The *Machigonne* made two trips a week under Captains Bill Olsen and Dan Backie, both of whom had skippered the *Malahat* and the *James Carruthers*. The route was often through very rough seas in an area famous for unpredictable and stormy weather. All the passengers disembarked after a trip on the *Machigonne* with a healthy respect, even dislike for the sea. Some vowed that they would never again venture off dry land.

Our agent in Port Alberni tried to drum up a little tourist trade to bring in more revenue. He advertised a two-day round trip up the west coast featuring magnificent scenery and the fine relaxation to be had on the gentle, soothing roll of the Pacific Ocean. Our advertisements made it sound like a wonderful holiday.

Among our first customers was a family of four from the prairies who had never before been to sea. As luck would have it, the trip was one of the worst the skipper could remember. The *Machigonne* cleared the Alberni Canal about eight o'clock on a calm, sunny morning, and after sailing past Ucluelet, headed north for the two-hour run to Tofino. Although the seas were rough on this part of the trip, they were moderate compared to the conditions we encountered after we cleared Tofino and ran the forty miles around Estevan Point at 15 knots with a stout westerly blowing.

Our skippers were on a tight schedule and no little storm from the Pacific was going to put them off their run. But even an experienced sailor would have felt queasy, because the sub chaser had a particularly nasty shudder on the crest of a big wave and would roll, twist and dive in a single sickening movement. The passengers endured four hours of this punishment, hanging on in terror to anything that was bolted down, as the *Machigonne* plunged and corkscrewed through 30-foot waves. One in every six trips was god-awful. If seat belts are considered necessary safety equipment in automobiles, then every passenger aboard that ship should have been lashed to the deck in a straightjacket. When the family from the prairies arrived back in Alberni, they almost sued us for false advertising because we had used the words "gentle roll of the Pacific." If ever a vacation package was misrepresented, ours was.

On many occasions the *Machigonne* brought to Tahsis workers who had been hired from Skid Row in Vancouver. Usually they had been plastered before getting on board ship, but after twelve hours on the *Machigonne* they were sick but very sober men. Rarely would any of them feel strong enough to work the next day. About the only virtue I could see in bringing workers up on that ship was that most of them were scared to death to make a return trip and were willing to put in a few months' hard work before going through the same misery to get back to Vancouver. In fact, the *Machigonne* had very few passengers on her return trips; people preferred to fly back even if it meant waiting a week or two for airplane reservations.

We maintained this service for about a year while Tahsis was being built, and until a stable crew of workmen had been established in their own houses. The gold-mining boom at Zeballos had slowed down and we felt that the *Machigonne* could serve us better elsewhere. At the time we were running a passenger service between Horseshoe Bay in West Vancouver and Gibsons Landing but our two 40-foot boats were too small for comfort or safety and couldn't handle the rapidly growing volume of traffic. The *Machigonne* took over the run, leaving Horseshoe Bay and travelling in behind Bowen Island and across Howe Sound to Gibsons Landing. The waters there are calm compared to those of the west coast of Vancouver Island. The *Machigonne* gave excellent service to the people on the Sechelt Peninsula for a couple of years until a ferry became necessary to transport automobiles to the hundred miles of road on the peninsula.

We did not want to get into the ferry business in addition to running an outfit as large as Tahsis, and therefore offered the franchise for the Horseshoe Bay-Gibsons Landing run to two Canadian companies, Canadian Pacific Steamships and Union Steamship Company. Neither of them were interested. Captain Peabody, who owned Black Ball Ferries in Washington, bought the franchise and put a large car ferry on the run. The residents of the Sechelt Peninsula have an excellent boat service thanks to the foresight of Captain Peabody and, later, the Government of British Columbia.

Not all of the boats we owned were as good a buy as the *Machigonne*. The blame for our first bit of folly, the *Odalisk*, must go to Clarke, for he concluded the deal before the rest of us laid eyes on her. She was a well-designed contemporary yacht, about 50 feet long: a yachtsman's dream in inside waters, but unsuitable for rough seas because she rode low in the water and had a very narrow beam.

Clarke and I decided to take a trip on our new boat from Vancouver up the coast. We were both good seamen and should have known better than to attempt such a trip without a test run. We cleared First Narrows at 12 knots and then foolishly opened the engine right up and headed for Active Pass at full speed, taking a great deal of abuse in the heavy seas of the gulf. The waves were so high that many of the *Odalisk*'s windows were smashed in and we were forced to slow down a little, though we kept on our course. The storm increased after we got through Active Pass. We should have used some sense and turned back, but instead we headed past James Island in very rough seas.

The winds were gale force, at least 60 miles an hour, so we swung in behind a big sandspit jutting out from James Island to take shelter until the storm abated. I threw out our anchor but it was almost useless since it was far too light to hold. The *Odalisk* drifted with the storm despite all our efforts to hold our position. Seeing that the anchor couldn't hold her, Clarke ran her up on the sandspit, while the waves broke all around us, pounding the hull and scaring the hell out of us. With a searchlight I was able to pick out a telephone pole about 100 feet up the beach. I jumped ashore with a rope and secured the boat to the pole, then we found shelter for ourselves.

After the storm had died down the next morning, I said to Clarke, "You can have this damned boat as a plaything to run around the harbour in Vancouver. As far as I'm concerned, that's all she's good for. The *Odalisk* isn't a west coast vessel. I want to be rid of her." We sold her, vowing that never again would we own a boat so useless.

I believed I had learned my lesson, but it wasn't a year before an enterprising salesman convinced me that we should have a speedboat to run between our camps. This was before we had a company airplane. To be of any real use the boat would have to be capable of making 40 knots.

The boat he had in mind was the *High Hatter*, a speedboat, 18 feet long with a 300-horsepower engine. I took it for a quick run around Vancouver harbour. It skimmed over the water as if it would take flight. I thought it was a marvellous boat and paid cash for it on the spot. It was loaded on the *James Carruthers* and carried up coast.

Most of our camps were very isolated. The post office

was 30 miles from Muchalat, and the *High Hatter* could easily make the trip in an hour. Even the time needed to get to our camp in Zeballos was cut from four to one and a half hours.

The *High Hatter* made five trips during the time we owned her and three of them were memorable. Clarke and I took her timber cruising to an area about 20 miles from our camp at Muchalat which we reached in half an hour. We cruised the timber, then headed home. The engine stalled and wouldn't start again.

It started to rain. There was no cabin on the boat for shelter. The *High Hatter* was twenty times heavier than a canoe and much more unwieldy making it extremely difficult to paddle. The two of us paddled all night, making not more than a mile an hour. We were damned hungry as we had brought only a couple of sandwiches figuring that the trip wouldn't take more than four hours. A fish boat picked us up the next morning and towed us into camp. That first trip dampened my enthusiasm a little but not enough to make me seriously doubt the wisdom of our purchase.

The next trip could have been fatal. I left Muchalat and made the 40-mile run to McBride Bay where we were selling logs to the Nootka Logging Company. A British freighter was in port loading lumber and the crew invited me aboard for a few drinks. It was Saturday night. About nine o'clock, encouraged by my liquor, I suggested that I take them to the beer parlour in Zeballos, twelve miles away. The *High Hatter* could make 40 knots an hour carrying one passenger, but with six husky men aboard her speed was cut to about 10 knots. She rode low, pushing her way through the water like a scow. This was fortunate because we were only three miles from shore when we hit a huge log. The night was pitch-black. The *High Hatter* ran right up over the log, losing her rudder and propeller. By the grace of God she didn't sink. There was no lifesaving gear aboard and I doubt that any of us could have swum to shore. We took turns paddling back to the ship, and five hours later we were seven very sober men. I'll bet that none of those British seamen ever again took a boat trip with a crazy Canadian logger.

The third trip in the *High Hatter* was with my wife, Louise. We left Muchalat to make what should have been a two-hour trip to camp in Zeballos. We cleared Muchalat Inlet and struck out across the open waters of Nootka Sound before entering Tahsis Canal in the protection of Nootka Island, a three-mile stretch of sea that can be extremely rough.

Louise and I were in the forward cockpit, the engine just behind our seat. Our body weight was distributed so that with the following seas, the forward deck of the speedboat seemed to slant nose down. It was a very wet passage, the seas hitting the windshield and spilling over into the cockpit. I figured that we should try to run a little faster and opened the throttle full speed ahead to 30 knots, hoping to hit the tops of the waves rather than wallow in the troughs. The *High Hatter* seemed to pound her hull from crest to crest on the black swells with an even and rhythmical thrust. Suddenly, the boat paused in the air for a split second before her bow plunged into the trough of a 10-foot swell. The seas rushed over the gunwales and poured into the cockpit. Our engine was swamped and stopped dead. Only the watertight compartments kept us afloat.

I have always believed that the instinct of self-preservation is so strong that it asserts itself over any other in a moment of danger, as it did in this instance. In the next few seconds the boat seemed to flounder. The story Louise told was that I put one hand on her shoulder and the other on the gunwale and thrust downward, forcing myself free and above the torrent of water. I always maintained that I did it in order to get in a standing position to help her out over the side like a gentleman, but I don't think she ever believed me!

Miraculously the boat stayed afloat, her gunwales just a few inches out of the water. When we gathered our wits about us, we bailed as fast as we could with a big bucket. Fortunately, the engine compartment was dry and I was able to restart the engine. We turned back for Muchalat.

I decided to get rid of the *High Hatter* as fast as I could, figuring we had pushed our luck far enough. The *James Carruthers* was in port and I had the speedboat loaded aboard her that same day and sent back to Vancouver. The *High Hatter* had belonged to me for ten days: I hope her new owners fared better.

CHAPTER 22

Other poets have warbled the praises of the soft eye of the antelope, and the lovely plumage of the bird that never alights; less celestial, I celebrate a tail.
　　　　　　　　　　　　　Herman Melville, *Moby Dick*

In September of 1947 Clarke telephoned me at Tahsis to tell me that the Consolidated Whaling Company of Victoria had four or five old whaling ships that were going to be sold at public auction. He wanted our company to put a bid on them since we were always interested in acquiring more ships to assist our fishing and towing operations. The whalers were at least fifty years old and steam driven, but we thought we could replace the steam engines with diesel power. I suggested to Clarke that he should bid no more than $5,000 to $10,000 a ship, which was a hell of a lot of money but far less than it would take to build a hull from scratch.

The next day, Clarke told me that all the assets of Consolidated Whaling were being sold as a unit and no bids for individual ships would be considered, so he had tendered $5,000 for the whole shebang: two whaling plants, four whaling ships, tanks, wharves, guns, ropes and cables. There were no other offers. Who in the hell wanted whaling plants in 1947?

Clarke had acquired four whalers, the *Blue*, the *Gray*, the *White* and the *Brown*, two run-down reduction plants at Sechart in Barkley Sound and at Rose Harbour in the Queen Charlotte Islands, as well as all the old whaling equipment. We were delighted with the deal but Clarke had also secured the whaling rights for British Columbia waters, which had been granted by the Canadian government to the Consolidated Whaling Company some sixty years before. We had bought the right to lose money and were more than pleased with ourselves.

Our cannery in North Vancouver handled herring, salmon and anchovies. Richie Nelson, owner of Nelson Brothers Fisheries, and Bob Walker, general manager of B.C. Packers, met Clarke and I for lunch one day at the Terminal City Club. When they heard about our purchase they wished us good luck, and Bob Walker said, "If you do well we might have a go at it ourselves next year, but we'll let you do the pioneering." I replied, "You're crazy to think you have a chance, because we control the complete franchise. You can't go into whaling without us. Your ads boast that you can everything from sardines to salmon, but we'll be able to advertise anchovies to whales."

Until that moment we had never seriously considered going into whaling, but the four of us talked about it far into the afternoon. Richie Nelson figured it was a venture we'd be sure to lose money at since we didn't know anything at all about whaling, and he suggested, "How about us going in with you? We'll pool our fishing experience and split the expenses three ways." We agreed. A three-way shot. We set up a company called Western Whaling Corporation and began to plan for the coming season.

Whale meat was occasionally on the menu at the Terminal City Club. The best meat comes from the same area of a whale as choice beef from a steer, just in the protection of the ribs. Because it tastes strong and somewhat gamy it is usually cooked like a pot roast.

Our Tahsis operation was running well because I had very good superintendents and Clarke was in charge of the sales. Consequently I had a little free time, and volunteered to start work on the plant. We chose the whaling station in the Queen Charlotte Islands to start our whaling operation, though not one of the whole bloody bunch of us had ever seen Rose Harbour, or had any idea of the tremendous amount of work ahead.

Jack obtained us a little free advertising, a piece by Kenneth Cragg entitled "Harpoons Replace War Cannon," in the Ottawa *Evening Citizen* of 24 December 1947:

Whale hunting in war surplus United States mine sweepers, luxurious craft with a telephone in every room and electric motors to flush the toilets, is described by John L. Gibson (Ind., Comox-Alberni) as the most recent west coast industrial development.

When the season opens on April 1, the new company, the Western Whaling Corporation of Vancouver which purchased the assets of an earlier venture that closed in 1943, will send three mine sweepers out to the whaling grounds, from twenty to fifty miles off the islands. These craft were converted for the hunting of whales by replacing their deck cannons with harpoon guns and adding the appropriate harpoons and cordage. They are diesel powered, 145 feet long and have a speed of 16 knots. They come equipped with asdic and radar and the new owners will try this equipment, intended for hunting subs, on whales. No one has much idea if it will work, but there is a report from wartime operators that asdic was used to scare whales away. They felt or sensed the asdic impulses.

Almost 90% of the whales to be caught within easy tow of the processing plant are the oil-rich sperms and each, at present market prices, is worth between $3,000.00 and $5,000.00.

Under the rules, each boat must tow back its own kill to the main plant, which will be located at Rose Harbour at the extreme south end of the Charlottes. There, in the modern practice, the whales will be tapped of their free oil and the rest obtained by rendering the blubber, like getting lard from a fat ham. What is left will be converted into edible meal for poultry and other feeds. The firm, Mr. Gibson says, has no present intention of canning whales for human consumption but he recalls eating canned whale meat during the last war and finding it appetizing.

"If the C.C.F. in Saskatchewan can convert surplus horses into good canned meat there is no reason, certainly, why West Coast ingenuity and skill cannot do the same with whales," he said.

I decided that our first priority was to build a wharf and some bunkhouses, so I loaded the required amount of lumber on a scow to be towed by the *Joan G*. I struck out from Tahsis with an amateur crew and a couple of carpenters. The *Joan G*'s only power was a 125-horsepower Atlas Imperial engine that made 6 knots an hour.

The contribution from B.C. Packers was a pile driver, but we were still operating without any money, just damned hard work and any materials at hand. Only the crew were being paid. After hooking up the B.C. Packers scow carrying the pile driver at Namu, we headed for the

Queen Charlottes towing both old scows at 4 knots an hour.

Sept. 3, 1947
Heckate Straights
Joan G

Dear Mother,

This is just after lunch and we are about half way across to Rose Harbour from the Mainland. Left Namu about 4 p.m. yesterday with a big Pile driver and a scow of piles, also a full load of lumber on the Joan G. We should get in about 8 p.m. tonight. The crew arrives tomorrow morning, then we have to arrange a camp and get started to build. It looks like a lonely place to be going from Choice. Guess there is something in me that I want to be the first to start. It's something like the feeling that Columbus must have had when he saw North America.

I don't seem to think in the terms that the rest of the world does—they're thinking of the money that's in this venture. I think I like it just from the adventure standpoint.

In a joking way I always said that when the West Coast got too many people on it we'd have to go to the Queen Charlotte Is. . . .

I feel sorry for Louise that she married a man who has so much Gypsie blood in him. . . .

I don't know what kind of a crew I'll get tomorrow but if they're no good guess I better stay here for a week or so and get the Docks built.

We took a load of Machinery into Jeune Landing on a scow this trip then loaded the same scow with Piles for Rose Harbour. We left there Monday morning, loaded a Pile Driver that day on a scow and put it behind the one we were towing. It was Rough last night but not too bad now.

Hope you are feeling well, next year I'll take you out and we'll shoot a whale.

Love Mother
Your Gordon

The Rose Harbour station was unbelievably run-down. Piles had fallen over and the wharf was down, but we were able to bunk into one or two of the buildings. The tubs used for rendering the blubber looked very old-fashioned to me, though I didn't know the first thing about a whaling operation.

Life was a little lonely. Because we didn't have a radio telephone in the *Joan G* there was no way to communicate with the outside world except by tying a note on a seagull. Our first task was to build a wharf. We had driven about a hundred piles when a very minor accident occurred. I swung the pile into position between the leads, barring it with a stick to keep it from moving before the pile driver drove it into place with a 2,000-pound hammer. To ensure that the pile was well grounded I signalled to the rigger to give it another little tap. Foolishly, I forgot that my thumb was in the path of the hammer. It took off nine-tenths of my nail and the tip of my thumb—just an inch down one side to the quick, shearing it as thin as a piece of cigarette paper. The thumb had been hit so goddamned hard that it came to a point. Strange as it may seem, my thumb wasn't bleeding and didn't hurt at all so we continued driving piles and I forgot all about the accident.

After the wharf was completed I left part of the crew in Rose Harbour and came back to Vancouver to report on our progress and to decide the next step with my brothers. After a lengthy meeting we concluded that it would be a good idea to have a look at a whaling operation before going any further. The closest land-base station was the Eureka Whaling Company in California, as most whaling operations were carried out at sea on floating factories.

While we were sitting round the meeting table someone asked me about my thumb, so I took the bandage off and told them the story. My brothers thought I was nuts not to have seen a doctor. The thumb wasn't hurting me at all and it had given me very little trouble in the ten days since the accident, but the nail was now hanging by a flap of skin at the base and getting in my way. I cut off all of the nail I could with scissors but it was still catching on everything. When I finally saw a doctor he said, "Gordon, we'll have to operate. I'll arrange it for tomorrow because we just can't leave it that way. We've got to go in and get that nail off. It's a bigger job than you think because the nail goes in pretty deep."

I reached down on his bench and grabbed a pair of snips from among his surgical instruments. "I'm sure as Christ not going to have an operation to pull that little bit of nail off there. You give me a pain in the ass talking about how painful it will be, because if the thumb didn't hurt when it was smashed I can't see how it will hurt now. There's only about a tenth of it left, just a piece at the cuticle."

Not thinking, I clamped onto the nail with the snips just as I would with a pair of pliers, pulling my arms in opposite directions. I landed flat on my backside completely knocked out. There is nothing in the world so painful as pulling out that part of the thumbnail. It hurt so much that I fell unconscious. When I recovered the nail was hanging at an even worse angle and we had to take a second pull to get it out.

The finish of this little story is that the doctor tried to give me some sedation, but I said, "Doc, I'll go over to the Army and Navy Club just across the street and have a few shots of rum." After knocking back about four doubles I felt no kick whatsoever because my senses had been thrown all off balance from pulling out that damned thumbnail. That's the only time in my life I was ever really hurt and I knew that I'd been a fool.

The next day we headed for Eureka with Richie Nelson and Bob Walker. Because I had come from a part of the country where I was well known, and my credit was good at places like the Devonshire and Vancouver hotels, I had plum forgot to take any money with me to California. There was no such thing in those days as credit cards or that sort of nonsense. I went to the manager at the hotel and asked if he'd lend me twenty dollars as I had to have some cash to tide me over the next day. He said, "No, Mr. Gibson, you can eat all you want here and we'll honour your bill but we have a policy that we don't cash any cheques."

I hadn't a lot of business experience at that time and didn't know that I could have gone to the bank and got them to call Vancouver. I went a little short of money for a few days while I was a guest at the hotel, though my food was paid for and I had my fare back. But that time I found out I was a nobody when I went away from Vancouver and the idea has stayed with me ever since. It's better to be a big frog in a small puddle than a little frog in a great big pond.

After only a few days in Eureka we had enough information to open our plant yet we had had to go that far away because all the whalers had been a whole generation before us. The captains were dead. The boats had been tied up for twenty years. There wasn't even a tradition left along the B.C. coast.

A whaling plant has the goddamnedest smell. The only reason anyone can stand it is that the rotten odour is making money. The plant at Eureka was no exception. Clarke, Bob Walker and I assisted in the operation and learned the fundamentals of whale reduction.

The whale was winched up a long wooden slip where one of the reduction crew jumped on top of the whale cutting an 8-inch strip along the soft fatty underbelly to release the tension on the skin, then rolled him on his side, and slit the entire length right down to the inner skin. The blubber can be from 4 to 8 inches thick depending on which part of the world the whale comes from. He will have twice as much blubber if he is caught before the pod leaves Japan to come across the ocean because up to 4 inches of fat is consumed during the long journey through cold waters. They fill up their bellies on the Japanese coast and then make a straight shot across, just like geese leaving the north.

Parallel strips were cut lengthwise along the whale at 1-foot intervals. Then each strip was hooked with a choker or chain and winched off as you would peel the skin off an onion or a huge ham. The strips were cut into pieces and cooked in a steam vat; the rendered oil rose to the surface as the residue collected on the bottom.

A hundred years ago the old whalers would catch a whale at sea and tie him to the side of the ship, leaving him there for a week or so while they cut off all his blubber and boiled it in their pots. Part of the blubber would be used to fuel the fire under their pots to produce sufficient heat to render the oil. The process was efficient as far as it went, but in those days the whalers just took off the blubber, cut out a little meat to suit themselves and then let the carcass sink.

When we got operating we used everything. The blubber was rendered into oil. The rest went through a press and huge grinders to be processed into meal: even the bones were ground up. Nothing at all was wasted. The only way a whale could be wasted was if it died without reproducing and contributing to the natural food chain.

There was no question that the Eureka operation could be duplicated easily, but as yet not one of us had seen how a whale was caught. While our party prepared to go back to Vancouver Richie said, "You go out, Gordon. You're the general manager. We'll look after sales; you find out how to shoot a goddamned whale." Clarke, the president of our new whaling company, remarked, "There's nothing to catching whales. It's like shooting cows in a pasture."

The whalers in Eureka were an amateur lot if there ever was one. All the equipment they had on board was an old gun unearthed from God knows where which was mounted on the bow and a little donkey engine to pull in the line. Attached to the end of the line was about 100 feet of 1¼-inch rope fastened to the harpoon.

A harpoon is around 4 feet long with three flukes lying along it, like a bird with its wings tucked in by its side, and right on the very sharpest point is screwed a cast-iron ring full of powder with a detonating cap that explodes approximately ten seconds after the trigger is pulled. In other words, it's in the whale for a few seconds before it explodes, throwing open the flukes and making a 3-foot hole inside the whale so the harpoon can't come back out.

The next day we managed to shoot a whale. We were in 2,000 feet of water when the whale sounded and it seemed as though it would break all our gear just to raise him up the first 20 feet. As we winched the whale in I found that when he was 1,000 feet up from the bottom the strain was only half what it had been at 2,000 feet; when we got him close to the surface I could lift him myself by pulling on the last 10 feet of cable. This meant that the whale didn't weigh more than 100 pounds when it was 100 feet underwater, and I could actually lift the whale up with a pike pole on the surface.

In 1947 Jack was in Ottawa as the Member of Parliament for Comox-Alberni and contacted the Crown Assets Disposal because he had seen an air force base at Coal Harbour in Quatsino Sound that he thought might be of some use to our whaling operation. He and John Buchanan of B.C. Packers remembered the huge concrete ramps where the seaplanes had been brought up during the war, and it occurred to them that it would be easy to drag the whales up these ramps to be butchered. The base wasn't a viable peacetime operation and we were able to purchase the entire plant extremely reasonably even though the government had spent over $2 million to build it. There were accommodation for the crews, winches and machinery. Nelson Brothers, B.C. Packers and Gibson Brothers made a three-way deal. Our whaling business suddenly started to take on big proportions.

We changed our whole concept after acquiring Coal Harbour and never looked again at the Rose Harbour station. Our men were brought down to work on the Quatsino Sound station. It was well worth the effort as the base was acquired for one-tenth of what it would have cost us to duplicate it.

Now the money had to be put out. We got some expert advice and started looking for gunners, crew and ships. Each company had spare ships in the summertime which were used seasonally for catching and packing herring. Our captains for the whaling ships were imported from Norway, but we broke in our crews up the coast.

The old whaling ships that we had bought from the Consolidated Whaling Company were sold to a junk dealer in Victoria by the name of Morris Greene. As a joke I kept an old harpoon gun from one of the whalers. I thought that for fun I would mount it on the bow of my boat while I was watching what the other captains were doing. Although everyone warned me that the gun was dangerous, I decided to test it. All the guns used on those whalers were muzzleloading whereas nowadays you just stick a cartridge in a harpoon and fire it off like an ordinary shotgun shell. This old gun was rusted and had a big trick hammer like a hunting rifle. It was cocked with the finger. The powder came up through a tiny aperture about the size of the eye of a large darning needle. It was as old-fashioned as the cannons of 200 years ago.

Clarke and I went out two or three times but we had no luck at getting a whale. Every time we fired a shot I usually landed flat on my ass at the forward end of the ship, principally because the gun would misfire seventy-five per cent of the time. It turned out that the aperture had been sealed for at least fifty years and the inside of the cartridge had been filled up with tallow to keep the air and dampness out. We didn't know enough to cut out the tallow, so when we pulled the trigger the powder would only pass through the hole about one time in ten. Whenever we got into position to shoot, we'd pull the trigger and nothing would happen. I guess those old whaling captains resented Clarke and I going around with a cannon on the front of our boat: they didn't bother to tell me why everything was haywire.

Early one morning we sighted a whale up forward. He came up perfectly, a great big beauty. I pulled the trigger: nothing happened. I was so mad that I picked up an 8-pound sledge hammer lying beside me and slammed it down on top of the shell. This time the gun fired. The tallow must have been jarred sufficiently by the blow to be shaken loose. Thirty seconds later the whale had travelled about 100 feet ahead of the ship carrying our harpoon and line with him.

The harpoon that I had carefully aimed at the whale's main section just back of the neck hit him about 10 feet from the end of his tail where it skinnies down to about 3 feet through. The whale thrashed wildly and with a great spew of foam he sounded into the depths.

Being shot in the head or in the lungs slows a whale down a lot and often kills him. But a whale has got some hundreds of horsepower of strength in his tail and that damned animal just got mad and pulled our 130-foot ship along at 6 knots all day and all the next night. We didn't want to slow him by reversing our engines because that might have pulled out the harpoon. We didn't know what to do except tire him. He always swam up to windward and the smell from that thing was god-awful—halitosis from the wrong end. He was furious. He kept on towing and sounding.

When a whale is shot the harpoon is left in place and a

second one is used to secure him. Unfortunately, I had only one line and it was in the whale. The other boats had seen me going all over hell but I was too proud to ask any of those old skippers what to do when you've got a whale shot in the tail. Perhaps I am the only man in the world ever to have roped a whale by the tail. When he got tired I winched him in a little and tried to get a good clean shot through the head. But that just woke him up and made him wilder than before. Now I had two harpoons in him but only one line. The second harpoon had excited him all the more and once again he towed our boat in circles.

Losing my pride and dignity at last, I called to one of the Norwegian captains. "Goddamn, I've got one harpoon in the tail of this damned whale and I've got another one shot right up through his head and I still can't get him. What do I do next?"

"Gibson, you've got to learn that there's only one place you can shoot a whale and that's right between the fins and into the lungs. When the water gets into his lungs he loses all his strength. A shot in any other part won't be fatal."

With a third shot I got him in the lungs and he turned right over. This one was 90 tons. A beautiful finback. We pulled him alongside but we had no gear in our boat to secure him. I found out the secret though. We stuck an air hose on a pipe into his belly which made him float a foot or two above the water. I tested out my theory by shoving the whale up and down with the pipe. We lashed him to the side of our boat. Because his body was pliable like rubber, we towed him backwards so his mouth wouldn't fall open and fill his belly up with water.

It had now been thirty-six hours since my first shot and we were all a little tired when we headed for port. Fighting the whale for so long with only four crew had been quite an effort, but we then managed to tow him 100 miles to the head of Quatsino Sound and into Coal Harbour.

One of my crew was a college kid and on the way to Coal Harbour we realized that no one had seen him since we lashed the whale alongside. Everyone got excited. We turned the ship back and cruised around, looking all over for some sign of a kid swimming in the water.

At last one of my men appeared and said, "He's asleep right under the cannon." The boy had sneaked into the fo'c's'le and was asleep on the bunk up forward. Perhaps he was tired but so were we all—bone weary. I was furious to think that a young kid of sixteen had so little ambition or life in him that he would let a little tiredness get the best of him during all the excitement of shooting his first whale. I damned near threw him overboard. When we got into port I let him go and said that he might just as well go home to his mother because any boy with that little spunk was no use to me or anyone else, including himself. I wonder if he ever amounted to anything.

An expert manager was put in charge of the operation when the whaling season was over. We got the plant running fairly smoothly, but at the end of the year, when the books were balanced, we found that we had lost $100,000 to $300,000 apiece. Another $1 million was needed to modernize the plant. B.C. Packers had put substantial amounts of money into new freezers and machinery, and were more than pulling their weight financially. They were prepared to expand, though the other partners were less optimistic about future prospects. Both B.C. Packers and Nelson Brothers became unionized and labour problems began to be a major pressure in the Western Whaling Company. I believed it was unrealistic to continue to whale in a country where labour costs were so high that we couldn't compete in the world market. Gibson Brothers figured it was time to sell out.

One big factor in our decision to get out of the whaling business was that whales caught on this coast were worth half what they would be if caught in Japanese waters. The sperm whales have little left of the sixty to eighty barrels of oil that they carried in their heads, and the other whales such as finbacks and humpbacks have lost much of their blubber and are very lean from the long trans-Pacific journey to our waters.

H. R. MacMillan held a significant block of shares in B.C. Packers. When B.C. Packers had had financial difficulties in the early 1930s he was offered a large number of shares to reorganize it. He fancied being known as the sardine and whale king of the world and now offered to take over our operation as of the first day and assume all our debts. We accepted immediately. B.C. Packers brought in whaling ships from Japan with Japanese gunners, and went into freezing of whale meat for the export market. Even then they couldn't make it pay.

The whaling industry had been viable until the beginning of this century, but we have depleted the reserves of whales coming up from the Antarctic where there was a tremendous food supply for them. Whaling really ceased to be economically feasible when we started to use factory ships for reduction and manufacturing.

When there are insufficient whales to support an industry, they won't be fished anymore. Economic factors are a natural conservation agent. It's much easier to catch a ton of herring and process it than it is to obtain the equivalent amount of whale meat. Would it pay to raise elephants instead of sheep? Although an elephant's bigger he takes a hundred years longer to reach maturity. Moreover, a whale was much more valuable to the economy a hundred years ago, when women needed bone for corsets and oil for soap.

The whales will be protected completely by economics. In my seventy-five years of experience I haven't found that the world has run out of anything that nature has provided for man's survival. We are told that man will run out of oil, timber and places to grow food. It's all bunk.

When we were in partnership with B.C. Packers and Nelson Brothers I was invited to Japan to take part in an international whaling conference. Jimmy Sinclair, the minister of fisheries, asked me to accompany George Clarke, his deputy minister, as the Canadian representative.

The Honourable Mr. Mayhew, the Canadian ambassador to Japan, picked us up in his limousine and took us to the Imperial Hotel in Tokyo. Our Japanese host had arranged for us to spend a weekend in a villa, about a hundred miles down the coast. We arrived at our destination after a ride on one of Japan's trains that are famous for service and precision. Twenty exceptionally beautiful geisha girls met us at the door of the villa and helped us to remove our shoes. For the next few days these girls looked after our every comfort, and it was indicated that each of us should pick out one as his personal companion.

As soon as I was in my room, the geisha I had chosen helped me to disrobe and put on a kimono before giving me a splendid scrub-down in the bath. With great delicacy she brought me a drink and served my dinner, and then knelt down on the floor beside me. My thoughts raced ahead to what I considered the other duties of the perfect geisha girl. After I made a sly advance or two, my geisha disappeared, arriving back a few minutes later with what she thought I wanted: an English-speaking Japanese girl whose profession was certainly of a lower standard but just as well appreciated as that of the geisha.

Her English was exceptionally good but her commercial ambitions seemed a little too high. I had a drink with her and paid what I figured the going rate might be, but I had my geisha girl stay to sort of protect me. That night I slept on the floor with a wooden block for a pillow. The geisha was still sitting in the same position at the foot of my bed when I awoke the next morning. We communicated quite successfully by sign language while I had my bath and breakfast.

That day George and I and the geishas were given a tour of the countryside by our Japanese host. Our driver spoke English and acted as translator when necessary. We returned to the villa that evening and set out the following morning for Tokyo where our meeting was to be held.

George and I were put up at the Tokyo Grand Hotel which had just opened, and because we were the first guests, we were invited to attend the opening ceremonies. Both of us were given magnificent suites as were all the representatives attending the conference.

Japan is the only place where I have ever taught a class. All the menus for the conference were in Japanese with a translation underneath for every country represented. Each floor had its own staff; if you ordered breakfast in the room, it was brought by the girls on your floor who always travelled in pairs. The two little Japanese girls who brought mine appeared to have little else to do, probably because the hotel had just opened and there were no other guests on our floor. Neither of them understood a word of English but were anxious to learn and spent hours in my room each morning. They would giggle and joke as I pointed out my breakfast order on the menu, repeating each word in English. After a dozen or so tries at the sound they would disappear and manage to return with the meal. I thoroughly enjoyed their company, especially since I had nothing to do until the meetings began. The girls were so tiny that if I held my arms straight out they could have run under them with 6 inches to spare.

I was in the hotel for ten days and the classes became a ritual. As many as ten Japanese girls would congregate in my room each morning for a couple of hours. After my breakfast had been served, I would start the English lessons. They all sat around in a circle, pointing out an object so they could learn to say its name. The geishas were warm and loving girls.

The meetings started at two in the afternoon. Many nations were represented around that 30-foot conference table. George Clarke did most of the talking for Canada as he was the deputy minister of fisheries. The only occasion I spoke up was when the Russians seemed determined to dominate the Japanese in the North Pacific. One afternoon the debate came to a head.

Russia had sent the commissar of fisheries as its representative. He was a man even bigger than myself. He was accompanied by a deputy who weighed at least 230 pounds. The Russians appeared to resent Canada siding with Japan and during the debate our eyes seemed to clash as if saying "watch out."

The reason I added my voice to George Clarke's was that I felt the Japanese truly needed the whales for food. Japan had a population of over 90 million people and they were the only nation at the time who were using whales for human consumption. They wasted nothing, whereas many of the other countries were merely rendering the oil and reducing part of the carcass for animal food and fertilizer—some not even that.

The session lasted until six o'clock. George Clarke was busy for the evening with his reports but I was free and went on the town. About seven I stepped out of the elevator alone and ran into the Russian commissar, his deputy and their lady secretary.

I thought that rather than have any misunderstanding about the day's proceedings I would clear the matter up right away. As all three spoke fairly good English, I shook hands with each of them and said, "Come up to my room. Have you time to accept some Canadian hospitality?" They looked at each other wondering what that might involve, but decided to accept the invitation.

It turned out to be a very interesting evening. Rumour has it that the Russians are great drinkers. I believe that it is quite so. No one had eaten any dinner. We broke into a case of V.O. and after a few drinks the Russians seemed much friendlier and responded quite openly to my questions about their country. It was not long before they invited me to come to Russia.

As the conversation moved along they indicated that they considered me to be a Capitalist, that is, a man whose money had been handed down through generations and who had never done a day's work to earn his wealth. But in fact, the commissar and I had both made our own way up through the ranks, and when he realized this he became very talkative. As the liquor flowed, we made some comparisons between the socialist and capitalist systems. I found the commissar was being given much more in the way of security, power and a home than I had in Canada. He told me that he would have complete security for the rest of his life if he handled his affairs with due regard for the society in which he lived. If he did not, he would be destitute. It took me a while to convince him that I was in the same position. He could lose prestige; I, my money. Many a man has made money by age fifty to be broke again at seventy.

One major difference is that in Russia a man doesn't worry about death duties because the government takes a large percentage in taxes all along. Children have to be successful in their own right in Russia whereas in Canada we might spoil them by leaving money for the next generation to spend. This probably ruins their chance of reaching their potential because they aren't forced to depend as much on their own initiative.

A few hours later, the liquor was really beginning to talk. The commissar and his deputy asked me some questions about our military power appearing to believe that I would know something about the subject. I played right along with them, brushing their questions aside with broad generalities and sweeping statements about Canada's association with the United States. I could see them lean forward when I mentioned the word "uranium," which was a very controversial subject in Canada at that time. Plastered as the three of them seemed to be, they were all ears. So I led them on a little more. "Uranium, why we have so much that we burn it like coal in our homes and factories!" They had no idea what sort of substance this might be but appeared to appreciate my evident frankness.

By now it was eleven o'clock. More drinks seemed to be in order. The Russians sent their secretary down to their room to get us a bottle of vodka. She returned with the liquor and presented me with a number of delicacies, including caviar.

When the evening drew to a close the Russians were completely plastered and passed out one by one. I managed to carry them back to their rooms with the help of a couple of the Japanese hotel staff. After they were all in bed, I went out and had a wonderful evening on the town. I consider that Canada won the first round in that instance.

The minister of agriculture in Japan was second only to the prime minister. One evening he held a marvellous affair for all the delegates to the conference. The food, liquor and geisha girls were excellent. I had an opportunity to speak to our host alone and was extremely interested by his remarks to me. "Mr. Gibson, we would just love to be left alone," he claimed. "America is spending over a billion dollars a year in Japan. That's about twelve dollars per person. This is doing our people a lot of harm. We would be better off if we got nothing so that our country would be forced to get back on its feet by its own efforts."

During my visit in Tokyo I went to the fish docks one morning at four o'clock. Hundreds of tons of fish arrive by boat at this hour every day and are auctioned off by eight o'clock. The fish are then distributed by refrigerator train all over Japan.

The fish are contained in bins or baskets. The best fish go to the highest bidder. Every morning a large crowd gathers in the market hoping that there will be fish left over. Everything must be sold. If a herring boat has had a lucky catch that morning there will be a glut on the market and the price will fall to rock bottom. The heads and tails are sold in separate baskets at a price established that day.

The bidders arrive in waves. Fast four-wheeled trucks carry out the best fish; then come vehicles with one wheel in front and two behind. The next to arrive are men and women on bicycles with carriers fore and aft to bid for the less expensive fish. Last comes the man with no wheels at all—just baskets slung on a pole! Even when there has been a tremendous catch there isn't a single scale left behind in the market.

Later in the morning I had a look at some of the fish boats in the harbour. The crews were having a meal. On deck eight or so men sat around a small charcoal stove cooking fish and rice, and eating from a central pot with chopsticks and little bowls. Except for some tiny bunks up forward I could see no sleeping quarters. They appeared to have a lot harder life than the fishermen on this coast though they looked wiry and capable. Most of the fishermen were half my size and weighed about 110 pounds. The fishing boats, engines and gear seemed to be in good shape.

The day of our departure came all too soon. My plane time was two o'clock in the afternoon, so at about one I left my room after tipping the girls and went down to pay my bill at the front desk. I stood in the lobby for at least five minutes because I could see a red carpet had been rolled out in front of the hotel. Thirty hotel employees were lined up on either side of the carpet. The manager of the hotel took my arm and escorted me to the door: I realized that the honour of the red carpet was mine for Canada. I turned back to get about thirty-five one-dollar bills and asked the manager to give one to each of the employees. As I stepped into the limousine half a dozen of the little girls I had been teaching gave me a kiss. It had been a wonderful experience and I knew that I had met some very fine people.

CHAPTER 23

It is not necessary that we should adopt the Biblical principle "For whosoever hath, to him shall be given, and he shall have more abundance; but whosoever hath not, from him shall be taken away, even that he hath."

H. R. MacMillan
Royal Commission on Forestry, 1955

Our family had taken a very strong stand since 1945 against the policies of the Socred government in the granting of Forest Management Licences. Many large companies such as MacMillan Bloedel, Canadian Forest Products and the Powell River Company were opposed to them in the early years, but they began to sing a different tune when they realized a little profit. Some overambitious operators began to lobby the government to allocate the province's timber resources without regard for the public interest. It was my belief that in time the industrial giants like MacMillan Bloedel would absorb most of the Forest Management Licences, putting the small truck logger out of business altogether.

Every company that held a Forest Management Licence began to cry famine in our forests and promised that if future reforestation were to be put in their hands, the public would benefit from their private control.

In 1937 Mr. F. D. Mulholland of the Forestry Department published figures in the "Forest Resources Report" showing that B.C. had a total of 155 billion board feet of timber on the coast and 100 billion feet in the interior, a total of 255 billion. When I read these figures I knew they were wrong, as would anyone who was knowledgeable about our timber resources. At the first inquiry into Forest Management Licences in 1945, evidence was presented before Mr. Justice Sloan that the correct figures were 200 billion board feet of timber on the coast and 150 billion in the interior, a total of 350 billion board feet. Our timber resources were still greatly misrepresented, since B.C.'s annual cut was running at least 3.5 billion feet, that is, about one per cent of the total supposed inventory. The reason for this inquiry was not only to establish how much timber the province had but also to plan for the future control of our forests by deciding how and to whom the cutting rights should be allocated.

By 1952, at the second inquiry into Forest Management Licences, a figure of 500 billion board feet was set. I gave evidence in a brief submitted by our company that the province had at least 1,000 billion feet, but our report was rejected as overly optimistic.

To show how out of line the government and other estimates were, the government re-evaluated these figures in 1955 to 800 billion feet; in 1963, they were doubled to 1,600 billion feet. That was six times the original estimate. The people of British Columbia were led to believe by the figures in these early reports that our forests were in danger. It was on this false premise that the timber of British Columbia was delivered into the hands of the few companies who are now in control of our resources and who are in a position to make vast fortunes out of a heritage that rightfully belongs to everyone.

Judge Sloan had been appointed by W. A. C. Bennett to listen to submissions from both sides in the controversy. Half the tree licences were to go to big companies and half to small truck loggers. At first there were about twenty representatives of the truck loggers, but they dropped out one by one as time and finances ran out. By 1952 I was the sole voice for the small logging concerns and was still speaking out against the briefs presented by at least ten highly paid lawyers on behalf of their corporate clients.

The real fight began when Chief Justice Sloan asked me to sit down and be quiet during what I felt was a particularly poor presentation by one of the corporation lawyers. "Mr. Gibson, I've heard your case a hundred times. I know it and I don't want to hear it again. Please sit down."

I was enraged by the unfairness of the situation and continued to speak. "I demand the right to rebuttal with each one of these men. I'm the only one here to represent the small interests. You are all on one side. Every other man in this room, including yourself, is charging $200 to $400 a day for his time. I'm going to have my say!"

Judge Sloan threw me out for contempt of court. Turning towards the bench I shouted, "I'll get myself elected and this matter will be judged by a higher court: the opinion of the people of this province. The true facts will not be hidden forever. I'll never rest until this matter is before the legislature."

I was not alone in my criticism. One of the most respected and best-known lumbermen in British Columbia, H. R. MacMillan, opposed for years the granting of Forest Management Licences. In a brief submitted to the Royal Commission on Forestry by MacMillan Bloedel Limited, in 1955, he remarked:

The total annual growth of pulpwood in North America exceeds the annual consumption. We no longer need to fear the timber famine preached to us in the early years of this century. . . .

It will be a sorry day for British Columbia when the Forest Industry here consists chiefly of a very few big companies, holding most of the good timber and good growing sites to the disadvantage and early extermination of the most hard working, virile, versatile, and ingenious element of our population—the independent market logger and the saw-mill man.

My chance came later that year when a delegation of men from the Lillooet riding asked me if I would stand for nomination to the Liberal Party. There were two other candidates and the delegation felt that my name would round out the campaign and give the voters a third choice. I figured that if I were elected I would have an opportunity to shoot down Judge Sloan's recommendations. In my opinion he was ill-equipped to make an informed judgement on an industry about which he had no first-hand knowledge. A seat in the legislature would also enable me to speak out about corruption in the granting of Forest Management Licences without fear of libel.

I won the nomination. After the meeting there was a coffee party and a dance, at the end of which I was expected to make a speech. I said that the issues to which I felt I could make my best contribution were Forest Management Licences and a much-needed road system for the Lillooet district.

Late that night about twenty of us were having a little party in my hotel room when there was a knock at the door. I was told there were two Indian ladies outside who insisted on seeing me. I thought they had come to wish me well so I stepped into the hall and thanked them, thinking that was the end of the conversation. But one of them said, "We are not here to help you in your election campaign, Mr. Gibson. We just thought we would tell you that if you want our votes, you had better give us both a drink seeing that you are giving liquor to the rest of your friends." I didn't, because at that time an Indian could drink in a beer parlour but couldn't consume liquor off the premises and it was illegal for me to give them a drink in the hotel room. But they were at least candid which is a refreshing quality.

The campaign started two weeks later. My plan was to drive as far as Lytton and electioneer through the northern end of the riding to Lillooet, then board a train to Shalalth, and travel up the valley to the Pioneer and Bralorne mines, back to Lillooet and down the PGE to Squamish.

As I was preparing to leave home Louise came out to the car and gave me some good advice. "Gordon, don't drink too much on this trip as you can't get votes that way." A few minutes later she came back to the car again and said, "Gordon, just one more thing. Please don't show undue attention to any one woman in these small towns. The few votes you would get that way won't amount to much but the criticism of the rest of the women could defeat you."

My first meeting was at Lytton where I hardly knew a soul. The hall could hold a hundred people but fewer than ten came out to hear my speech. After spending three or four days meeting the voters, we went on to the town of Lillooet. The meeting there was not much more successful, but at least I was able to introduce a personal note by telling them how my mother had come to Lillooet from Ontario with my grandmother after my grandfather had died. It had taken them at least a day to make the journey by wagon from Ashcroft to my great-uncle's ranch. To give me a little local involvement I told them that my grandmother was buried in the graveyard below their town.

I knew I had to create a real issue and promise the people of the district something they truly wanted and needed for prosperity. The road system ended at Lillooet and to get into the Bridge River valley and the Bralorne and Pioneer mines you had to load your automobile on a railroad car for an hour's run to Shalalth where the road picked up again. There had been talk of putting a road through this area for fifty years. I made this my election issue. I promised I would try to get a road built from Lillooet to Bridge River, and to create a little public interest I walked the entire seventy-five miles of trail with one of the local old-timers. My father had been over the same country some sixty years earlier.

Since our family had a lot of experience in building roads, I suggested that Gibson Brothers start building one right away and arranged a meeting with the management of the Bralorne and Pioneer mines and their employees as well as anyone else who was interested. The townspeople were very enthusiastic about the project. They were to supply the cats while our company supplied the foremen, the knowhow and the money to meet the payroll. Four routes had been debated but we agreed on one along the riverbank. The committee and I walked over it. I am sure that it was because I showed such initiative that I later got the vote both in Lillooet and in Bridge River. Road construction had become the central theme of my election platform.

The next stop in my campaign was Pemberton, a farming community just thirty miles from Bridge River. Bridge River had a population of a thousand, most of whom were employed in two local mines, the Bralorne and the Pioneer. I pointed out to the Pemberton audience that a new road in their district would not only provide an excellent link with the other towns in the area, but would also help Pemberton to sell its produce to Bridge River. The new construction would allow cattle to graze on the high ground in summer. I next told the people of Squamish that I would work for a road into Vancouver.

In 1952 I was elected representative for the Lillooet district and determined that in my maiden speech I would acquaint all the members of the House with my riding by taking them on an imaginary bus trip. I hung a 4-foot by 10-foot map of the Lillooet area on the wall behind my desk and it well illustrated our need for roads. The speech went well, and everyone seemed to enjoy the imaginary journey.

About six months after I had been elected to the legislature, the town of Lillooet invited me to attend a ceremony in honour of my maternal grandmother. Clarke, my mother and her sister, Lucy, came to join in the festivities. Aunt Lucy was very high-strung and had several drinks to steady her nerves, taken when mother was out of the room for she thoroughly disapproved of liquor.

I had purchased a wreath to lay on my grandmother's grave, but when we arrived at the cemetery I found that all the graves were marked by numbers rather than by names. One of the local dignitaries was sent to the registrar's office to find the location of the grave and came back with the information that it was No. 26 by the river. We wandered in the graveyard for half an hour searching for the site. At last we found No. 20, and then No. 25. But No. 26 was not to be found. Apparently the grave had been washed away by the river in the eighty years since grandmother died. Aunt Lucy, overcome with emotion and spirits, threw her arms around Mother's shoulders, sobbing, "Oh, God! She's been washed away. Isn't it terrible!" We all made a great fuss over her and finally got her calmed down, but from that time on I had to change my story about my roots still being in Lillooet.

In 1953 Premier Bennett and Public Works Minister Gaglardi were determined that the PGE Railway be brought from Squamish to North Vancouver. At that time it was necessary to travel to Squamish by ferry, and I argued that it was essential to build a road before a railroad, or at least to construct both of them at the same time so that the road ran along the shoreline. I believed that $10 million could be saved by building both together, because if the railroad were put in first, all the debris would have to be handled twice and the blasting would interrupt the rail schedule.

In a big meeting at Squamish, Mr. Gaglardi said that the road was not a priority and that the railroad should be put in first. I insisted that the whole project would cost four times as much if the road were built after the railway. Gaglardi claimed that the road would cost only $6 million even after a railway had been constructed. I said I was prepared to take on a contract guaranteeing that if a road were built before the railroad, or even at the same time, it would be done for $2 million.

A man stood up during the question period. "Mr. Gibson," he said, "I admire both you and Mr. Gaglardi. You are both competent and fair men. Now, you say you can build the road for $2 million and Mr. Gaglardi says it will cost $6 million. I'm afraid the cost will be about $4 million. If you take this contract for $2 million and it costs $4 million, will the people of this province have to find the other $2 million to pay for it?"

It was then that I told the biggest lie of my life and scared the hell out of my banker. "If I take a contract for $2 million and it costs $4 million, I'll write a cheque for the $2 million debt."

Bennett and Gaglardi, in their wisdom, decided to put the railroad in first. The road, instead of costing $2 million or $3 million, cost around $12 million when they built it five years later. All the rock had to be handed carefully across the railroad tracks below. Anyone driving up Howe Sound can see for themselves how much cheaper it would have been to build the road first and the railroad later.

As an MLA, I felt it my duty to make public some of the facts in the Forest Management dispute. These licences had become so valuable that companies which held them—and so were entrusted with the province's resources—began to sell them to American concerns at huge profits. The ability to hold Forest Management Licences was treated as a right rather than a privilege.

Many licences were being handed out even while the case was under review by Chief Justice Sloan. The right hand of the government would not acknowledge the deeds of the left hand, and the people of the province paid a high price for what was then a straight drive for power by the Bennett government.

Moreover, by October 1953 the Socred government proposed a yearly tax on timber held under pulp and timber licences and leases that had been granted many years previously. As far as any sensible person could make out, this tax was a confiscation imposed by irresponsible men with their first whiff of real power and it was designed not just to get revenue but to force companies into applying for government-controlled Forest Management Licences. No independent company or truck logger could stay in business under such punitive taxation.

I asked in the House that all forestry taxation proposals be delayed until the subject could be referred to the Forestry Committee of the legislature, chaired by Cyril Shelford, which was wasting valuable time on trifles while allowing real problems to remain unchallenged. If the government wouldn't follow this suggestion, I said, it could certainly refer the question of taxes to a royal commission.

I charged that the small logger was reluctant to come to Victoria to oppose the tax because he was afraid of losing the market for his logs if he stood against legislation that was in the interest of large companies such as B.C. Pulp and MacMillan Bloedel. Defending the tax, Lands and Forests Minister Robert Sommers said the tax had nothing to do with the small logger because few of them held pulp and timber leases. Of course they didn't: they were already being squeezed out!

The *Vancouver Sun* of 18 January 1954 summed up my fears:

The Social Credit government has hitherto opposed the holding of a new inquiry until the ten years period mentioned by Mr. Sloan expires. Its ground for opposition is that the new inquiry would be all the better for a full ten years' research. But in view of the present discontent in the industry it would be unwise to be too finical.

One of the fears constantly expressed is that there is danger of the forest resources of B.C. falling into the hands of the few great companies. This is a questionable trend from the public's viewpoint—and from the viewpoint of the government which stands dedicated to a freedom of enterprise. It is not only that the gathering of all forest resources in relatively few hands is bad but also that the growth of this trend towards monopoly may give rise in the future to a worse evil—the transformation of private monopoly to state monopoly.

There was one Forest Management Licence granted that will forever be a disgrace to this country. Mr. Sloan had recommended that half the timber be set aside for the small logger in what were to be known as Public Working Circles. Generally speaking, however, this meant that the men with money also got their choice of the best areas in the Public Working Circles, leaving the poorest land for the rest.

Now almost all the coastal timber was either in Public Working Circles or under reserve for Forest Management Licences for some company, pending decision or political lobby. B.C. Forest Products, which had been late in taking advantage of this great giveaway, found that there was little choice of timber left and lobbied in Victoria. Against the advice of the chief forester, Dr. Orchard, and with the opposition of every small logger, the whole of the Public Working Circle in Clayoquot was taken from the public sector and given to B.C. Forest Products. Within a few days the company's stock jumped from $7 a share to $15 a share. There were 3 million shares of stock on the market; that was $24 million clear profit, which was more than enough to finance the new B.C. Forest Products mill at Crofton.

I raised this matter privately with Sommers, who told me to mind my own business. The next morning I went to the premier and told him the same story. He would not listen either; in fact, his comment to me after a hard half hour of talking was, "You had better mind your own business, Gordon. You Liberals started this. We're no worse than you are."

That was 11:30 in the morning; the House opened at 2:00. In a roaring speech that could be heard outside the House without any amplifying system I challenged Bennett to put the whole method of awarding Forest Management Licences before the Forestry Committee, which had representation from all four parties. I said, "We've got to find out what's going on around here. You backbenchers on the government side must demand that this be done. Learn what is going on. You are sent here by the people. Show some backbone.

"You've no chance of running a fair government so long as your cabinet ministers, in awarding Forest Management Licences, will only talk to men with $20 million or more.

"There is something that the premier and his cabinet are afraid of. They know things will be divulged before the committee that they are afraid to have divulged.

"I firmly believe that money talks and that money has talked in this: I want that answered by the ministers. We are not going to let this go unanswered. Evidence will come out showing wrongdoings by this government. If everything is fine, surely you will take the misapprehensions from the minds of a lot of people by taking the matter into the Forestry Committee.

"I will be ashamed of every one of you over there on the government side of the House if you don't take this thing into committee. I will have a bone to pick with all you gentlemen in your own ridings. If you gentlemen don't accept this challenge, I then—and the public—will know that you are afraid to look into your own government."

The House sat stunned—then all hell broke loose. Arnold Webster of the NDP, Arthur Laing, and members of the Socreds were shouting at the top of their lungs. In the midst of all the bedlam, the Speaker adjourned the House.

The next day my charges against the government were published in the papers: that money had talked and that the government had mismanaged funds. The Socreds were caught where the hair is short by the public outcry which followed publication in the newspapers.

When the House opened at 2:00 P.M. the next day, Attorney General Bonner demanded that I retract my statements. I refused to do so. The Speaker of the House demanded that I retract. Then he said, "Honourable Member from Lillooet, I asked you to retract your statements. I shall read your name three times. You must leave this House or be forcibly ejected."

He read my name three times slowly and deliberately. "J. Gordon Gibson, I name you and must ask you to withdraw from the House until the Members decide what to do."

To make my point I deliberately stormed straight up to the Public Gallery which was off limits to Members while the House was in session. This rule was originally intended to prohibit Members from taking council with advisers or attorneys and then returning to the floor of the House. I figure that the law must have been made to control characters like some in the Social Credit who needed an extra brain or two to keep them abreast of the proceedings below.

One Member yelled, "Mr. Speaker, there is a stranger in the House," which means that the business of the House must stop until a Member is removed from the gallery. However, anybody else in the world is allowed to sit up there.

I roared down to the premier from the gallery, "I'm either a Member on the floor of this House, or a private citizen up here in the gallery. I demand to be in one of those two places." Two policemen came to escort me from the gallery, but I just laughed at them. There was a lot of shouting on the floor of the House as the Members argued about what was to be done.

The crux of the trouble was that the government looked bad to the public and so they blustered and acted arbitrarily to cover up their precarious position. To my mind it was like calling a man a "bastard" when he doesn't know who his father is. He's apt to be a bit touchy.

The Socred government knew they were on soft ground, and instead of suspending me, Attorney General Bonner moved a motion that was adopted allowing me to reconsider my position with no time limit. The point could only come up again if it were introduced by another Member.

Quite simply, this was a manoeuvre to allow the government to worm out of the charge with the least embarrassment. The House clerk invited me back, and since I had been the last speaker to hold the floor, I took up where I left off, telling them what a crooked bunch they were and that their reaction proved the cap fit—a little too snugly. I was so enraged with the whole situation that I resigned my seat, but I was still determined to fight for the right of the small logger to a fair share of the timber resources.

The Vancouver *Province* published the following editorial on Friday, 18 February 1955, by which time the government had submitted to pressure and ordered an investigation.

The government's decision to hold an investigation into MLA Gordon Gibsons's suggestion of impropriety in granting of forest management licences belatedly retrieves a bad blunder.

It is a decision that should have been made when Mr. Gibson made his remarks last Tuesday. The attempt to rule Mr. Gibson out of the House until he withdrew his charges was a highly questionable effort to silence criticism under the guise of enforcing proper parliamentary rules.

Silencing critics with a parliamentary gag is no substitute for investigating and answering criticism.

Now the government is doing what it should. Only a thorough examination of Mr. Gibson's charges will satisfy the public. That should have been instantly apparent to the government benches last Tuesday.

When Mr. Gibson made the charges, or near-charges, to which objection was taken, the senior minister in the House should have been on his feet instantly to demand retraction or proof.

This was NOT the time to sit in silent contempt. It is not the sort of charge that should be allowed to simmer for 24 hours. . . .

Mr. Gibson's offending speech was made on Tuesday and halfway through it Premier Bennett left the House. As far as we have heard there was no objection to what Mr. Gibson was saying from either the government benches or the Speaker.

The next day, apparently after digesting the full import of the Lillooet member's observations, the attorney-general and the Speaker, with the implied sanction of the government, took steps to banish Mr. Gibson.

Beauchesne's Parliamentary Rules and Forms, the accepted authority on parliamentary practices, specifically says that if there is to be interference with a member's speech it should be made at the time, not 24 hours later.

Quoting authorities, Beauchesne says: "The proper time for interference is when the offensive expressions are uttered, and NOT AFTERWARDS; and it may take place, either on the Speaker's voluntary motion, or on the call to order of the member assailed, or of some other member, or the general call of the House."

Furthermore Beauchesne's rulings indicate that while members cannot impute bad motives, or adopt unparliamentary language with respect to other members of the House, they have much greater latitude in attacking a government as a whole.

"If a member should say nothing disrespectfully to the House or the Chair, or personally opprobrious to other members, or in violation of other rules of the House, he may state whatever he thinks fit in debate, however offensive it may be to the feelings, or injurious to the character, of individuals; and he is protected by his privilege from any action for libel, as well as from any other question or molestation."

There is no reference in this section to attacks on a government. It is generally accepted that opposition members will attack governments. Mr. Bonner's position that Mr. Gibson's remarks bordered on a patronage charge against the government hardly shocks those accustomed to far more vigorous allegations against men in office.

The charges still hung heavy over the government, which had made a very foxy political move: they threw the case to the courts and appointed Judge Lord to investigate the "money talks" charge immediately if I would consent to appear before him. Being an amateur in legal and political life, I didn't foresee what would happen. I was inexperienced enough to accept the condition, not realizing until the very day of the court case that if I gave evidence I would have no protection of any kind and could be sued for slander by any of the forest companies who were making millions of dollars and could afford to fight the case right down the line. This issue could have broken my family, involving us in a legal battle for years to come. I decided not to testify because I had lost the immunity of an MLA. The case then got tangled up in efforts to define "impropriety." Did it refer to a government policy or to actual cash changing hands?

When Judge Lord found no evidence of out-and-out bribery the case was closed on 9 March after a three-day run. Only one-tenth of the evidence had been presented and as far as I was concerned the proceedings had been a government mop-up job.

Next day I declared, "Because I consider this denial of justice of such vital importance to the people of British Columbia, it is my intention to take the issue to the people, and I therefore advise you that I will seek reaffirmation in a by-election on the issue. It is repugnant to me that such poor principles are exercised in our parliamentary system." To the people of the Lillooet constituency I made this statement:

> Two years ago when I stood for election I stated that I was unalterably opposed to Forest Management Licences. I predicted then that if the policy continued, eventually all our timber resources would be controlled by a few large companies. This would result in economic and political domination of the province by a few government-selected concerns. Small operators enjoying no such government advantage would be forced out of business. Local merchants would suffer as the business formerly done by the small operator in his own community moved to Vancouver.
>
> In January of this year the government appointed Chief Justice Sloan to investigate government forestry policy. For a moment I thought that this was a sincere move by the government to seek the assistance of the Chief Justice. It soon became apparent, however, that the government had no such intention. In February, therefore, I decided that nothing short of an election could stop this government "give-away" policy even long enough to permit Chief Justice Sloan to report while there were still some horses in the barn. I resigned so that you, the electors of Lillooet, representing all the people of the province by your ballots, could decide this issue.
>
> The particular aspect of the government forestry policy which the Chief Justice was appointed to investigate was Forest Management Licences. It must now be obvious to everyone who has followed the events of the past few months that the appointment of the Chief Justice was nothing more than a government political

move designed to still the growing public protest against the granting of these licences to giant monopolies at the expense of the public. Having appointed Chief Justice Sloan, it was the government's clear duty to him and to the public to grant no more licences until the Chief Justice's report was finalized. The action of the government in granting four new licences since the appointment of the Chief Justice, involving untold billions of feet of public timber, has made a mockery of the Sloan Commission and is a contemptuous insult both to Chief Justice Sloan and the people of this province. It must now be clear to all that if the Commissioner continues in this investigation, the Sloan Report will be nothing more than a very expensive historical document and the Sloan Inquiry a colossal waste of public and private funds. What is this government trying to do—force Chief Justice Sloan to resign? As matters now stand the government has left Commissioner Sloan no other alternative.

You and I have a heavy responsibility in this election. The issue is the government forestry policy with particular emphasis on Forest Management Licences. The government will try to change the issue. They are relying on the oldest political trick known in the business. They hope that by spending millions on public works in Lillooet they can successfully appeal to the electors. I don't need to remind you that I campaigned last time on the Vancouver-to-Lillooet road and that because of my constant pressure, parts of this road are now under construction. If re-elected, I shall continue to press for the construction of the remainder of that road.

The issue in this election is simply this—will you join with me in fighting for the fundamental right of every citizen to buy our timber resources at open competition? The small operator wants and is entitled to nothing more than the right to compete at public auction against all comers big and small. The big operator wants his timber guaranteed forever at noncompetitive prices. Do you favour Forest Management Licences which guarantee timber forever to the few government-selected operators, or do you favour equal opportunity for all? This is the issue you, by your votes, will decide for all time to come.

No more vital issue was ever considered by electors anywhere. The big operators and the government will spend money like water to defeat me.

If you support me, I urge you to join with me now in the fight to preserve this fundamental principle in our way of life.

It cost the government millions of dollars to defeat me in that riding and every cabinet minister in B.C. spent two weeks around Lillooet promising the constituents all kinds of schemes that could never be carried out. Every baby within the radius of twenty-five miles was kissed at both ends.

On 2 June I charged that hired "contract men" of B.C. Forest Products had threatened Vancouver Island's residents with unemployment, loss of a $25,000 paper mill and no new access roads unless they supported the company's application for a Forest Management Licence.

The fight waged on and on, and the list of accusations was endless. It was another two years before matters came to a head when a Conservative government came into power in Ottawa. The case came to the attention of the new minister of justice, Davie Fulton, who considered that the matter had been hushed up under the former federal government because there were a few Liberal senators and back-room boys with interests in the B.C. lumber industry who stood to gain financially by the granting of Forest Management Licences. By this time the RCMP had made a report to the federal cabinet and Attorney General Bonner to the effect that money was indeed talking—that there was trouble within the ranks of the Bennett cabinet.

In December of 1955, all hell broke loose when lawyer David Sturdy appeared before the Sloan Forestry Commission and stated that he had a "certain body of evidence that, if proved true, could form the basis of an inference that the Minister of Lands and Forests, Robert Sommers, had received considerations for the issuance of Forest Management Licences." The commission refused to hear his "body of evidence." Mr. Sommers launched suit against Mr. Sturdy for libel and slander. The saddest part of the affair was that Attorney General Robert Bonner had already seen the RCMP report and had protected Sommers, calling the evidence "far-fetched."

Sommers publicly denied allegations of bribery. "The past while has been the era of the great, great political smear. . . . I challenge any Liberal to place a charge against me." Bennett claimed that David Sturdy had gone to the Sloan Commission just to get "the dirt" into the papers. Art Laing and I were accused of being a couple of professional hatchetmen.

Two years after the first allegations against Robert Sommers, preliminary hearings started, and on 14 November 1958, the former minister of lands and forests was sentenced to five years in Oakalla prison. Penalties: conspiracy, one year; receiving rugs worth $707, one year; receiving $2,500 cash, one year; receiving $2,000 in bonds, one year; receiving $1,000 in bonds, one year.

The Sommers case was absolutely exhausting and emotionally draining for everyone. It is my contention that Sommers should not have taken all the blame. Each member of the cabinet was equally guilty in his own way and if any of them had been men at all they would have stood up to be counted. As far as I'm concerned that was the first really sleazy act of the old Bennett government.

The editorial in the *Province* of 6 November 1958 speaks far more cogently and to the point:

A Minister of the Crown in British Columbia has been found guilty of crimes of which none other in any parliament of the Commonwealth has ever been convicted before. For it Robert Sommers is to be punished by the due process of law. But what of the government which for nearly two years refused to believe, or at least to admit, that there was any wrongdoing on Sommers' part; which rejected repeated demands from inside the Legislature, and from outside, that there be an inquiry to clear up the matter?

It was in December, 1955, that the breath of scandal publicly touched Robert Sommers' conduct of his department. . . .

Robert Sommers was not dismissed. After three months he resigned his cabinet office, but not his seat in the Legislature.

From December 7, 1955 until November 14, 1957 the Attorney General of British Columbia, Mr. Robert Bonner, the chief law enforcement officer of the Crown in this province, refused to act against his colleague although on the first of those dates the essential charges on which Sommers has now been convicted had been laid before him. He refused, also, to divulge the contents of an RCMP inquiry into the charges.

From December 7, 1955 until October 31, 1957, the Premier of British Columbia, Mr. W. A. C. Bennett, who must have been privy to all that Mr. Bonner knew, refused to act. On the latter of those dates he announced the appointment of a royal commission to investigate the charges. But the commission sat only one day. Two weeks later, Mr. Bonner finally ordered criminal prosecution.

If ours is indeed a government in the parliamentary tradition, all this has to be answered for.

An individual is tried, as Robert Sommers has been, in a court before a judge and a jury of his peers.

A government has to answer at the bar of a different justice. It is tried by the people in the polling booths.

It gave me great satisfaction to be returned to the legislature in 1958 as representative for the riding of North Vancouver after the Sommers case had run its course. I can honestly say that the happiest I have ever seen Mr. Bennett was the day in 1965 when I announced that I would not be running in the next election because of my wife's ill health. He could breathe a sigh of relief that the Sommers case was finally dead. It had haunted his government throughout its life.

CHAPTER 24

Recalling my years in politics puts me in mind of the young Scot who moved into a village and showed such enthusiasm for religion that he was immediately appointed deacon of the local church. Two months later the community found out that he had been a murderer and a rapist. When the clergy tried to strip him of his office he said, "Look here, gentlemen, there are some souls in this parish who have committed the same sins as I, and they too need representation!"

There is no doubt that politics attracts men and women of many diverse characters and ambitions. Because a government must represent proportionately all citizens, honest and even dishonest, of every colour and background and every financial circumstance, I suppose that there is room for all kinds of politicians.

W. A. C. Bennett appeared to put ambition and personal power above most every other consideration. During his tenure his motto seemed to be, it's *right* if it will get me votes and *wrong* if it will lose me votes. Because he held immense power over a period of twenty years in the B.C. legislature, this policy was often detrimental to the future good of the province. The forest management policies of his government were not good for this country and gave him such power over the industry that he was guaranteed inexhaustible campaign funds that could be called upon by threats like higher stumpage rates, which were completely under his control.

On the other side of the coin, it must be said that he was a man who was completely loyal to those who were loyal to him, though equally cruel to those who opposed his schemes. Except on very rare occasions when we had some pretty tough words, he was always pleasant to me socially and in the House.

The Honourable Philip Gaglardi added a great deal to this province. We needed his sort of vigour, enthusiasm and bombast. He and I certainly competed in one respect: for the loudest voice. I very much admired his church work with Sunday School children because it was to the benefit of the community as a whole. I would never trade my own five years of Sunday School for time in any other school because it undoubtedly instilled in me a sense of fairness which is so fundamental to good citizenship. Gaglardi brought many into the fold of the Lord. During his tenure as minister of highways he invited contractors to attend the opening of one of his new churches. His shining example of Christian spirit moved some to renew their commitment to the Lord with astonishing vigour.

He was not without a sense of humour. On one occasion, he and I were having dinner in the Empress Hotel. At that time I was a heavy drinker and smoked a few too many cigars. Gaglardi had neither of these vices as he had stopped drinking and smoking long before I did, and more credit to him, but I saw a glitter come into his eye when a trip to meet some attractive señoritas in Italy was jokingly suggested: he and I did have interests in common.

Gaglardi as a Social Creditor went along with a lot of things that I don't think a man of the gospel should have. It must have caused some conflict of interest to have God as one of his bosses and Bennett the other.

One of the outstanding men in the Social Credit party was Cyril Shelford, who always put public interest before his own. I admit that my own efforts in the public interest came after years of building a stable foundation for my own life. By the time I was elected I could afford the luxury of being concerned about community matters. Harry McKay, Alan MacFarlane, Art Laing and Ray Perrault of the Liberal Party have also made very real contributions to this province. Although biased, I do believe that my son, Gordon, has contributed to the future of Canada.

Over the last thirty years, I would have to say that Dave Barrett and Alex MacDonald have worked for and represented the people of this province more than any other two men in the legislature. If I were asked to name the politicians of the highest integrity who have sacrificed personal gain, I would pick these two. Either of them could have been financially better off if they had directed the same energy and talents into business.

A voter could well decide how to cast his ballot according to his own economic class. The Conservatives do a good job for the wealthy, who would like even more. The NDP in this province are trying to advance the poor and the blue-collar worker at the expense of the corporate rich; while the Liberals, who represent middle income, are determined to make life attractive to all three levels. Social Credit, however, is a bastard party which has widened its perimeters to embrace wheeler-dealers, car salesmen and, latterly, stockbrokers. Those who are really dedicated to Social Credit rather than self are destined to suck the hind tit.

In my years of experience as a politician, I have found that the Conservatives, Liberals and NDP have in their ranks many who should be respected for their personal and financial sacrifices, especially if one keeps in mind that these men and women have just one chance in four of getting elected, and a fair prospect of being fired every four years.

The priorities for our federal politicians should be keeping the country together and balancing the budget. I believe that although we hear a great deal of bitching from minority interests, most Canadians are happy with our parliamentary form of government. Our country has great prosperity and freedom in a world where these two fundamentals are in increasingly short supply. Anyone who isn't sure that we are one of the most favoured nations on earth will gain some perspective from comparisons with the revolution-torn countries of Central and South America, the famine- and drought-stricken Third World, the dull and suppressed USSR and Eastern Europe. Even the Americans have to cope with virtually unsolvable social strife and corruption of high government officials. It is essential that we maintain a strong federal government to safeguard the future stability of Canada, and it is in the best interests of the whole country that neither the west nor Quebec nor any resource-rich province dictates policies to the federal government that unfairly advance one group of citizens over another. The battle of the Plains of Abraham is over: we must look to a confederation of faith. The provincial governments should contribute to the decision-making process at the federal level, by working towards an equalization of economic and social opportunity for all regions of the country. To do more would be like branch managers trying to control the head office of a bank.

We must look to economic self-sufficiency in world trade to enable us to make a better contribution to global stability as a strong and financially independent nation that will not be pressured by the politics of other countries and that will not ride on the coattails of more powerful friends.

To achieve this goal we must attract into government men and women who have ambition and ability. I suggest that these public servants should be drawn from the financial world where they have had to compete to survive and are used to making decisions under pressure. Before a man can be a competent politician, he should be successful in some other endeavour.

It has been my experience that professionals such as doctors, teachers and lawyers have been trained to think in a single direction and lack the perspective to make sound judgements in areas other than their own field. Our politicians should come from senior management and be used to making corporate decisions. A man, like myself, who has built up a small business is too independent to negotiate as a member of a team, and isn't used to being scrutinized by a board of directors. Members of Parliament should act as though all Canadians were shareholders in a corporation selling its goods on a competitive world market. This would keep them on their toes, for a successful businessman must establish his credit and spend less than he makes in order to balance his budget and get ahead. If he does not, the bank will call in his notes and he will be forced out of the marketplace.

Unfortunately, it seems that many of those who have the greatest contribution to make either don't want to run for political office or can't get elected. No one likes to lose, and a successful man often can't stand the humiliation of losing to someone who, in his opinion, has poorer credentials.

Popularity at the polls has little to do with real ability, since intelligence and personality don't necessarily go together. H. R. MacMillan would have made an efficient prime minister but he would have had trouble getting elected.

We need to attract public servants like Ian Sinclair, head of the CPR, who have the ability and experience to run our federal government as they would a corporation, having the public interest at heart just as if every Canadian was a shareholder and each provincial premier a member of the board. Governments create inefficiency because the people who run them are ill-equipped to cut down on unnecessary expense and red tape. The public has been conditioned to accept inefficiency that would never be tolerated in private enterprise. Government should be run as well as most of our large companies, with respect for a balanced budget and a sense of corporate responsibility.

Anyone with average ability can make money in a rising market. A single quick success is comparatively easy to achieve, but only experience can bring the kind of judgement needed to stay on top. There are nine innings in a baseball game and it is necessary to win most of them to take the honours. If Joe Clarke had as much business experience as political know-how he would have had the wisdom to be more humble until he had a majority in the House. Although many of his policies were sound, he was like a general who marches out of reach of his supply line: he ran out of ammunition at the critical moment. He didn't have the kind of background that taught him when to bid and when to negotiate. I admire Prime Minister Trudeau's showmanship and political intelligence, but I feel he could make an even greater contribution to this country if he had had the privilege of running a business and meeting a payroll.

CHAPTER 25

Gordon, when are you going to say something? If you sit there much longer they will call you Sitting Bull instead of Peddling Some.

Phil Gaglardi

I had some fun as an MP between my fights with Premier Bennett. To publicize the need for roads in the riding of Lillooet, I attempted twice to make the thirty-five-mile trip from Bralorne to the coast with packhorses. Each time I encountered heavy snow or ran out of feed for the animals.

My partner on one trip in 1952 was Fred McNeil, now chairman of the board of the Bank of Montreal. At that time he was a newspaper reporter and an expert horseman, a fine outdoorsman and a great man to spend time with in the bush. He will probably retire in a few years to his own cattle ranch in Alberta.

Now I have no claim to being a great horseman, and was foolhardy enough the following year to attempt to make a safari from Squamish to Pemberton, up the Pemberton Valley, across Railroad Pass and down into Bralorne. All my attempts starting from the other end had failed and I figured I might have better luck setting out from Squamish. It was July when I started out with three horses: Prancer, an exceptionally strong horse; Mainbrace, a heavy hunter, and Lady Evelyn, a three-year-old mare.

Ray Street and Buster Marks, two loggers from Squamish, and their wives set out on the trip with me, each with their own horse. We also took along a four-wheel-drive jeep hoping that it might be able to get through if the trail were not too rough. The first day we got as far as Garibaldi where we camped overnight quite comfortably in two tents. The next day we travelled through beautiful country to reach Alta Lake, then made the long hard ride to Pemberton. That is where trouble started; the jeep, which was following us, got mired, and we decided when we pulled it out to send it back to Squamish. Unfortunately, I was foolish enough to leave a large part of my clothing, including my boots, in the jeep. We decided to stake out our horses and give them a good feed before enjoying a little partying, for the next day was the First of July when a great celebration was held at the Indian village in Pemberton.

There were to be at least ten horseraces at the Indian festival, run with small Indian ponies ridden bareback by the young braves. I asked the Chief if we could have an open race and offered to put up $100 as a prize to make a little competition. I presumed that the first prize for the race would be fifty dollars; second prize, thirty dollars, and the third prize twenty dollars. The race was to be a quarter of a mile long with the finish line about 100 feet away from a creek on the other side of a fence. Ray Street and his wife entered their horses in the race and I put in Mainbrace, who weighed more than any other two horses in the event by the time he had my 225-pound weight on top of the 40-pound saddle. Moreover, there were at least 20 pounds of spare horseshoes, nails, and cinches, as well as a hammer in the saddlebags.

There were ten horses in the race. My heavy horse was slow to get away from the starting line. At the beginning of the race I was in tenth position, then ninth, eighth, seventh, sixth, and then up to third. I now felt I had a chance and spurred my horse on: he was gaining all the time. As I crossed the finish line in third position old Mainbrace was just getting his steam up and refused to rein in. We headed straight for the fence where he stopped just short. Over his head I went, landing in the creek on the far side. I wasn't hurt but had to crawl under the fence in a very undignified fashion and return to the finish line with my clothes soaked and covered in mud. I still figure Mainbrace would have won the race if he hadn't been carrying such a heavy load.

The prizes were presented in the true spirit of free enterprise: fifteen dollars for first position, ten dollars for second, and five dollars for third. When I asked the Chief what had happened to the rest of the money, he explained, "Oh, that's my percentage."

That night I tried to find a couple of men to go through to Bralorne with me because the rest of my party, having more common sense, had decided to turn back. There were two volunteers, a bartender about sixteen years my junior and a young fellow of eighteen who had been born in the Pemberton Valley. The boy knew the mountainous area that we were going to travel through reasonably well as he had a contract to register the depth of snow in that part of the countryside, but we were to find that going through the area on skis or snowshoes in winter was a completely different matter than trying to go through in summer with packhorses.

About ten o'clock the next morning we packed enough supplies for seven days. It was only a thirty-five mile trip and we figured we could make it easily in three days. We loaded our horses on a raft and pulled ourselves across the Lillooet River by an old cable. If we had had any sense we would have realized that the going would be easier if we turned our horses loose to find their own way back and continued on foot. They kept bogging down in swampy ground, and this should have been a warning to us of what lay ahead.

The next day we started up through the pass where there was supposed to be a trail, but we seldom if ever found it, as it had not been used for at least ten years. We gradually climbed up one side of the valley to get clear of the windfalls and onto better ground. We made three miles that day and camped for a second night. The boy from Pemberton had bought a sleeping bag, but the bartender and I had just one blanket apiece and when it rained we became soaking wet and had to huddle around the fire all night. How I envied that boy with his sleeping bag. I would have paid a thousand dollars a night for it. When a man meets raw nature head on, money no longer counts, just self-preservation. I didn't have the guts to offer to buy the sleeping bag from him and toughed it out through the cold night.

Daylight comes about four o'clock in the mountains at that time of the year. We had an early breakfast and continued our climb. The weather was thick and foggy, and although it was raining, we kept climbing. We knew the pass was well below us but we were unable to get to it because of impenetrable windfalls. By afternoon, we were all in and so were our horses. It is much harder for horses to descend a steep slope than to go up one. By now we were in the snow belt, at least 1,000 feet too high. Our trail lay in the valley below. We had run out of food for the horses and it was virtually impossible to get any wood to light a fire. The only way out was down a snow slide that extended at least 500 feet below us to gravel, which went right down into the valley. Our situation was so bad that there was no alternative but to take the horses down the slide. The young lad pulled a horse by his halter while I took a big pole and hit the horse's rump. Down he went, slipping and rolling right to the very bottom. We got three horses down this way, sometimes skidding 100 feet at a time. But in the process we lost our blankets as well as our provisions except for one side of bacon and a can of dried vegetables.

By great luck, we managed to find a 6-foot by 6-foot trapper's cabin containing a small stove about the size of a 4-gallon can. We staked our horses in the grass, lit a fire and, after a bit to eat, all three of us slept until ten the next morning. We were exhausted from three days of continuous travelling and three nights of sitting up in front of a fire for six goddamned hours.

For some perverse reason we continued to use bad judgement, pressing ahead when we should have had the brains to go back by an easier route. But we were sure that the going had to become less difficult and that we would complete the trip in another forty-eight hours. We were wrong.

We found that if we stayed in the bottom ground we ran into swamps where the horses sank to their bellies, and when we went on higher ground, we ran into windfalls and had to chop our way through. We made only three miles the next day even though we worked our fool heads off. That night we set up camp again.

By now the horses were in such poor shape that we had to prod them to get them going. Their hooves and fetlocks were cut and their legs bruised and swollen. Every time we stopped it was much harder to get them started again. We couldn't put them out of their misery by shooting them as we didn't have a gun, and we couldn't leave them behind to die in the wilderness.

The next day we again made only three or four miles, and now our meals consisted of a little bacon and a few dried vegetables. For breakfast we cut some chunks of bacon into a billy can and fried it, then added six cups of water and two handfuls of dried vegetables. All this was brought to a boil for ten minutes and was eaten with whittled sticks—hard rations for that kind of travel.

I must confess that I hadn't anticipated how hard this trip would be and was wearing a pair of low-cut oxfords, though my partners were sensible enough to have worn heavy shoes. On the sixth day out we were leading our horses through the swamps and came to one spot, approximately 200 feet across, which was particularly soft. I started on foot to pull Mainbrace by the halter while he lunged through mud well up over his knees. Unfortunately, one of his front hooves happened to hit my right foot and I felt my shoe come off. It was impossible for me to stop until we got to firmer ground because the horses could hardly make it across themselves. On the other side of the swamp we made camp and I spent the next four hours wading through the mud, or crawling across on my hands and knees, reaching my arm as far down into the mud as it would go to search for that damned shoe. It took me four hours to find it; I was soaked to the skin and up to my hips in mud. Two or three miles ahead, we came to a fair trail.

It had been raining so heavily that the rivers were swollen and our horses could not make it across. The bartender stayed behind with the animals, provisioned with a quarter slab of bacon and our few remaining dried vegetables, while the young boy and I started out at daylight to walk into Bralorne. It was still a twenty-mile trip and we had to cross rivers and wade through swamps. By four o'clock even the young fellow was tired, while I was absolutely done in, just forcing myself ahead step by step.

Half an hour after dusk we straggled into the Gold Bridge Hotel in such poor shape that the clerk on the desk wasn't sure what to make of us. Our clothes were torn and dirty and when I asked for the best room in the house with a bath, he thought we were plum crazy. Later I phoned my friend Cy Manning, manager at the Bralorne Mine. He had heard of our attempt but had felt certain that we had turned back, whereas back in Pemberton our friends thought we had got through at least two or three days before. It was now eight days since we had left Pemberton.

I went to sleep that night at Cy's after a party and a lot of liquor and didn't wake up until noon the next day, by which time he had sent out guides with a pack train to take oats and hay to the horses, and food for the bartender. It was ten days before the horses were in good enough shape to make it to Bridge River. I had lost twenty pounds on the trip, but felt convinced that I had shown enough spirit to publicize the need for the road.

To add to the foolishness of the whole venture, I had made a very one-sided business deal with Buster Marks. On an evening at the beginning of our trip, Buster and I had sat around the fire talking about the outdoor life and how much we enjoyed it. Buster said he would like to own a couple of horses and at this my ears pricked up, for I had four of them. My son, Gordon, and my daughter, Louanne, had become interested in other pursuits, and I was keeping these four horses at Spuraway at a cost of $75 per month each.

"Buster, how would you like to buy four horses?" I asked, and started to deal. I found out that he was a hell of a lot better horsetrader than I was. I started first at $100 a horse though I had paid at least $1,000 for them. But he began to beat me down mercilessly until I finally said, "Buster, I'll give you the four goddamned horses."

Buster lived in Squamish and had a good place to run horses, but they would have to be shipped up by railroad. Taking full advantage of the situation in a good-humoured way, he dickered, "Well, Gordon, since I am saving you $75 per horse per month, it only seems fair that you should pay the freight to Squamish." I guess I had had enough to drink that I acknowledged the advantage and conceded I would ship them to Squamish.

We had another drink or two, and I'll never know how I

ever made a dollar in this world because I managed to lose again. Buster had sized up my condition pretty accurately and said, "Gordon, I have your horses, and I am saving you $75 per month, per horse. Now doesn't it seem fair to throw in your tack?" and I answered, "Surely, Buster, you will buy the tack?" to which he replied, "No, Gordon, my family prefer to ride bareback but if you want to send your saddles up, I'll look after them for you and that will clinch the deal."

Now I would not mind that little story at all if it were not for a raffle at the timber industry's Hoo-Hoo Club. Two hundred and fifty people had bought tickets on a Cadillac at $50 apiece, and I was lucky enough to win it. A year later there was a similar Hoo-Hoo party at the Vancouver Hotel with a raffle for a $7,000 Cadillac. There were already 200 to 300 guests in attendance before Buster Marks made his entrance. He was feeling no pain whatsoever. He came over to my table and wanted to buy a ticket on the raffle but all the tickets had been sold and in fact were now being drawn out of a hat. The owner of the last ticket drawn was to win the Cadillac. To keep Buster quiet, I offered him half of my ticket but warned him that I had won the year before and felt that I had no chance this time.

There was a lot of speculation going on as to who would be the last man out. I gambled that my ticket would not be among the first half drawn, then among the last twenty, then the last ten, then the last five. When there were just two tickets left in the drum, Buster and I were offered $3,500 for our ticket. But we were both good gamblers and decided to hang in. I won the Cadillac for the second year in a row. Buster and I were co-winners. I suggested that we take the $7,000, but he wanted to keep the car.

Each time we met, I would say, "Buster, what are you doing with our car? Do I own the front or the back seat, the left or the right side?"

One day I said to him, "Buster, we must get this settled," and he replied, "Gordon, that's easy. Do you remember the horses that I was kind enough to take off your hands? They have eaten so much that I have saved you $3,500 in hay. Why don't you give me the car?"

I knew he was just teasing me: a week later I received a cheque for $3,500 and he kept the car since I had no need for a second Cadillac.

In 1960 a nudist colony which owned a square mile of land in the centre of Burnaby was causing quite a controversy as the area became more densely populated. These nudists felt that the general public did not understand their way of life, and therefore they invited members of the legislature, the local mayors and aldermen to be their guests at a picnic. The invitation included our wives, and we were to be at the camp at noon on Sunday for lunch with the privilege of joining them in the nude if we chose.

I asked Louise if she would like to go. "Absolutely not," she said, "and I don't want you to go either. I thought that trip to Paris would have cured you."

I let the matter drop but I have to admit that I was so overcome with curiosity that I got in the car and headed for Burnaby. I stopped at a gas station and asked directions to the camp. The attendant knew me and said, "Mr. Gibson, surely to God you aren't mixed up with that outfit?" I assured him I was only a guest but I saw that the residents of Burnaby had a low opinion of nudists.

After being stopped by a uniformed guard at the gate, I drove down a dirt road into a beautiful parklike area with magnificent trees. I noted several naked families walking along the roadway and several riders on horseback. Everyone was as God made them.

I parked my car at the camp headquarters and was greeted by a naked woman who escorted me to the office. I felt quite comfortable as I have always appreciated a beautiful woman. Her breasts and backside were the same colour as the rest of her body which somehow took away from any impression of nakedness.

A man, also in the nude, introduced himself as president of the camp. I don't know what his intellectual capabilities were, but I could clearly understand why he had been chosen for this job. He inquired whether any other members of the legislature were coming. I said that the matter had not been discussed. My host looked downcast. "We've put on a buffet for them. We hope that at least a few will arrive."

It was obvious by one o'clock that I was on my own, and I could see the nudists felt that they had been slighted. The president turned to me and said, "Mr. Gibson, I had hoped that the premier or one of the cabinet would address us. Would you be the guest of honour?"

"Certainly," I said, "delighted." We left for the swimming pool where 50 children and at least 200 adults were congregated around the buffet table.

"Mr. Gibson, would you care to speak to us with your clothes on or would you like to join us?" I took a quick look around and thought to myself that in such a crowd I would be at least average, and that I'd probably be more conspicuous with my clothes on.

I stripped and tossed my clothes through the car window. I wore my running shoes and the cigar I was holding between my teeth cast a shadow at six o'clock.

In my five-minute speech I praised their natural way of life, saying nothing could be more pleasing than to see all of them nude as the Lord made them, and soundly condemned the narrow-mindedness and lack of courtesy of the other Members for not answering their invitation. They all clapped and then formed a line to shake hands with me.

At first, I was a little embarrassed at being naked, but after seeing the number of people whose bodies needed more exercise and less fat, I concluded that nudeness, if anything, would go a long way towards making men and women take more pride in their physique. The greatest spur to general fitness would be to force everyone to go naked for a few months.

Although there is no harm in nudity, there are times when it can be quite inconvenient. During my tour of the camp I saw some carpenters up on a roof hammering, one with a nail sticking out of the corner of his mouth and a shingle in his hand. A carpenter's apron would have been helpful. Later we passed a sports field where four people were playing volleyball. There was a man and a woman on each side of the net. I watched in amazement. I had never before seen four tits and five balls flying in the air at the same time.

On the way home I dropped in to see my long-time friend and secretary, Helen Richards, and her husband, Reg.

They were entertaining some guests and invited me to join them for a few drinks. I told them all about my experiences at the nudist camp, and drank a considerable amount of liquor.

It was getting late by this time and I was a little nervous about going home to Louise, so I asked everyone to come with me and vouch that I had been with them and not the nudists until eleven o'clock. Otherwise she was apt to become a little suspicious.

When I got home we had a few more drinks and possibly my judgement was a bit impaired because I dove into our pool when it was only half-filled with water and had to get stitches in my head.

It was a moment of real pleasure when I told Premier Bennett and the legislature what they had missed. I painted a vivid picture of the carpenters and the volleyball game in the nude, until the Speaker, losing all patience, told me to sit down and stick to the order of the House.

CHAPTER 26

I told the tennis pro that I played a fair to middlin' game, thinking of the games played at Ahousat on the mud flats in rubber boots. Up there I was a fair to middlin' player.

More than once during our years together Louise told me that if I used by brain as often as my mouth I wouldn't get into so many tight situations. It was during a holiday after we had been married about two years that she decided it was time to cut me down to size.

We had made reservations in San Diego at a resort called Del Coronado, one of the great tennis centres of California. The taxi driver who picked us up from the airport seemed doubtful when I gave him our destination, remarking, "Are you sure about the hotel, sir? Generals and admirals and people of that type stay there."

That afternoon we soaked up the sun for a few hours with one of Louise's friends who was travelling with us. The two girls couldn't be coaxed to go in the water more than a few times and were content to have a rest after our long trip, but I was boiling over for a little action. Impatient for some exercise, I went to the tennis courts and asked to see the pro, little realizing that this man was to tennis what Arnold Palmer was to golf.

"My name is Gibson and I'm from Canada. I'd like to have a game of tennis tomorrow. Can you arrange a game with one of the other guests for me?" He felt sure that he could and asked me what kind of game I played.

I was about thirty-five years old at the time, and felt myself to be a strong athlete. Of course, I didn't have the faintest notion how to rank my game, so I told the pro that I played a fair to middlin' game thinking of our years in Ahousat playing on the mud flats with Earson and the Baldwin boys.

The pro promised he would arrange the game for the next morning. That night Louise and I went dancing and arrived back in our room well after 3:00 A.M. At 8:45 the telephone rang. It was the tennis pro. "Mr. Gibson, I have found a man who would be delighted to play with you. He apologizes that he is fairly rusty, but would enjoy the workout." The game was arranged for 11:00 A.M.

By the time I got up I was rather wishing that I had kept my mouth shut. For one thing, I hadn't brought any sneakers, but at least I had the sense not to turn up in my oxfords, or in bare feet. It was 10:45 by the time I bought a pair of tennis shoes, and I felt so tough that when I got back to our room I figured a good stiff gin and tonic was in order. At five minutes before 11:00 I was feeling much more cheerful, and sauntered over to the tennis courts. The pro was looking for me with two other gentlemen tagging along behind him: the manager of the hotel introduced himself and the assistant pro. Everyone greeted me with extreme cordiality and directed me towards the pro shop. "Mr. Gibson, we know that you did not bring any equipment. We hope there is something here that will suit you." There were fifty rackets laid out in a line.

Unwittingly I threw them into complete confusion by saying, "Hell, any of these will do." They looked at each other in bewilderment. That was the first time I had ever seen three balls tied together in one bag. One sufficed on the mud flats in Ahousat, and when that was gone the game was over.

I was introduced to my opponent, a Mr. Jacks from the University of Peru. He looked about twenty-five years old but at that moment it made no difference to me. His apologies started immediately. "Mr. Gibson, I hope you realize that it is a few months since I have played, as I have been in the army and am just brushing up now."

It would have been much better for me if I had told him right then that I hadn't played for ten years. However, I said nothing and we all walked towards the middle court. Thinking that this was where we were going to play, I tried to show a little life and jumped over the net to the far side.

The men just looked at me very oddly, so I joined them again and walked towards the next court, hoping to drop the four or five people who had come with us, and said, "Let's play here. God knows, all we want is a little fun."

When I looked up I discovered there was a crowd of 500 people in the grandstand around the last court, and two umpires sitting up in high seats. A horrible sinking feeling ran all through me. I might have turned back right then but suddenly I saw my wife and her friend sitting in what could be termed the "royal box"; I decided that this was not the moment to lose face.

The game started. I didn't even know how to keep score. Jacks served the ball and it flew past me so fast that I didn't even see it. After three serves and no returns, he saw the joke and started to lob the ball over easily. At least I was athletic enough to return these slow balls, but he could place them from one corner of the court to the other at will. No one has ever seen a 235-pound man take as much abuse as I did in that next half hour. Sweat was pouring down my face, but I hung in until the finish which was mercifully swift.

Mr. Jacks and I shook hands. I said, "Jacks, someone has played a dirty trick on us. I think I'd have a better chance competing with you in my own line. Come on back to the hotel and have a drink with me."

"Mr. Gibson, I haven't ever taken a drink in my life," he replied. No wonder he was in such great form.

At the swimming pool I met Louise and her friend who told me the story. The night before the match Louise had telephoned the manager and told him that she hoped he could arrange a good game for me as I was a great player from Canada and she would like it to be a sort of international match. She had so impressed the management that they had mimeographed a little announcement, placing it on every table in the dining room and under the door of every room, so that when the game started I had been billed as one of Canada's best tennis players.

That was one of the most embarrassing days of my life but I was glad that I had played the game to the finish. It certainly took away any conceit I had about myself as an athlete.

The next day I thought we would get away from the hotel so I took the girls to the greyhound racetrack just over the Mexican border. We left San Diego about noon in a new Ford convertible that we had rented for the occasion.

After visiting most of the bars, and having a great day, we crossed the border again to start our drive back.

Louise saw a couple of sailors thumbing a ride and asked me to stop and pick them up. Her brother was in the navy and she had a soft spot for the uniform, so I agreed and we put the sailors in the back seat. The traffic was moving about 80 miles an hour, and the boys had pulled their greatcoats up over their ears. Louise thought they were cold and taking pity on them asked me to stop and put up the roof. The kids looked warm enough to me, but I asked, "Boys, do you want the top up?" They replied yes and I said, "That's alright with me, just lift the goddamned thing up."

The two sailors looked at me, then turned around and made what I thought was a very weak effort to raise the top. Getting in the back seat, I impatiently pushed each kid aside, saying, "Let's not fool around any more, let's lift this damned thing." I grabbed the roof, which seemed to be stuck, and ordered the boys to heave on it. They both were looking at me as though I had drunk too much on the other side of the border, but gave a mighty tug just the same. I felt the bottom springs go down about 6 inches and the hood come up about 6 inches.

There was a pause while I thought up my next set of orders when one of the boys said, "Don't you just press that button in the front seat, sir?"

I didn't even answer, thinking to hell with it, a kid wasn't going to tell me what to do. I got back in the front seat and we drove off. Louise and her friend tried to explain to me that it was necessary to push the button on the dash, but I wouldn't hear of it. I was just that goddamned mad!

The next morning, I drove over to the station where we had rented the car and asked them to fill up the tank. While the attendant was working on it, I said casually, "By the way, what would I do if I ever wanted to put the top up?"

With a smile, he answered, "We thought you would know, but since you don't, I'll show you." He jumped into the front seat, started the motor, pushed the button and the roof began to move. As I watched it make a great arc up in the air and then start down, I could see that it was going to overshoot the windshield by at least a foot.

That was not the end of the mischief, because just before the hood shot out past the windshield, the canvas split down the middle and tore all the way across.

If I was surprised, the attendant was absolutely stunned. He asked me what had happened, and I told him the truth, that I had not pushed the button to put the top up. He shook his head in disbelief, but gave us another convertible. This time he made sure that I knew how to operate the goddamned top.

CHAPTER 27

After all our boasting I managed to mount my horse from the wrong side. The cowboys started to laugh like hell, but I said, "You amateurs just get on from one side, whereas I can mount from any goddamned direction."

About ten of us had been invited on a hunting trip to Big Bar Ranch in the Cariboo. The first three days of the hunt we spent in camp, telling stories and having a few too many drinks. We were staying at the ranch guesthouse which was located at the bottom of the valley with very steep surrounding hills. The roundup was in progress, and after a few scotches I figured it was time to try my hand as a cowboy. I asked the foreman if I could help round up some cattle, and I shot him quite a tale about my ability. He was kind enough to lend me his own lasso, chaps and spurs, and a fine-looking mount rigged with saddle and bridle and ready to go.

The hill up to the plateau was so steep that the only way to climb it was by a trail that "zigged" a quarter of a mile in one direction before "zagging" back that far in the other direction. All went well during the roundup, until my friend Allan Spencer decided to join me. He was riding a horse that was a little wilder than mine. Spencer was a good rider and jumped on the horse bareback using nothing but a halter and a rope.

I have to admit that neither of us was feeling any pain, and looking down at the camp 1,000 feet below, he challenged me, "Anyone can ride a horse with all that gear, saddle and bridle, but it takes real horsemanship to ride bareback."

I couldn't resist the bait and immediately demanded to change mounts. When I got on his horse, it refused to move forward, backward or sideways despite the direst threats muttered in its ear. One of the cowboys came alongside and said, "Be careful, Mr. Gibson. That horse is mean."

Brushing aside his warning, I dug the horse in the ribs with my spurs, took off my hat and waved it in front of the animal's eyes. The horse made one great jump. I should have bailed out then. Instead, I grabbed his mane and we took off at a full gallop down the hill.

The barn lay 1,000 feet below us and there were six zig-zagging roads to cross on the way down. The cowboys started to yell and their voices carried behind me as the horse raced down the slope.

My friends at the guesthouse were amazed to see a horse and rider fly past, making about 20 feet a stride heading hell-bent for the barn door. Suddenly the horse stopped dead about 2 feet short of the barn, throwing me head first into that soft stuff that animals are good enough to leave around the barnyard. It's lucky I did not have hold of his tail or I would have torn it out. As it was, the horse was missing part of his mane, and my wrist was broken.

The boys picked me up and took me into the house. After pouring a little whiskey down my throad to kill the pain, the foreman shook his head, saying "I have been around horses all my life, and have seen them clocked at races. There have been all kinds of records broken by fast riders, but this is the first time that it's taken *two* men to clock a horse: one to say 'here he comes' and the other, 'there he goes.'" It happened that fast.

After that incident any sensible man would have been too discouraged ever to get in the saddle again and it would have been the end of my riding career if I hadn't been told about an excellent guide who would show me how to shoot an elk.

The two of us spent the first night in a cabin in the mountains east of Princeton, and started out on horseback the next morning. We had gone only a short distance from the cabin when the guide asked me if I had brought along any liquor. I said that I hadn't because I didn't plan to take a drink until we had done some shooting. A few minutes later the guide pointed out that we were in the wrong spot to find elk since he hadn't seen any tracks and suggested that we head back to our cabin and start out in another direction. I agreed. When we arrived at the cabin he suggested that we go in and warm up. We tethered our horses, loosened the saddle cinches and had a few drinks in front of the fire.

I have to admit that both of us felt better when we came out. As the snow was 4 or 5 feet deep all we had to do to mount our horses was to pull them over to a fence, climb up on a post, then swing a leg over into the saddle. About 200 yards down the trail we met a hunter on foot and stopped to talk for a few minutes to be hospitable. I offered him a drink, which seemed to offend my guide, as though it would mean less liquor for him. He started down the trail without me. About ten minutes later I thought I should try to catch up with him and spurred my horse to a pace. I figured I cut a fine figure on horseback until we took a sharp turn in the trail. Being a greenhorn, I had forgotten to tighten the cinch, and as the horse swung into the turn, the saddle slipped sideways until I was being dragged through the snow upside down under the belly between the horse's legs. Twenty yards farther on I managed to get control of the horse and rein him in.

My guide was still not in sight and after a while I found myself on a main highway. About 50 feet ahead of me was a game warden I had known for years, setting up a road block to check game licences and guns. I thought I would have a little fun with him so I rode about a quarter of a mile farther down the road and set up a road block of my own. The game warden shooed me away. I simply moved along another half mile and continued to check cars until he came after me again. By now the game warden was beginning to lose his sense of humour and by the time we reached Princeton, five miles away, he was goddamned angry. I met up with my guide and we decided to find a bed for the night before I got into any more mischief.

The guide was well known in town because he owed money to many of the residents. I guess he thought that this might be a good opportunity to re-establish his credit—with me paying the bill. When we checked into the hotel, he ordered the best room in the house. During the evening he brought all his friends and creditors to the hotel room. Squaws, half-breeds and layabouts caroused and sang until three o'clock. With the help of the management I was able to get rid of them, but not before my reputation had been completely ruined.

A week later, after bagging an elk, I went back to the same hotel and asked for a room. The manager took me down to the basement. After looking around the room, I said, "This is not as nice a room as the one I had before. There are eight beds here and I would prefer to be alone." He replied, "Mr. Gibson, this is the bull pen, and it's the only kind of room you will ever get in this hotel."

The last time I went hunting was for moose, with two close friends, Howard de Qui and Carl Gentry. Our Norseman airplane was so heavily loaded down with food, ammunition, warm clothing and liquor that it couldn't take off. We were carrying a case of liquor for each member of the party, and the suggestion was made that two cases be jettisoned which would lighten our load by at least 100 pounds. After due consideration, it was decided that we could do without some of our blankets and food rations. We flew to a small lake in the Chilcotin district of British Columbia, an area that was almost uninhabited and is called the "Grass Beyond the Mountains." We asked the pilot to return to pick us up in a week.

That evening we fished for trout, catching at least ten apiece within an hour of putting our lines in the water. The fish were cooked over an open fire in front of a cabin belonging to Jack Belan. The duck hunting season was just beginning, so after dinner we hid in a little pass, 20 feet away from each other. The ducks flew over our heads in such great numbers that our guns heated up from the constant firing and we had to lay them aside in the grass to cool off while we had a couple of drinks to restore our energy. In a short time we had thirty ducks to feed us for the coming week.

The next morning we started out to track moose with a young guide, Jimmie Holt, and three Indians and four packhorses to carry the supplies. Jimmie was a white boy of about nineteen who was married to a young Indian girl. He certainly knew the country we would be travelling through but the largest city he had ever heard of was Williams Lake about 150 miles away. Jimmie was so full of energy that I never saw him walk anywhere. He either ran or rode a horse.

That day we made fifteen miles on horseback, camping just outside the trading post of Anaheim. A full blizzard had blown up by daylight the next morning. Jimmie Holt and the Indians said that it was too stormy to leave and we agreed. We started to drink hot rums to pass the time, and swapped tales of our ability to hunt and ride. By ten o'clock we started to get impatient, telling Jimmie that the storm was nothing to men like us from the great city of Vancouver. Young Jimmie and his companions were making their first trip as professional guides and it wasn't long before we had talked them into loading up the packhorses.

We had taken a few more swigs of scotch and reassured the guides about our experience as hunters. Carl Gentry and Howard de Qui were expert horsemen, but I was not. After all my boasting the guides were amazed to see me mount my horse from the wrong side. They burst out laughing. I had to sell my story so I said, "You amateurs get on from just one side. I can mount a horse from any direction." Jimmie was so naive that he was taken in. With a dozen drinks under my belt I figured that what I lacked in skill I could make up in confidence, and dug my spurs into the sides of the horse.

We had a six-hour ride ahead of us before we would reach our next camp. The storm was blowing straight into our faces. The snow was at least 3 feet deep so that the trail was almost obliterated. Howard, Carl and I took the van rather than let our guides take charge. The rate of travel with packhorses is usually 3 or 4 miles an hour, but we started up over the mountain at a gallop. I can still recall the look of astonishment on the faces of those guides. They had never encountered anyone like us before.

We made our next camp in less than four hours, two hours less than expected, at a one-room shack owned by Jimmie Holt's parents. They had come to this part of the country forty years previously, and had established themselves through a lot of hard work, building up a herd of 200 head of cattle. Upon our arrival, Mrs. Holt excused herself saying she would like to put on some good clothes. She changed from a pair of old, worn-out dungarees into a newer pair of dungarees and a shirt with a full set of buttons. I guess we were the first guests from the outside in a few years.

At daylight the next morning we started for our next camp twenty miles into the woods. About four o'clock that afternoon we were settled in a 12-foot by 12-foot log cabin belonging to a trapper. The following morning we were to start moose hunting but not before we made a pact that none of us would take a drink from his flask until he had shot something. Jimmie and I were hunting partners. To this day he will never believe what happened.

We looked for moose, but didn't see any fresh tracks. I figured it was about time for a drink, but reluctantly kept to our agreement and decided to wait. Then we jumped a jack rabbit on a fairly steep hillside. I wanted to get a good shot at it and leapt off my horse, gun in hand, but my jackat caught in my saddle horn, hanging me up so that my feet were off the ground. My horse got pretty excited and started off at a gallop with my body close-hauled at the neck and my feet dragging. Jimmie managed to catch up with us and reined in my horse, whereupon I tried to explain away the incident as a silly accident. But he had become suspicious of my abilities since I had mounted my horse from the wrong side. Now he was convinced that I was no horseman.

The rabbit had not run away but paced with me as though he was enjoying all the excitement. To redeem myself, I figured I would take a shot. I simply swung my rifle up and fired. The rabbit was bounding through the grass, and I'll never know by what grace I managed to hit him. Jimmie shouted, "That's a great shot!" I said, "Hell no, it's just as easy to hit them running as when they're asleep. I always shoot 'em in the middle of a jump."

We felt that getting that rabbit was reason for a drink. Half an hour later we ran into some tracks that were so fresh they were still steaming. We spurred on our horses. A few moments later I saw a magnificent bull moose on the far side of a river. He had just swum across it and stood on the opposite bank facing us. I took careful aim and fired: once, twice, three times. The moose fled towards the woods. We knew he had been hit and we forced our horses to ford the river. After following the tracks to a knoll with a few overhanging branches beside the river, Jimmie motioned to me to follow the moose while he circled behind, to head off any escape. Laying my head along the horse's neck, I rode under the trees. The smaller branches broke against my shoulder, the larger ones scraped and bruised my back.

Three times I saw the moose about 100 yards ahead, and each time I took a shot at him. I was sure that he had been hit more than once and I wanted to put him out of his misery. After fifteen minutes of circling each other, the moose charged, his huge rack of horns pointed right at me. The horse reared up on his hind legs, throwing me off balance.

I will never know how I managed to hang on. The moose was not more than 50 feet away when I fired three times from the back of the rearing horse. The moose fell to the ground 10 feet from me. The horse was terrified and reared again.

I slipped out of the saddle and tried to lead him away but my legs were shaking so that I couldn't walk more than a few steps. I sank to the ground, feeling completely drained, as if the death of the moose had drawn out some of my own strength.

I was sorry I had shot that moose because he had put up such a gallant fight. The hardest part lay ahead, skinning, cleaning and cutting up the carcass so that we could pack it onto our horses. We walked all the way back to camp. I wished that I had missed my first couple of shots. It was the instinct of the hunter in my blood that had caused me to kill for sport rather than for the meat. I have not shot a moose since nor do I ever want to. It was a cowardly act, one that I am not proud of.

CHAPTER 28

Hawaii was like heaven to a man who had been wet up to his ass all his life.

The first time I heard of Hawaii was from Miss Chambers who had been the government nurse in Ahousat and Tofino when I was a kid. She had left the West Coast to take a post at a school in Honolulu. In those days we knew so little of the outside world that receiving her letters was like getting a message from another planet.

In 1947 Louise planned our first trip to Hawaii. We flew to San Francisco and made a four-day crossing by ship, arriving in Honolulu at the Aloha Towers wharf at eight o'clock in the morning. We disembarked in brilliant sunshine to the rhythms of seductive native music and the sight of beautiful flower-laden wahines performing a graceful dance of welcome. What a change it was from the rainy west coast of British Columbia. It seemed to me to be a paradise. From the moment I set foot in the Hawaiian Islands I knew that they would become a part of me.

For the first few days I was content to lie in the sun, but it wasn't long before I was helping some of the other guests to carry their surfboards into the water. After a lesson or two I learned what a marvellous feeling of freedom comes from riding the crest of a wave on one of these boards. I have to admit that most of all I enjoyed looking at the women and I might have been tempted had Louise not been there to keep an eye on me.

Our accommodation was superb at the Moana Hotel, which was situated right beside the famous Royal Hawaiian. Gus Guslander, the manager, sparked my interest in the island of Maui, referring to it as a frontier compared to the more cosmopolitan Honolulu. He regaled me with stories of how Capt. George Vancouver had anchored in Maalaea Bay in Maui before visiting Friendly Cove in

Nootka during his historic search for a northwest passage from the Far East to Europe. When Guslander asked me to accompany him on a trip to Napili Bay on Maui I welcomed the opportunity. He was planning to buy several acres and build his own hotel. The island was so beautiful that I vowed to return.

The fourth year that we holidayed in Honolulu it rained steadily for two weeks. I figured we had enough rain in Vancouver and asked whether any place there was dry all year. The answer was Kihei on Maui. The next day Louise and I flew to Maui aboard an eight-passenger airplane and were met by Andy Freitas, the chief of police and a friend of Guslander's.

Andy chauffeured us around the island, and showed me a 50-foot lot in Kihei. The area was residential, and most of the homes were expensive second houses of the wealthy. A lot was worth about $30,000. It was so dry in this area that no natives lived there, for it was impossible to cultivate the land without extensive irrigation.

Our party drove a little farther along the leeward coast until Andy pointed out 30 parched-looking acres that he said were owned by a group of men, of which he was one. He explained that the land was useless because there was no fresh water. "Let me out and I'll look around," I said. I strode up a sandy hill into the kiawe woods. About 500 feet from the road I turned to look out over Maalaea Bay. Before me lay a breathtaking panorama of the Pacific Ocean. A gentle slope to seaward looked like an excellent site for a house, with protruding volcanic rock for a firm foundation in the surrounding sand. Most of all, I liked the dryness and the sunshine.

As I walked over the land I spied a narrow strip about 200 feet long where the trunks of the kiawes were 3½ feet thick, ten times the diameter of the trees around them. Moreover, they were lush and green, and 25 feet above sea level. Having spent so much of my life in the woods, I knew that these trees were being fed by an underground stream or water pocket. I made up my mind right then that I would transform this desert into a tropical paradise.

Back at the car, I said to Andy, "What's your price?" He

answered, "Gordon, this land is not for sale. The club is going to keep the land for two or three years until the price doubles. It will take two years to pay for it as we put only ten per cent down."

I was not going to be put off. "What do you want for it right now, Andy? Name your price."

"We want to double our investment, but we're not shysters," he said. "It's not for sale until our debt has been paid in full. The total price was $17,000 to be paid over a five-year period with no interest charged."

"All right, Andy," I said. "I'll give you $34,000 cash for clear title. If it's not worth $1,200 an acre, it's not worth anything." I could see that Andy thought I was crazy. My purchase caused a stir on Maui because the next day the headline in one of the island newspapers read: "Eccentric Canadian doubles land values in Kihei."

I promised Louise that our home would be the most comfortable on the island despite the desert and kiawe trees. Our first plans were drawn on a piece of cardboard for a 24-foot by 24-foot Panabode with a wide overhanging roof to provide shade, a lanai in front, and windows all around so that the wind could blow straight through the house. A 24-foot living room was planned, with two bedrooms and two bathrooms along one side, and another bedroom, a laundry room and a kitchen along the other side.

Rather than excavate a foundation, I decided to set the house well above the level of the surrounding ground so that Louise and I could enjoy the splendid view of Maalaea Bay over the low kiawe trees. Within a few days a 10-foot mound of sand and rocks had been bulldozed by one of the local contractors. The natives were mystified. Andy Freitas paid us a visit one afternoon and asked, "What on earth are you building, Gordon?"

"A fort to keep you out," I joked. From that time on our neighbours in Kihei referred to the project as "Gordon's Fort." The word "fort" had sprung to my lips but when I heard it repeated it grew on me. I added "Vancouver" thinking of our home in British Columbia and also of Capt. George Vancouver who had first landed in sunny Maui. No mansion in Acapulco or Waikiki could have given us one-tenth the pleasure and companionship that we were to find in this log home.

I hired a contractor and six helpers to pour the cement floor for the Panabode. To my amazement, the contractor arrived on the job dressed in a white shirt and tie, and paced around the site with the plans in his hand. To have a little fun and get some exercise, I helped the labourers lay the floor. The contractor couldn't understand why I wanted to work, but I explained to him that it was impossible for me to just stand on the sidelines when something needed to be done.

He was convinced that I was nuts when, a week later, before the roof had been nailed down or the finishing touches added, Louise and I moved into our new home. Louise bought a few pieces of unpainted furniture and varnished them herself. The contractor came to me and said. "You can't fool me anymore. You work for some man who is paying you to get this house finished before he comes to Maui."

The mystery surrounding me continued for some time. I bought a run-down old car which we later nicknamed "Blue Bonnet" for $200. At first, they figured I must be poor because I had not bought a better car; later it could have been said that I had to be wealthy to keep the blasted thing running since it needed so many repairs.

A swimming pool was built from rocks between Fort Vancouver and the beach. The labour was done entirely by ladies and children who were picked up each day in an old truck. They worked for eight hours every day, the oldest children looking after the little ones, who never bothered their mothers.

Some of the women planted grass at the rate of an acre a week. In Maui the Kona winds blow steadily in one direction, northwest to southeast; the seedlings were placed in the ground in 1-inch clumps so that as the roots grew the plants would be firmly anchored.

I stayed there for about a month after we started to build, and then left for Victoria as the legislature was now in session. When I arrived back in Kihei some months later, I was asked by the local Chamber of Commerce to look over the mountain forest on Maui and give them some advice about logging it. I suggested that it would be sensible to leave the timber as ground cover because most of it was little over a foot through the stump, knotty and well over a hundred years old. I advised them instead to plant lots of cocoanuts, banyan and monkey pod trees along the ocean, boulevards and highways into town so that in years to come they could be enjoyed by tourists. The monkey pod tree would provide employment for woodcarvers as each tree could produce enough wood for a thousand tourist items.

I took this advice myself and planted cocoanut palms in clumps of three every 20 feet along the driveway to our house and watered them by running a pipe from our well.

About this time I was approached by the leader of the Boy Scouts at Kihei for a $500 donation to help them with one of their projects. I figured it would be far more beneficial for both the troop and myself if they did a little work to earn the money instead of my giving them a handout.

I'll tell you what I'll do," I said. "Get your boys to dig me 1,000 sprouted cocoanuts growing in the wild. I need them for shade and decoration, and I'll pay 50 cents apiece so that you can earn the $500." It was a generous offer, because I could easily buy them for half that amount.

To my disgust, a farmer from Hana with two big Hawaiian helpers delivered the 1,000 sprouted cocoanuts. The bill was $250. The Scout leader had ordered the palms at the price of 25 cents apiece, figuring to net $250 profit with no effort. Instead of teaching the children the ethic of earning their own money, he taught them to double their money by taking a cut on the contract.

I expressed my disappointment to the Scout leader: "What kind of leadership are you giving these boys? Couldn't you see that I wanted to help them? Besides, now you have only half of the $500 for your project. The boys had better come over this week and plant the sprouted cocoanuts so that at least they will feel they worked for the money." The Scouts planted the 1,000 cocoanuts around the perimeter of the grounds, 10 feet from the property line at 12-foot intervals. I ran a water line around the trees with a drip to each palm.

As time went along, I cleared the kiawe woods with a bulldozer and replaced them with a profusion of palms, hibiscus, ironwood and other ornamental trees and shrubs. It was a challenge to me to turn that land into a tropical garden.

Because Kihei is so dry, all these plants needed water and loving attention. One of our caretakers, a happy-go-lucky Hawaiian, obviously felt that the cocoanut palms planted by the Scouts were watered by God, for when Louise and I were in Vancouver, the water pipe broke and the caretaker did nothing about it. By the time we arrived back in Maui two months later most of the trees were dead. Those that survived were near the sea, where the tender roots reached sand dampened by the salt ocean waters. If the palms had been a year more mature, it is quite possible that they would have survived. Fortunately, the palms along the driveway flourished.

As the palms grew, so did the number of guests at Fort Vancouver, as we loved to share our sunny home with our friends from the West Coast. Louanne and Gordon also brought many of their companions for a holiday. The house was in such demand that sometimes it was hard to find a place to bunk down ourselves.

Rather than disappoint our friends we decided that we would build a guest house about 24 feet by 36 feet a fair distance from Fort Vancouver. I arranged that sufficient lumber be delivered to Maui from Vancouver. A few months later, I received word that the lumber for the guest house had arrived at the Kahului dock. To my astonishment, I found not the 5,000 board feet I had expected but 50,000.

I figured then that we might as well build ten guest houses, which later became known as the Maui Lu cottages in tribute to Louise. Instead of plain sloped roofs, they were built with upswung gables and peaked Polynesian eaves to salute the many Japanese Hawaiians in Maui. The lanaiis, 24 feet wide and 12 feet deep, opened onto a tropical parkland. These cottages were always full and the idea seemed to work beautifully for the first year.

Our friends had been encouraged to enjoy our swimming

pool, but soon the sounds of splashing and laughing started at seven in the morning and continued until well after midnight. Finally, Louise could stand the commotion no longer. "Gordon," she said, "either you tell your guests to keep away from the pool and our house until after lunch, or I'll surround Fort Vancouver with barbed wire."

I told her I would build another pool for the guests next to the cottages. The bulldozer started to dig at a spot halfway between Fort Vancouver and the guest houses. I had intended that the pool would be 60 feet by 40 feet by 12 feet deep. We dampened down the sand with water from our hoses and completed the 12-foot hole. Unfortunately, the bulldozer was very old and had no cleats on the treads, so that it needed a gradual slope to be able to climb out of the hole. I figured this was an opportunity to do something a little creative. I instructed the driver to follow a mark I made with a stick in the sand and to scoop out sloping sides so that he could easily drive the machine out of the hole.

The crowd of guests and neighbours could only wonder at what I was drawing in the sand. Soon it became apparent that the contours of the new pool resembled the outline of the island of Maui. The bulldozer had to cut out another 40 feet to make the climb so the final measurements of the pool were 100 feet by 40 feet by 12 feet. We painted a map of the local attractions right onto the floor of the pool. Roads, mountains, towns and craters were marked in the cement. Our guests could relax by Kihei, visit a pineapple plantation or cattle ranch, go to the top of Haleakala and swim around the entire island. Later a mosaic walk bordered the pool, with signposts indicating the mileage to twenty cities such as Tokyo and London.

Over the next few years, many of our guests insisted that I allow them to pay something for their accommodation. Strangers assumed that the cottages and pool were part of a hotel rather than a private estate.

Charging for accommodation was a great mistake because it put us in the hotel business. I wished we had never done it because when people pay they expect service. It wasn't long before I found that we were going to have to invest more money: it was uneconomical to hire a manager and staff to operate just ten guest houses. That year, in a semicircle outside the ten Maui Lu cottages, forty "Roundhouses" were added. A few near the gate were built on higher land and nicknamed "Nob Hill" by our staff. Now we had fifty rental units, and although each of them had cooking facilities, I opened a small restaurant at the end of the Maui Lu pool.

Louise and I could see that we needed a place to ourselves so we built a new home, Luika's, three miles along the shore. This was to be our last home together.

When a small lump developed on Louise's breast, we both took the matter casually. Even our doctor seemed to believe that it was nothing to worry about, but a year later Louise announced that she was going into the hospital to have it removed and expected to be home the same night.

A few minutes after seven o'clock in the evening the doctor told us that the lump had been malignant and that it would be necessary to perform a mastectomy. That was the beginning of the end.

By this time our family was grown and Louise and I were spending a great deal of time in Victoria. We decided to sell Spuraway, our big home in West Vancouver, because Louise wanted to have the pleasure of running the Maui Lu Hotel. She told me that she wished to live in Maui until she died because it was as close to heaven on earth as anyone could find. She died in 1967.

After Louise's death I threw myself into work and started to drink too much. I have always found that hard work helps to get my mind off my troubles.

I started to improve the recreational facilities at the hotel and built a small golf course, though I knew nothing about the game or how a course should be designed. One putt was the maximum anyone took and many played the course with five holes-in-one, because I had unwittingly sloped the greens towards the cups, which were 8-inch-wide jam cans. Almost every ball landing on the green rolled into the hole. My golfing guests soon persuaded me to rebuild the greens more conventionally.

When the first restaurant became inadequate for the number of guests, I built an elevated dining room and bar, called the Longhouse, above the west end of the Maui Lu pool.

In 1964 a tidal wave hit Kihei. The beach across the road from the Maui Lu was badly eroded by the torrential waters. At one place, a 100-foot-wide cliff was reduced to 16 feet by the pounding seas. The beach homes on the top of the cliff seemed to be about to fall into the sea. The owners figured they were a total loss. I bought these houses and the beachfront, and brought in rocks from my acreage across the road, thereby adding seven units and a beach to the hotel's assets.

The Maui Lu Hotel was becoming very popular and in 1967 I built four four-plexes by myself, naming them the Quadras as a reminder of Capt. George Vancouver's meeting on Vancouver Island with Señor Quadra who had given the island of Maui a gift of highly bred cattle.

In the fall of 1968, I found that we had sold twenty-four more rooms than we had available for the Christmas season. Most of these guests were friends, and I decided that rather than disappoint them I would build a comfortable apartment building and have it ready a week before Christmas. Each room would be 36 feet by 24 feet. My staff and neighbours said it was a crazy undertaking. The contractor told me the building couldn't be ready until February.

The first day of November arrived and I still hadn't reached any agreement with the contractor. Finally we made a deal. I said, "Give me ten good men from your crew and I'll pay you ten per cent of the costs." We started work on 6 November and finished the apartment in thirty-three working days. The only time missed aside from sleeping was a couple of Sundays and an hour or two during torrential downpours. The carpets were still being laid as the first guests arrived. I believe we set a record for building that type of structure on the island of Maui.

By this time the restaurant had grown so that it could seat 400 people. We had a very popular native entertainer, Jesse Nakooka, who is now a great star in the Hawaiian Islands. When I first met Jesse he was driving a tour bus, and playing piano and singing for his guests while they refreshed themselves at the bar. Upon learning that he earned $250 a month I offered him $500 a month plus his room and board to be our entertainer. He was free during the day to continue driving the bus. It turned out to be a splendid deal for both of us.

It was in the bar of the restaurant that I hung a polar bear hide, where it looked down at the guests. Later the bar became known as the Polar Bar. My bartenders got so that they could tell the story of how I shot him and packed him through the streets of Vancouver better than I could.

In the years that followed I built 2 more apartments and 50 units on the beach bringing the room count up to 150. The Maui Lu Hotel was a wonderful success, but it started to require too much of my time to operate. My roots are in Canada, in British Columbia, and I missed my home. Canada has four beautiful seasons whereas Hawaii has only one. Sir Walter Scott's words from "Last Lay of the Minstrel" kept running through my mind:

Breathes there the man, with soul so dead,
Who never to himself hath said,
This is my own, my native land!
Whose heart hath ne'er within him burned,
As home his footsteps he hath turn'd
From wandering on a foreign strand!

In 1977 we sold the hotel to a group of Canadians. I had never planned to be in the hotel business, and that became my greatest sales pitch. "Hell, boys, it's making money and I didn't even want to run a hotel. If you can't manage it better than I have, and make a lot more money, you had better throw the towel in right now."

I still have some financial interests in Hawaii, but my heart is here at home among my own people.

CHAPTER 29

You can't really blame the taxi-driver for being startled. He was hailed at noon yesterday by this great hulking man carrying a great hulking polar bear skin and ordered to make haste to the Terminal City Club. Once there, the great hulking man hauled out the remains of the beast, yarded it across Hastings St. and plunked it down in the foyer, where it stopped traffic all lunch hour and cut into the usual demolishments of the rye and soda. The man was Gordon Gibson, former bull-of-the-woods, two-fisted Liberal MLA who broke the first forest scandal in this province, present Hawaiian Island squire, councillor of the Northwest Territories, and latter-day polar bear killer. How did he slay the bear? "Easy," says Gordon in his usual bellow. "Just went 500 miles north of Yellowknife up to Baffin Bay Island, went out from an Eskimo village for three hours on a Skidoo till we found the bear. Nearest censored post office up there is the North Pole. Bear comes at you—if you want to survive, you shoot it." He shot it. It stretches 11 feet. "The reason it's got a smile on its face is I told it just before it died I was taking it to Maui Lu." . . . A little gag to help publicize the Northwest Territories' centennial. What's a 65-year-old man doing carrying polar bear remains around by himself in downtown Vancouver? "I do things myself. Nobody else thinks so, but I still figure it's a do-it-yourself world."
Alan Fotheringham, *Vancouver Sun*

In 1967, Arthur Laing, federal minister of northern affairs and a great personal friend, invited me to attend a conference based in Yellowknife to discuss the future development of the North with twenty other men, some of whom were prominent bankers, industrialists and economists. My only credentials were the years that I had spent among the Indians.

The guests and press travelled in chartered DC6s which flew all through the Northwest Territories, stopping at towns and villages where a landing could be made so that we could familiarize ourselves with their problems. Our first layover was at an Indian school on the banks of the Mackenzie River, where we trolled for salmon. The catch was excellent and we decided to add the fish to the dinner menu. To my surprise, the cooks, who were elderly Englishwomen, asked me how to prepare them, whereupon I spent an hour showing them how to clean and fillet salmon. Evidently all their fish was sent from Vancouver. It seemed a shame that no thought had been given to developing a local industry in an area where there was such an abundance of fish and cariboo that it had to be sheer laziness to import high-protein food products.

On our final evening in Yellowknife, Arthur Laing thanked us for taking an interest in the project and asked that each man give his ideas about how the life of the Indians and Eskimos could be bettered, so that he could go to the cabinet with our suggestions.

Most of the guests were enjoying their liquor, which could account for some of the impractical solutions that followed. I listened as suggestions on how to create opportunity and a cash flow in the North were thrown out by men who should have had more sense. Some talked about underground sewage systems and treatment plants with costs running into millions of dollars. I figured it would be cheaper by far to send every Indian and Eskimo in Yellowknife to stay in the Chateau Laurier and keep them there for the rest of their lives than to implement the proposals being discussed.

I had lived among the Indians and had seen how government interference had done nothing but damage their way of life. Native people became wards of a government that seemed to promote them as first-class citizens but in fact took away their initiative and pride.

Finally I could stand this fanciful talk no longer. Most of the men had been speaking from their seats in the hall; to make an impression, I strode up to the front beside Arthur Laing and gave them my opinions in a voice that was loud enough to guarantee that they wouldn't sleep through my speech.

I told them that I had never heard so many clever men,

experts in their fields, suggest such foolishness as constructing houses suitable for a city with a temperate climate like Vancouver's. I said that before the days of snowmobiles and airplanes, the Indian lived off the land and migrated with the seasons. The number of people in any given area was limited by the amount of food that the land could supply. The natives were used to moving their whole camp each year, taking all their household goods with them and leaving a season's accumulated litter such as tin cans and waste. I urged that federal policy should be to send a well-trained and practical teacher to each village to assist the Indians to adapt to the changing circumstances in the North.

Many of the Indians were living in tents or prefabricated government houses which had been built by contractors from Edmonton. I felt that it would be far better for the Indians to become self-sufficient by giving each village a diesel-powered portable sawmill. There was lots of timber along the banks of the Mackenzie River which could be logged and floated downstream. The Indians should cut the timber, mill it and then be paid to build their own houses. They could benefit from the construction experience, add some comfort to their lives and have more cash in their pockets. As it was, the white man contracted all the work, often at huge profits.

The Department of Northern Affairs apparently thought it was helping the Indians by doing everything for them. Instead, the government was doing more harm than good by putting the Indians in the position of accepting alms rather than earning their own livelihood.

When I had finished, Arthur Laing thanked me for my comments and I figured that was the end of the matter, but a month later I received a telephone call from the prime minister, Lester Pearson, who asked me to accept a four-year appointment as a councillor of the Northwest Territories. He told me that my suggestions had been the most helpful to the Department of Northern Affairs, and that my participation would make a real contribution.

I accepted the challenge, and made my home in Yellowknife for two months of the year, the last half of January through to mid-March. It was quite a change leaving the sunny beaches of Hawaii in 80-to-90-degree temperatures and arriving in Yellowknife twenty-four hours later where it was well below 30 degrees and there were less than five hours of daylight. I used to joke that I got my hot flushes in Hawaii and my cold flushes in Yellowknife.

The commissioner of the Northwest Territories, Stuart Hudson, and his deputy, John Parkes, both wonderful and capable men, worked very hard for the advancement of the North. They tried to cut down the interference and red tape from Ottawa.

The North is fine if you are white, not bad if you are an Eskimo, but downright discouraging if you are an Indian. The problem is the white man's welfare system: the advent of the relief cheque in the North signalled the end of a proud people. Often the whole welfare cheque would be spent on liquor and the health nurse would have to scramble for more money to buy food for the family. What the Indian people need is education, and the ability to earn a living by developing a great fishing industry and by attracting hunters and nature lovers to spend their money in the North.

As long as the Indian people are allowed to stay on reserves they will be segregated from the growth of society. It would be to their distinct advantage to intermarry with the rest of the population instead of remaining isolated.

The Eskimo seems more adaptable, probably because he has not been pampered like the Indian who, living farther south, came into closer contact with the so-called benefits of civilization. The Indians used to hunt and fish but now they can go to the store with their welfare cheques to buy pork chops wrapped in paper, or salmon imported from the coast.

The North is coming into its own now but unfortunately the beneficiaries are the shareholders in mining or exploration companies rather than the native people. I always believed that the oil and minerals of the Northwest Territories would provide a basis for a lasting economic boom as soon as a way was found to get ships into the Arctic and sub-Arctic waters, some of which are iced over up to nine months of the year.

I believed that the government in Ottawa was squandering the taxpayers' money on outdated and impractical icebreakers. If we could put a man on the moon, I argued, surely we could find a way to cut a northwest passage through 10 or 12 feet of ice. I set my mind to discovering a practical solution to this problem, as Pat Carney reported in the *Vancouver Sun*, 15 April 1968:

But what really bothered Gibson were the icebreakers, the key to opening up the Arctic and transporting its mineral riches to market. Canada has more than $100 million worth of icebreakers, and Gibson says: "There is everything wrong with those blank-blank ships."

They are uneconomic. The bigger ones cost $20 million to build, and require 80-90 men crews, costing millions annually to run. "You could not move freight economically on the damn things if you had 100,000 tons," says Gibson.

They're built wrong. They ram their way through the ice, which is pretty slow. And they are built as wide in front as in the back, which means they are difficult to manoeuvre. "If they hit an obstruction, they have to back up," says Gibson.

Thirdly, they are used inefficiently. "They pack a doctor on the SOB and tie up $20 million worth of ship while he tends to someone on shore," Gibson shakes his head.

What upset Gibson was that nobody—NOBODY—cared. "When I got North, I found they hadn't changed in 50 years, nor have they thought of change, or do they WANT to change," he says sadly.

So Gibson, a practical man, designed his own icebreaker. His model was one he invented when he was a 14 year old kid on the wild west coast of Vancouver Island, with a two-cylinder, 14 horsepower fishboat. It was the most powerful boat on his coast.

A mine was frozen in that winter, and they asked Gibson to try and break the ice so that the Maquinna could get to the wharf to offload the crew. The prize was $100, "a hell of a lot of money in those days," said Gibson.

Young Gibson lashed some logs forward and rammed. He didn't get far. So he and the Indian kid with him went to the beach and got three boomsticks.

They lashed one along each side, angled downward, heels out of the water. The third, a cedar stick, they lashed across the front, resting underwater. Around this cross stick, they hooked several boom chains.

When they started the 14 hp engine, the cross log pressed up against the ice and the chains sawed their way through. They needed only power to push the chain through the ice.

Gibson and the Indian kid chewed their way through two miles of ice at three or four knots and went home.

Fifty years later Gibson was down on his knees, unrolling his sketches on the carpet to show how he has adapted the cedar stick and boom chain principle for the north.

The key is to rig the ship's bow with knives, like a bulldozer blade with teeth, to chew through the ice. "This is a road building piece of equipment, because we're building a road through the ice," explains Gibson.

His blade is 100 feet wide and 11 teeth spaced roughly ten feet apart and thickest at the leading edge. The blade cuts the ice and lets the water come up. "It is the water under the ice that stops you," says Gibson. "You can't just shove something down unless you have some place to put it."

Ideally, his icebreaker would taper from 100 feet at the bow to 30 feet at the stern, to give it lots of swinging room with a boom jill-poked out the side to sweep the ice aside and keep the channels clear. It would have 15,000 horsepower.

Gibson figures his ship would require only ten men working so many days on, so many day off, like B.C. towboat men. It would be guided from shore. A helicopter would plot the course and the icebreaker would follow it.

It would not be much different from laying out a road between here and Lillooet, says Gibson. The Arctic freezes at the rate of one foot a month, and regular ploughing could keep the channels clear. "When drift ice comes down, just cut it like a mudslide on a road."

Gibson took his idea to a local shipyard to get it on paper. He went to Yellowknife to get authority to represent the Northwest Territories Council.

Then he went to Ottawa. The following is his account, with only the language changed to protect the innocent.

"I figured it would take a day to give them the idea," said Gibson. "But they said it would take quite a while maybe a month—to get it through the Department of Transportation."

So he went back. "There were two fellows there, one of them an admiral. He said: "Mr. Gibson I don't know if you realize the horsepower needed to push this . . . seadozer, or whatever you call it . . . through the ice. There is not enough power in the world to push that 100 foot blade."

Gibson said "Have your naval architects studied it?"

Gibson held his cigar like an elegant teacup, little pinkie curled and mimicked the admiral. "I have given the matter a certain amount of thought."

"You so and so's never even studied it," roared Gibson. "I wouldn't hire either of you in my camps and I'm not going to allow you to play around anymore."

"But, Mr. Gibson, we haven't the money—better leave it until next year—there's a new government coming in—the minister's busy—there's no appropriation—" tattled the civil servant.

"Appropriation my eye," said Gibson. "You're building a $20 million ship right now that is not worth a gosh darn. I'm going to call in the press and tell them the department is the enemy of the north and that this is the most gosh darn inefficient thing I've ever seen in my life." He picked up his plans and left.

That night Vancouver MP Grant Deachman spotted Gibson in the Gallery of the House of Commons and asked him if he wanted to see Transport Minister Paul Hellyer.

Hellyer was cordial when Gibson met him in his office. "How nice to see you, Gordon. That is a great idea you've got there. I like it." (There's a politician for you, says Gordon. He hasn't seen it—knows nothing about it—but he likes it.)

He told Hellyer "I'm going to build this if I have to rig this dozer blade on a Japanese freighter and make the department look like a Gosh Darn fool."

"Why, Gordon," protested Hellyer. "Have you been running into any trouble?" (The minister knew I had, says Gordon.)

They all met the next day—minister, civil servant, and Gibson, and Gibson told them what was wrong with their icebreakers.

"Do you know what their defence was?" says Gordon. They said: "Gordon, they are doing much the same thing all over the world." (Unfortunately, that's true, says Gibson. The Russians are doing something but they are still doing the wrong things in the wrong way.)

So Gibson told them: "I'll make a deal, I'll put my rig on one ship. If it will go through the ice four times faster than yours, I want four times my money back."

Hellyer passed up the bet. Instead he turned to his deputy and said: "Do this. I'll find the money."

So in a Montreal shipyard, Gibson's seadozer blade—or whatever he calls it—is being fitted on a 3,500 ton ship, the Sir Gilbert Humphrey. It will cost the taxpayers around $30,000.00. "I'm not saying it's perfect. It's like a logging truck, or a donkey, or a spar tree. You keep improving on the general idea."

He blew cigar smoke toward the ceiling. "Our mental attitude is wrong. Everyone says we can't go through the north. I'm quite certain that we can keep it open if we want to, and I'm predicting we will use the northwest passage in five years."

So far as is known no admirals, civil servants, or transport ministers have given Gordon Gibson an argument on the subject.

The government had a model of the seadozer blade built, but it was so undersized that I concluded they did not want the project to succeed. Although I had asked to be present at the test run, the trials were over before I was even notified that they had begun. I certainly found out how unreceptive the civil service is to new ideas.

By 1970, at the end of my term in the Northwest Territories, there was a movement by the native people to have a stronger voice on the council. I stepped down gladly, as I believed that the best representation would come from the Indians and Eskimos themselves.

It is ironic that I finished my public life near the place where I was born. If I had been a young man during my years as councillor, I would have stayed in the North because there is great opportunity there for anyone who isn't afraid of a little cold and a lot of hard work.

CHAPTER 30

I am pleased to report that it is just liquor and tobacco that have become repulsive to me, and not the ladies, who seem even more desirable than ever.

I did my fair share of drinking whiskey from the age of twenty on. My friends and I drank all the liquor we could get, but it was a moderate amount since we were limited by finances. We drank mainly at parties or in the dance halls and none of us missed an hour's work because we were drunk or hung over. But as I got a little more money I could afford to buy more bottles of rye than I needed.

By the time we owned Tahsis, I often drank a bottle of rye a day, working on the theory that if there were any drinking to be done in our logging camps, I would be the one to do it. Our men worked an eight-hour shift, but I was boss and was on call twenty-four hours a day. There were only two occasions in all those years that I wasn't on the job before my crew and still at it after they had finished for the day. Even though I drank a bottle a day, I watered it liberally, and drank a quart of milk before I went to bed. Moreover, I ate and talked a lot along with the drinking, which probably helped to offset the effect of the liquor and to speed it through my system.

Luckily I wasn't argumentative while drinking so I never made an enemy that way. In fact, the wild west stories about hard-drinking, fighting loggers are myth. In the forty years I lived in logging camps I saw less than a total of ten minutes of fighting. It is the beer parlour or hophead loggers who do all the brawling; the logger who produces doesn't need to prove his credentials.

My doctor in Vancouver had told me for fifteen years that I was in great shape considering the fact that I was 20 pounds overweight, drank too much rye and smoked too many cigars. It was my physical strength and endurance that enabled me to cope with these excesses for so long. The liquor didn't seem to have any effect on me during the years of abuse, but by the time I was sixty it began to take its toll. After Louise died, I started to drink heavily: at least two bottles a day. But I never took a drink before eleven o'clock in the morning unless I was still carrying on with a party from the night before.

In 1967 I was spending the winter at the Maui Lu Hotel and didn't feel very well in the mornings so decided to see a doctor. I picked one at random out of the telephone book.

In the doctor's office the next day I stripped off my clothes and stood naked in the middle of the floor while he made disapproving noises about my physical condition. He was about 5 feet 2 inches, weighed around 130 pounds and was about twenty-five years my junior. I was caught completely off guard when suddenly he struck me in the stomach with his fist. "Gibson, look at that paunch. You need to take off 30 pounds. How much do you drink?"

When I told him that I drank about three-quarters of a bottle a day, he was shocked. Shaking his head, he warned me not to drink more than four ounces. "I spill more than that," I snorted, beginning to run out of patience. When he found out that I smoked at least twenty cigars a day, he looked at me in disgust, and gave me twenty-one pills to be taken at the rate of three a day for a week. He warned me sternly not to drink alcohol while I was on this medication. I took the pills as prescribed, but admit that I went on drinking as before.

There were five or six people in the waiting room when I returned to his office a week later. The doctor saw me as the door of the examining room opened and he yelled, "Get out of here, Gibson. You lied to me, saying that you only drank three-quarters of a bottle of whiskey a day. I telephoned your bartenders at the hotel, your great friend, the chief of police, and some of your old cronies. All of them say you drink at least two bottles a day. Don't waste my time. The next man you see will probably be an undertaker. You'll be dead for sure in five years."

I was humiliated and tried to bluff my way out. "Doctor,

get this clear. You don't call me a liar. How much do I owe you?"

"You don't owe me anything," the doctor replied. "I feel sorry for you, Mr. Gibson. God gave you everything, and you're going to drink yourself to death. Get out of my office."

If I had had a tail it would have been right down between my legs as I left that office. No one had ever dared tell me to my face that I was a liar, and worse, a drunk.

Sitting in my car after the doctor's tirade I began to think about what he had said to me. That five years bothered me. If he had said I would be dead in one year, I would have figured he was wrong. If he had said ten years, I would have been satisfied to go by then because I would be seventy years old.

Almost automatically, I opened the glove compartment and took out a bottle. At that time I always drank V.O. 83 which came in a flat bottle and lay still in one place whereas a round bottle rolled about with the motion of the car. Three times I started to take a swig before I screwed the cap back on and threw the bottle down. The doctor had really scared me. All my life I had given orders to other men and I knew that now it was time for me to take some of my own medicine.

As I sat alone in the car, I said aloud, "Gordon, you big son-of-a-bitch, you'll never take another drink as long as you live."

I tightened the cap on the whiskey bottle and from that moment I have never even thought of having a drop of alcohol. Once or twice over the years I've picked up a glass, put it to my lips and found that it contained liquor and immediately spit it out into my napkin. It was easy once I had decided never to have another drink. I'm not the sort of person who could have tapered off. It was all or nothing for me, and I now regret the years that I drank without regard for the people around me.

That doctor became a great friend. He would never allow me to pay him for any medical advice so I invited him to the Maui Lu Hotel as my guest. After dinner, as we sat on the lawn, he asked me how I had stopped drinking. When I told him that it was just a case of willpower he pleaded with me to help him break away from a drug dependency. For the last two years he had been taking heroin and he knew that he couldn't stop cold turkey.

Two weeks later I received a note from him. "Gordon, I'm sorry I haven't the strength you have. I know I'm going over the hill." He had taken his own life. It was so sad to think that a doctor who had devoted his life to healing others had so little faith in himself.

There is no doubt that an excess of liquor will eventually rob anyone of his vigour but drugs like heroin can degrade a person so that he loses complete control of his life. I believe we would get rid of much of our drug problem by bringing in such deterrents as the guillotine for the parasites who peddle heroin and cocaine on the street. A few public beheadings would clean up the streets very quickly.

Giving up smoking was much easier than giving up whiskey, and the circumstances were a lot more fun. I met a very attractive woman at the hotel and after she left we continued to correspond. She wrote that she was going on a cruise and I figured it might be fun to join her so I booked a stateroom on the *Queen Elizabeth II*.

The lady arrived in style with two large suitcases and a metal trunk. She was a high society girl who had been widowed twice. This made me a little nervous but I thought that a two-week romance wouldn't necessarily make me husband number three.

She had brought at least twenty different outfits and ten wigs in varying styles and colours. While I could place her without any trouble in the cabin, I couldn't always recognize her in a crowd. She loved to gamble and we stayed up late in the main salon at the gaming tables. I would often lose her in the crowd and have to go back to the stateroom to wait for her return.

One evening as we were taking a walk on the upper deck, I said, "This is the first time I've ever had a rotten cigar." In those days I smoked White Owls at ten cents apiece instead of dollar cigars, figuring at that price I could afford to give away ten for every one I smoked myself. I threw the offending cigar overboard in disgust and reached for another. It tasted just as bad so I discarded every cigar in my pocket and bought a bunch of new ones. That night I felt so ill that the ship's doctor was called. He asked me if I had been doing anything unusual. I told him about the two rotten cigars and the doctor said, "Mr. Gibson, there's nothing wrong with the cigars. Your system is just revolting against all the abuse it gets from tobacco."

I tried to smoke once or twice the next week, but I just couldn't. That was the end of my cigar-smoking days. I guess I had smoked more than my share for a lifetime.

The *Queen Elizabeth II* docked at 8:00 in New York on as miserable a January morning as I have known. It seemed impossible to get a cab and tipping the porter didn't speed things up. In frustration, I walked three blocks before flagging down a cab and then returned to pick up my girlfriend and the baggage.

After dropping her off in town, I headed out to the airport and was infuriated to be delayed for three-quarters of an hour more in heavy traffic. I checked my baggage on the 2:00 P.M. flight to Toronto as I was planning to go on to Ottawa to see my son, Gordon, who was chief executive aide to the prime minister.

I sat in the airport until 6:00 expecting my plane to take off at any moment, but I got so fed up that I took a taxi to another airport where it was rumoured there was a flight due to leave for Toronto. I left my baggage checked.

It was a bitch of a night. To make matters worse, I had slipped and fallen into a puddle of water getting out of the taxi and my clothes were soaking wet. If I had been stranded in any city on the West Coast, I could have called up a friend. I didn't know a soul in New York except the lady whom I had just left and we had agreed to end our relationship. I felt New York was one of the loneliest places I had ever had the bad luck to visit.

Every bed had been taken at the airport hotel but I was so tired that I growled at the night clerk, "I'll sleep on the couch in the foyer. Throw me out if you dare!"

I managed to sleep for about an hour. The illness that had plagued me on the ship became worse. My fever was so high that I was probably delirious. Eventually an announcement came over the loudspeaker that my plane was departing for Toronto. It was a flight that went through to Vancouver, and I was so miserable when we arrived in Toronto that I told the airline crew to go to hell, I would not leave my seat so that the plane could be cleaned. And I certainly knew that I was too sick to go on to Ottawa.

In Vancouver I was ordered to bed for a week by the family doctor, who told me I had emphysema. That means I was good for a 20-yard dash but would come in last at 200 yards: I have lots of strength but no wind. My lungs will give out before my heart.

In 1971 Louanne, who had been a nurse and was now married to an orthopaedic surgeon in Guatemala, Frederic Labbé, visited San Francisco to entertain some friends. I was invited as honoured guest with the privilege of paying the bill. I didn't want to attend the party alone. I asked Gertrude Schneider to come with me even though she was twenty-three years younger than I. To my delight, she graciously accepted. We had a marvellous evening together but I knew she had no interest in me other than as a friend.

Gertrude and I had met at the Maui Lu while she was playing a game of golf. In order to make her shot, it was necessary to move a sprinkler, and when she saw me move it back into place she said, "Be careful now, or I'll report you to the manager for interfering with my golf game." I guess she figured I was the gardener because I was wearing an old shirt, cut-off shorts and a pair of slip-alongs.

I was so ungracious that I said something like, "Who the hell ever showed you how to play golf?" and modestly showed her a couple of my better shots.

I can't say whether or not she was impressed with my golf but that evening when I had a drink sent over to her table with a request that she join me for dinner she seemed a little surprised to find out that I owned the hotel.

The morning after my daughter's party, the telephone rang. It was Gertrude. "Gordon, turn on the T.V. Prime Minister Pierre Trudeau and young Margaret Sinclair have been married." I had been a friend of Margaret's parents for years and my son, Gordon, was an aide to Trudeau. The announcement was not a complete surprise.

Gertrude seemed to be very excited as if it was terrific news, and I said, "Don't you think that thirty years is too much of a difference?" I was surprised when she answered, "Not if you are really in love and have a lot of interests in common."

All my life I've been a man to take advantage of a quick remark. "There's only twenty-three years between our ages. Perhaps we should get married."

From that moment on I planned to marry her. She was good-looking, single and had never been married, which was an asset as I didn't want to compete with former husbands or lovers. I didn't need a mother for my children since they were grown up. I knew that she would be a wonderful companion because she was lighthearted and hardworking, holding the position of freight account executive for American Airlines.

If she married me I would get the best of the deal, and I decided to present my case so well that she would at least consider it. I put my best foot forward from that time on and invited her to Maui and Vancouver so that she could get to know me and in time, perhaps, love me.

A few months later in San Francisco I gathered together enough courage to ask her to be my partner. Although I can be as tough as hell in other directions, when she said she would marry me, I was so emotional that I broke down and cried. It was like the time I wept so much at an Al Jolson movie that a kid tapped me on the shoulder and said, "Don't take it so hard, mister, it's only a movie."

Our wedding was in San Francisco and the reception in Vancouver. She came to me knowing that she was truly needed and she has made a great job of our marriage. I guess my biggest contribution is that I'm a good provider, while she brings most of the other qualities that make life worth living. I've mellowed considerably. Somehow I feel more of a gentleman.

CHAPTER 31

I'm at the stage when I wouldn't take on a job that would take me more than a couple of years or so to accomplish, whereas at thirty the whole world seemed ahead of me and I was thinking of forever.

I have always had a love affair with the sea and my brothers and I have owned some marvellous ships. One is the yacht *Norsal*, built in 1922. She is 132 feet long with 320-horsepower twin engines, and makes about 12 knots an hour; a beautiful ship having seven hand-crafted hardwood staterooms and four washrooms, two with full baths. The main salon is about 40 feet by 18 feet and contains a piano and a bar. The companionway leads to a galley on the main deck, just back of the dining room which is completely panelled in oak, with leaded glass windows on the serving buffet. The wheelhouse is large and well appointed for our captain's comfort. She is a seagoing yacht in the grand style, elegant and proud.

The *Norsal* was the only one of the fifty or more boats we have owned that wasn't bought as a commercial venture. She was built for the Powell River Company. It was Clarke's good judgement and salesmanship that convinced us to buy the *Norsal* for our fishing fleet. He made a fine pitch, telling us how cheaply she would run as a fish packer and that she used only 10 gallons of diesel fuel an hour at twenty cents a gallon. But as soon as we saw her we knew she was far too fine to be run as other than a yacht, so we kept her for pleasure—for fishing derbies with our friends. It turned out that fuel has nothing to do with the running costs of a yacht. If our engines had run on scotch whiskey and the guests had drunk diesel fuel we would have been better off. We owned the *Norsal* for twenty-five years.

In 1960 when I was an MLA for North Vancouver, I took a bunch of World War I veterans and their wives for a run up Indian Arm. When I left the wheel with one of the guests for a few moments, the ship ran aground on a falling tide at the head of the inlet just off the site of the huge Ioco refinery. As the tide went out, the boat listed badly. Although we weren't in any danger, I wanted the guests ashore because our generous liquor supply was beginning to take effect.

Most of the guests clambered smartly into the lifeboats for the 100-yard run to shore. A few of the old booze artists refused to leave the ship: they wanted to play the hero and go down with the ship. In order to entice these guys over the side, I grabbed all the bottles I could find and put them in the lifeboats shouting, "Well, boys, we're taking all the liquor ashore. Possibly that will change your minds." The drunks followed like wolves chasing a rabbit. It was a grand day. We made the event into a real shipwreck, picnicking and singing on the shore until the tide floated us free. It was midnight before we got back to Vancouver, the "wreck" having made the day one to remember.

Over the many years that we owned the *Norsal* I dreamed of taking her to Maui, for the winter months when she was not being used in Vancouver. We were spending so much time in Hawaii that it seemed a shame not to make use of the *Norsal* where she could be enjoyed by many people.

My brothers thought I was crazy to tackle such a voyage at my age; our insurance company was dubious about extending coverage on a venture that our captain and engineer declined to join for being foolhardy and risky. As the difficulties became evident, I became more stubborn, thinking that if Captain Vancouver and other navigators could take a little sailing ship across all that ocean then a man on a power vessel could certainly make Hawaii. I knew that the *Norsal* could go anywhere in the world, so I made a deal to buy the vessel from my brothers and take all the glory or blame for myself, and I rechristened her the *Maui Lu*.

I invited five couples to come with me, but quite strangely four of the couples had to leave town suddenly and missed the trip. They had talked to the old engineer who had been with us for fifteen years and who had told me, "Gordon, you scare me enough right here on the coast, having half-wrecked the boat ten times between here and the Queen Charlotte Islands. There's no way I'll ever go with you to Hawaii."

One couple, Eric and Betty Allen, either didn't speak to the engineer or were willing to take the chance. Betty turned out to be our strongest crew member and with the help of some of the others looked after the galley.

A dozen men who had papers and the ability to navigate wanted to come along, but that would have taken away all my fun. I decided to take a crew who knew less than I did—if that were possible: four young fellows from university, Betty and Eric Allen, and my grandson, Marc, who was fourteen at the time. Marc's parents weren't going to let him come until I said, "If you're going to make a sissy of him, make the decision right now." So with that threat, they surrendered and we started to make our preparations.

We took on enough dry provisions and fresh water to last us a month to six weeks. I took one extra precaution. There was a lot of canvas aboard—old awnings and hatch covers—so I got four lengths of 2-inch pipe and four T-joints just in case we got lost and ran out of fuel oil. That way we could convert her into a square-rigged Chinese junk and keep going south until we ran into something.

Ringing the bells and pressing the starting button was about the total of my experience with the ship's engines because we had always had an engineer aboard. Two of the university lads brought a sextant along so that they could locate our position if we got lost. They didn't know any more about operating a sextant that I did, but it seemed to make them feel a little better. They never did find our position within a hundred miles. We ran on time and dead reckoning, which came out right.

On the evening of our departure there was a celebration to send us off in style. Marc's parents looked pretty down in the mouth, figuring there was a good chance that their dear son would fall off the edge of the earth, and doubtless some of the crew's wives thought their husbands were goners also.

We pulled out at six o'clock that night. Everything was stowed away and people were assigned to their watches of six hours on, six hours off. I slept in the wheelhouse so that I could keep control of things.

That first night was long. As we went through Active Pass just before midnight, the weather thickened. We steered past Victoria, Race Rocks and Carmana Point. By then the ship was rolling fairly heavily and we started to hit some big seas. Suddenly one of the engines started to splutter and stopped dead. One of the college boys had worked on motorcycles and automobiles and helped me find the trouble.

It was sludge as thick as molasses in the filter system which had mixed with rust from the tanks because of the rolling of the ship. Between the two of us we cleaned the filter and managed to get the engine started. A couple of hours later the same thing happened again in the other engine.

The filters were made of very fine copper mesh and were difficult to clean. After they clogged up several more times I could see why the engineer had declined to come with us. He must have known that the tanks were dirty and that an ocean voyage was out of the question before they had been thoroughly cleaned. We had to stop the engines every six hours and clean one or other of the filters.

By this time we were fifty miles out to sea; I headed down the coast so that, if necessary, we could go over the Columbia River Bar for repair. After the fourth change we decided that rather than cleaning those bloody filters it would be much easier to punch big holes all around them and use a pair of socks to catch the sludge. This gave us about eight hours running time, and now it wasn't a case of cleaning the filters but of having enough pairs of socks!

We altered course to southwest by south, and saw the Hawaiian Islands on our tenth day out. Our course had taken us right in between Big Island and Maui. We were a gala outfit by the time we arrived and had become pretty adept at changing those socks. If there had been any doubt about our course, we could have navigated by the jet streams from the airplanes which flew between the mainland and Hawaii.

Someone saw our lights just before midnight and phoned the Maui Lu Hotel. Everyone in the restaurant of the hotel came down to the shore as we dropped anchor and put over the lifeboat. Gertrude came out in the water almost to her waist, and some of the waitresses splashed in to welcome us. It was like the Captain Father coming home.

We had more than our share of adventures on the *Maui Lu*. During the ten months that she was in Hawaiian waters, we took our hotel guests on day trips around the island, stopping for lazy picnic lunches and swimming parties.

On one fine morning we lifted anchor about ten o'clock to take a trip to the pineapple island, Lanai, with about sixty hotel managers and their wives. After a three-hour run, we took them ashore in small boats, asking that they be back by three o'clock that afternoon so that we could arrive home before dark. To make the landing back in Maui through the reefs against all the lights from shore was dangerous, and I wanted to drop anchor before dusk.

Liquor flowed freely both on the way over and on shore in Lanai while the hotel managers were visiting with their friends. I was one of the few people not drinking. As a result, most of them were two hours late for the rendezvous.

When we arrived back at Maui, instead of anchoring well out, I ventured close to the shore trying to pick up our permanent buoy. Quite a strong onshore wind came up, and we failed to pick up our buoy with the searchlights. One of the problems was that thirty or so well-wishers had come onto the bridge and were standing just ahead of the wheelhouse so that I couldn't see a goddamned thing. I couldn't get them to move so I stopped the engines and bellowed, "Until you fellows get the hell out of my road, we're going to drift around out here."

Just then I felt the boat kiss close up to a reef, making a nasty scraping sound on the coral. The tide was falling. We were stuck. It would be at least ten to twelve hours, a whole tide, before we could refloat. With the boat taking a heavy list and the possibility of a storm coming up, I decided to ferry all the passengers ashore in our large lifeboat which could carry about sixteen people. We had drifted sideways, and were being held against the reef by the strong winds. Unfortunately, the gangway was on the weather side of the ship, and as we filled the lifeboat, a huge swell swamped the outboard motor so that we couldn't get it started. That meant we had to row. Neither of our two Hawaiian crew had ever rowed a boat before: they were used to paddles rather than oars. We made three trips against the wind over that half mile to shore.

Rowing was a business I knew well from the old days in British Columbia, but I was getting damned tired by now. Gertrude had gone ashore on the first trip and had called the coast guard who were located just four miles away. She signalled back that they would be coming to pull us off the reef. All the rest of the passengers had been ferried ashore and just the crew and I went back aboard.

Three more hours had passed and we were stuck fast with the falling tide. I figured we would need a little pull to get us off the reef. The *Maui Lu* had gone on the reef just before high tide. The next tide would be lower still. She was grinding and bouncing and I knew she couldn't take much more of that kind of abuse before a hole was rubbed right through the hull.

A short while later we saw a flashing light on shore signalling to us to abandon ship. The coast guard had not sailed in his ship to help us but was gawking from the shore with the others. It had been three hours since Gertrude had put in her call to the coast guard station and the captain had driven over to our hotel in his goddamned car.

I rowed into shore. The captain asked what the problem was, and to my further disgust, insisted that the *Maui Lu* was too large a vessel to be pulled off the reef.

"Christ, you could at least try," I snapped, but it seemed that he had to get further instructions from headquarters. When the coast guard ship did finally arrive, it stayed so far off the *Maui Lu* that one of the crew and I had to row the lifeboat out 1,000 feet against the wind to pick up a little hand line so we could pull in his main towline. The captain could have brought his ship close to the *Maui Lu* and thrown the line to us, since his very powerful boat drew only 7 feet of water whereas the *Maui Lu* has a 12-foot draft.

We were now lying sideways on the reef and the only way to free the *Maui Lu* was to pull her bow about. The coast guard gave a halfhearted try after which I asked the captain if he would stand by for another four hours, holding his position with his anchor down until the tide came up and floated us off. I told him that the ship would be wrecked if he didn't stay with us.

The captain refused, sending word that he was a rescue ship and not in the salvage business. As he saw the situation, no lives were in danger, and so he was returning to his station. He suggested that we get a towboat from Honolulu, which would have taken about twelve hours to arrive, thereby causing us to miss another tide. By that time the *Maui Lu* would be a total loss. I found out later that the patrol ship was to take part in a sea-rescue stunt in Honolulu and apparently this was why the captain was so anxious to get back to port.

All the time we were waiting to get off the reef, I could hear the coral grinding into the belly of the ship. We tried unsuccessfully to pull her free by tying all our ropes together to form a 1,000-foot line and pulling it through our buoy with the forward power winch. It was no use. She wouldn't move an inch. The flood tide was almost at its height. This was our last chance. It was then that the idea occurred to me to swing the boom carrying our large lifeboat out over the side of the ship, and to open the sea cocks so that the boat half filled with water. We winched up the lifeboat as much as possible, until the *Maui Lu* listed about 15 degrees. I rolled her as far as I could without breaking our gear. In ten minutes the *Maui Lu* was free. I have never been so tired in all my life. I had been up since six in the morning and it was now five the next morning. For the last twenty-three hours I had been on my feet constantly with the responsibility and effort of getting all the passengers to shore and I had worried about losing my beloved ship.

I never really recovered my strength. It seemed as if that was the peak of my endurance. A man cannot attempt to do at seventy-one what he did easily at thirty without it causing him to remember his years.

During the next few weeks we tried to find a shipyard that could handle a vessel the size of the *Maui Lu*. My crew and I had dived under the ship and found a gash 2 feet long and 1 foot wide in the side of the hull. Her planks had been scraped so severely that some of them had to be replaced. The *Maui Lu* was 30 feet too long for any private shipyard and the naval shipyards were only equipped to handle steel hulls. We managed to put a temporary canvas patch over the damaged part of the hull while we searched for some alternative way of repairing her.

The warm waters of the South Pacific are hard on a wooden ship, and she was making a little water by this time. I decided to take the *Maui Lu* back to Canada for repair.

My first crew had flown back to Vancouver but word of our planned return voyage to Canada had spread. Quite a few people wanted to take part in the adventure. I selected most of my crew from my hotel staff. One was a man who looked after the grounds, an expert on lawnmowers. Unfortunately, he had just recovered from a broken hip. I had counted on his helping me run the ship but he couldn't climb the stairs to the wheelhouse and therefore spent most of the time in the dining salon.

One of our waitresses, Leona, a petite woman who weighed no more than 100 pounds, turned out to be one of the best quartermasters we had. Except for a man and his wife who were close to my age and good sailors, the rest of the crew of eight were Hawaiians who had never left the island before.

The *Maui Lu* still had the temporary canvas patch in her hull. The next problem was to obtain enough fuel oil, for there was an oil restriction in the United States at that time. There was lots of fuel on the island if you could get permission to use it, and I managed to get one of the contractors to buy a truckload of diesel oil on the quiet.

It was pretty certain that we would need more oil on our return voyage than we had used coming over so I took about thirty extra barrels on the afterdeck. While we were waiting to load the rest of the oil, my doctor ordered me into hospital because I had had a severe case of phlebitis in my leg. He told me that on no account was I to leave his care and that I was to lie absolutely still. The contraband oil had to be loaded in the dark and my mate was waiting for the go-ahead signal from me. I told him to provision and to wait for my arrival. The next day I sneaked down to the ship at 4:00 in the afternoon. The time for our departure had been set for 6:00 P.M.

The crew and the hotel employees thought we should have a good sendoff and prepared a luau in our honour. The party was at its very peak when I sent the guests ashore and gave the signal to pull out. We backed clear of the dock while everyone waved good-bye and sailed out of the harbour with the luau still spread on tables on the front deck. As soon as we swung out of the sheltered water we were hit with a real rough northeaster breaking water right over the bow. At least every third swell would come clean over and run the entire length of the ship.

Naturally, all the crew got seasick from too much partying. The food was skipping all over the decks and rolling around in the galley. I heard dishes breaking and everything going all to hell but decided to leave things as they were, and to let everyone take care of themselves—just as long as those two engines kept going and the ship headed for the mainland. I couldn't expect anything from the crew or any more from myself. My God, what a night that was!

I kept the ship heading home like a horse running back to the stable, figuring we'd hit the coast somewhere between San Francisco and Nome, Alaska.

The strong northeaster continued to harass us, but the crew got a little more used to the rolling of the ship, though most of them were still seasick. We were down at the stern on account of the extra thirty drums of oil, and that changed the rake of the ship. Unknown to me, we started to take on a little water because a manhole cover had been left open on the afterdeck: a lot of water was running through the manhole into the after companionway.

The seas were the kind that wear a man down, and our ship was just the wrong length for the 12-foot swells. We seemed to hit about every third wave, dipping our nose into the trough. Green water flew up over the decks.

Northeast winds of 30 knots an hour blew steadily from the time we left Hawaii until we reached the mainland. Our oil was limited, and in seas that heavy and bucking such strong winds, we couldn't slow down, since even at full speed we could make only 9 knots instead of 11.

On the sixth night the second engineer told me that there was a little more water than usual in the engine room and the pumps were having trouble keeping our bilges dry. I said to him, "We have an emergency fire pump which you know how to use. Just open the sea cock to the outside to prime it, and then open the valve to the bilges." He mumbled a few words and then went below. That was the last I thought about it. I was so tired that it was one of the few nights I slept more than a couple of hours. At the change of watch next morning, 6:00, I was awakened by a cry, "Captain, we're flooding!"

There was 3 feet of water in the after companionway: my first thought was that the patch on the outside of the ship had come off. I ran down to the engine room where water was flying all over hell, shifting up between the ribs, coming through the air vents and shooting out all over the engines.

Diesel engines don't stop in water like gasoline engines, but our generators were out which meant that the batteries were dead. I knew that we didn't dare stop the engines because we would never get them started again. There was a little 5-horsepower auxiliary gasoline pump aboard, but it hadn't been run for a year. There was only one man aboard who had a chance of starting it, the lawnmower mechanic, Adrian. He was so seasick that we had to move him out of his bunk and set him alongside the engine so that he could get it going.

After three hours of pumping we were running out of gasoline to run the auxiliary pump. The water was out, but more water was coming in from an unknown source. In another six hours we would have to repeat the process. There was only enough gasoline for one more pump-out and we were still six days from shore. I figured I had better get an auxiliary pump running on a V-belt off the main engines. Our electric power was gone since there was no more juice left, but a diesel engine runs without electricity. If I couldn't get another pump running we would be down to our last option which was to axe a hole in the deck of the main salon midway between the two on-deck doors, so that we would get at the water that was rapidly rising in the after companionway by the staterooms. We could carry the water up through the hole we had cut in the deck.

While this emergency plan was forming in my head, we were desperately trying to locate a suction hose. I thought of the fire pump and, reaching down to pull it out, found a 1½-inch stream of water running into the ship.

The engineer had forgotten to turn two valves when he started the pumps, making a direct connection from the outside sea cock through the valves into our bilges. We were taking on water directly through a 1½-inch pipe. That was the source of our trouble, not the gash in the side of the vessel as I had feared. We could all breathe a sigh of relief.

The trip became even more hectic. Our stove, which needed electricity to run the fan, quit working. There were no lights at night. Everyone just had to make the best of the situation.

We did have radar aboard but I never used it. Radio telephones ranked a little higher in my estimation. I had been at sea all my life and had never called for a tow.

The ship had used 2,800 gallons of fuel for the trip to Hawaii but we needed 1,000 extra gallons for the return voyage, because we encountered head winds most of the way. We didn't sight land until the eleventh day when one of the crew picked out the coast of Washington.

One of the crew managed to get our telephone working just as we rounded Cape Flattery. To my surprise, he got Gertrude on the line and told her we would be in the next day. We arrived at about noon and got a fine reception. No tougher looking crew had ever landed at the Royal Vancouver Yacht Club. It had been quite a voyage. The ship needed new reduction gears, generators and motors. The carpets and bedding were a total loss. I wouldn't have missed it for the world. That adventure was a special part of my life, and I believe that the crew felt the same way.

I have been asked why any man at the age of seventy-one would take on a voyage like the one I made to Hawaii. Was it the adventure, the publicity, or did I want to go down with my boots on? I guess it was rather like Ulysses striking out boldly on his own. It was the challenge of feeling alive and taking a risk. I'm at the stage in my life when I try to make the most out of each day and savour it as completely as possible.

For the next two years the *Maui Lu* was used for family outings, and for entertaining patients from G. F. Strong and Shaughnessy hospitals as well as taking Boy Scouts and handicapped children fishing in the *Vancouver Sun* Derby.

The ship was sold in 1977, and is now a charter boat running out of Vancouver harbour.

I plan to spend the next two decades of my life accomplishing something different and rounding off my career as creatively as I started it. I'm too old for politics and I don't care about money.

For many years I had admired the sturdy vessel *Cape Beale*, but I never dreamed she would come on the market. In June of 1980 she was offered for sale and my bid was accepted. The *Cape Beale* was built in 1924 by Menchions Shipyards, which had given life to the *Norsal* just two years earlier. She is 70 feet long, beamy, and sound as the day she was first launched.

Now, instead of spending hours in our offices or eating too much lunch at a club, I spend my time in the fresh salt air of False Creek helping to rebuild the *Cape Beale*. I feel more alive and vigorous than I did at sixty-five. I'll go back to my roots and haunt the west coast, challenging the seas of Quatsino and Clayoquot sounds. The folks who live up there are my kind of people, and in their company I will relive my early days in the fourth quarter of my life.

What I have liked about my life is that I have been able to survive poverty, and many years later to enjoy having a little extra money. I have been a sawyer, captain, pilot, fisherman, logger, hotel owner, politician, and councillor of the Northwest Territories. I have been lucky to have had many kicks at the can.

No man can live forever. Sometimes, like Walter Mitty, I dream of being a great international spy and, having been caught, stood against a wall in front of a firing squad. My captors give me a moment for my final words. Now, I would plead like anyone else if I thought it would do any good, but if I saw that the end was inevitable, I would say, "Shoot, you bastards, shoot."

Carol Renison spent eight years on the West Coast, during which time she came to know Gordon Gibson. She now lives in Toronto.

Gordon F. Gibson is son of the Bull, an author, columnist, businessman, former politician and current Senior Fellow in Canadian Studies at the Fraser Institute.

www.ingramcontent.com/pod-product-compliance
Lightning Source LLC
Chambersburg PA
CBHW032050220426
43664CB00008B/945